Medieval Bridges OF SOUTHERN ENGLAND

100 Bridges 1000 years

By Marshall G. Hall

WINDgather PRESS

Windgather Press is an imprint of Oxbow Books

Published in the United Kingdom in 2022 by
OXBOW BOOKS
The Old Music Hall, 106-108 Cowley Road, Oxford, OX4 1JE

and in the United States by
OXBOW BOOKS
1950 Lawrence Road, Havertown, PA 19083

Hardback Edition: ISBN 978-1-914427-13-8
Digital Edition: ISBN 978-1-914427-14-5 (epub)

A CIP record for this book is available from the British Library

Printed and bound in the Czech Republic by FINIDR s.r.o.

For a complete list of Windgather titles, please contact:

United Kingdom
OXBOW BOOKS
Telephone (01865) 241249
Email: oxbow@oxbowbooks.com
www.oxbowbooks.com

United States of America
OXBOW BOOKS
Telephone (610) 853-9131, Fax (610) 853-9146
Email: queries@casemateacademic.com
www.casemateacademic.com/oxbow

Oxbow Books is part of the Casemate group

Cover images by Marshall Hall
Cover design by Chris Sims

CONTENTS

Dedicated to the memory of Marion Townsend
(1956–2022)

FOREWORD

There are 210 medieval bridges in England with many more in Scotland and Wales, although these areas are not covered here. Even with the narrow definition of medieval that I have adopted, AD 410 to AD 1536, there are a lot more of these tenacious survivors than I had expected, and many are still working hard today on the modern road network. I have divided this work into three books that correspond to the governmental regions of England:

1. Southern England, defined as the regions of Southeast England and Southwest England, has 100 medieval bridges.
2. Middle England, defined as the regions of East of England, East Midlands and West Midlands, has 62 medieval bridges.
3. Northern England, defined as Yorkshire and the Humber, Northeast England and Northwest England, has 48 medieval bridges.

Each of these regions is further divided into tours that are listed along with their medieval bridges. Each tour can ideally be completed in a day, albeit that several would be long days. In every region and in each tour, there are diverse structures that all, in their own way, contribute to an understanding of life in medieval England.

INTRODUCTION

There is a wide range of medieval bridge structures, some very simple in their construction to amazing triumphs of design and engineering comparable with the great churches of the period. They stand today as proof of the great importance of transport networks in the Middle Ages and of the size and sophistication of the medieval economy. These bridges were built in some of the most difficult places, across broad flood plains, deep tidal waters, and steep upland valleys, and they withstood all but the most catastrophic floods. Yet their beauty, from simplistic to ornate, remains for us to appreciate.

Throughout history, rivers have been a hub for human settlement and have long been a key part of local livelihoods, history, and culture, as well as still playing a present-day role in providing services and leisure to people who live around them. It is no coincidence that all four of the earliest human civilisations were formed on great rivers: the Nile, Euphrates, Indus, and Yellow rivers all saw great human aggregation along them. The most ancient, and vital architectural structures linked to the use of rivers are bridges. The Romans were great bridge-builders, but they used timber for most of their bridges, which, of course, are long gone. After the Roman exit from England in AD 410, bridge building slowed considerably for nearly 700 years until the 12th century when major bridging projects began again across the country causing an explosion of population growth. Cities, towns, and villages sprung up at bridgeheads or where a river could be forded at any time of the year. Examples in the UK are London, Oxford, and Cambridge.

People hold a deep fascination for bridges. Who isn't captivated by them? Who hasn't held their breath as their parents (or they themselves) drove across a particularly high or lengthy span? Bridges have always maintained a lure for people and there is even a specific word for someone who loves bridges; pontist:

> *A historic bridge enthusiast who enjoys either lobbying for preservation and/or who enjoys visiting and photographing historic bridges.*
>
> **(The Urban Dictionary, 2010)**

Perhaps the allure of bridges is their essential nature, their ability to overcome a natural obstacle, their engineering achievement, their pivotal historical significance, and the views afforded by them, but also perhaps because they are a metaphor for so many things in life. Bridges connect two things that nature had no intention of connecting. They represent humans evolving in their relationship with the environment. The metaphorical bridge represents hope, opportunities, potential, and healing, because it is symbolic of an intentional connection only made possible by a mutual understanding between two separate sides, countries, disciplines, or people.

Medieval bridges served many purposes. Chapels and shops were commonly built on them, and many were fortified with towers and ramparts. Two examples are the Old London Bridge and The Old Tyne Bridge in Newcastle, neither of which survives.

An ancient engraving of the Old Tyne Bridge in Newcastle as it looked soon after its rebuilding in 1250 (Public Domain)

Some even featured a drawbridge, a medieval innovation. Rivers were often used as boundaries or formed part of town defences, so it would make sense to guard the river crossing with a strong gateway. Few survive in England but at Warkworth in Northumberland there is a late 14th-century stone gate tower at one end of the bridge. Other places like London, Bath, Bristol, Shrewsbury, and Stirling had bridge gates once. In fact, Bristol managed to combine both bridge chapel and gate in one massive structure.

Bridges have long been the subject of superstitions and legends. Because they are a literal passage between two places, perhaps they symbolise the fear

Old London Bridge – Looking North Before the Great Fire of 1666. *From* The Book of Martyrs *by John Foxe, first published in 1563, this edn published in 1865 (Public Domain)*

of movement from one stage of life to the next. Superstitious rituals are most powerful when there's underlying fear and anxiety involved. In many parts of the world, it is considered unlucky to be the first person to cross a new bridge; the belief is that the devil, envious of the human ability to create a structure so beautiful and complex, will take the soul of the first living creature to make its way across. Workers to this day will sometimes leave money in the mortar of a new bridge to protect it and ensure good luck, perhaps a remnant of a rumoured earlier custom involving human sacrifice. There is also a belief that you must hold the top of your head while crossing a bridge to keep the bridge from collapsing. While compiling this work I was told that if you say goodbye to a friend on a bridge, you will never see each other again.

Whether allure or superstition, bridges have for centuries been much more than a simple water crossing and, in many cases, became status symbols or political statements. Historically many bridges have been emblazoned with the crests of local families or parishes. Bridges have become the icons of cities and countries. Mention the bridge name and the city springs to mind; the Golden Gate, the Ponte Vecchio, the Bridge of Sighs, Gateshead Millennium Bridge, Tower Bridge, the Forth Bridge, the Brooklyn Bridge and many, many more. Bridges are symbols.

Because of the job they perform, the weight of focused traffic, and where they are located, bridges have always imposed a high financial burden of upkeep responsibility, and arguments have flourished throughout history about who was liable for payment. Sometimes the obligation fell to the local parish, occasionally private companies set up tolls to fund maintenance, and sometimes local authorities absorbed the cost.

All the bridges in this book, even the very old ones, are replacements for earlier versions. The very earliest bridges were simple structures that were built from easily accessible natural resources like wooden logs, stones, and dirt. Resultantly, they only had the ability to span very short distances, and their structural integrity was not high. None of these survives in modern England. Over the millennia, materials and techniques have evolved to produce the wonders of modern bridge engineering we see today, such as the elegant and beautiful Millau Viaduct Bridge over the River Tarn in southern France, or the Kylesku Bridge in Scotland. But the predecessors of these modern structures established the foundations (sometimes literally) of the modern structures which are so easily taken for granted. The building of our modern bridges was only made possible by the Roman perfection of cement, the cofferdam, and concrete, all of which they brought to England.

There are literally hundreds of bridges in England that meet the criteria for inclusion in this roll of honour for senior bridges. They vary vastly in size, style, and materials. Most are stone and a very few are brick. We have lost many of our older bridges to the ravages of time and the modern practice of culvertisation and urban development. A few of our older bridges remain though, and their beauty and pivotal role in our history is starting to be recognised.

> *If watching a bridge is more exciting than crossing that bridge,*
> *then you can be sure that it is a very beautiful bridge!*
>
> **(Ildan, 2005)**

The aim of this work has been to include all surviving medieval bridges in southern England where at least some part of an existing structure is thought to have probably been built between AD 410 and 1536. In Britain the medieval period is usually taken as extending to the dissolution in 1536.

DEFINING MEDIEVAL

The word medieval has its origins in the Latin term medium aevum (middle age) and first came into use in the 19th century. However, there is no agreed definition of the word because there are so many ideas among historians about where to begin and end the medieval period. What is certain, and generally agreed, is that after the Roman era, there are really three medieval periods: early, middle (medieval), and post-medieval.

Roman (43–410)	Traditionally begins with the Roman invasion in AD 43 and ends with the emperor Honorius in Rome directing Britain to see to its own defence in AD 410. The Roman empire eventually falls in AD 476.
Early medieval (410–1066)	This dates from the breakdown of Roman rule in Britain to the Norman invasion in 1066.
Medieval (1066–1536)	The medieval period or Middle Ages begins with the Norman invasion and ends with the dissolution of the monasteries in 1536.
Post-medieval (1536–1901)	Begins with the dissolution of the monasteries and ends with the death of Queen Victoria in 1901.

In understanding the definition of 'medieval' one must also recognise that diverse academic fields each describe the above periods slightly differently. For example, archaeologists, cultural historians, architectural historians, and the science community all characterise medieval using different criteria. Of course, as if all that wasn't complicated enough, all these periods differ with geography and alternate dates are used in Europe that are related to their own historical events. An example is that the Renaissance is usually accepted as starting in Europe in the late 1400s, while England was still firmly in the medieval period.

Medieval Period Overview

The early medieval period was a troublesome time for the inhabitants of England. Without the structure and discipline of Roman rule, areas of the early medieval countryside descended into regional warfare and without the protection that the Roman army offered, coastal areas were plagued by regular invasions, particularly in the northeast from the Nordic kingdoms and the Germanic Anglo Saxons, and in the south from the Normans *(Williamson, 2004)*. Both of these peoples would go on to become the English.

No Longer the 'Dark Ages'

In the 5th and 6th centuries, the period directly after the Roman exodus, England was initially thought of as being in the 'Dark Ages' because of the lack written records and scientific achievement. This period was dismissed as an age of brutality and ignorance as people scratched out a living trying to stay alive. However, in recent decades the attitude that scholars have taken towards medieval times has evolved and they have begun to appreciate medieval architecture, medieval philosophy, and the particular type of religious devotion that caused some later 19th-century scholars to label the era 'The Age of Faith'. Medieval historians of the 21st century are now recognising many ground-breaking developments in legal history, technology, economics, and education that took place during the medieval era. Many of our modern western moral viewpoints, some medievalists would argue today, have their origins (if not their full fruition) in medieval times, including the value of all human life, the merit of all social classes, and the right of the individual to self-determination.

Agriculture

Despite the frequent warfare, for most people life was dominated by living and working on the land. Most land was owned by the powerful noble families or the monasteries who often controlled large blocks of countryside made up of several separate estates. The landowners kept some of their acreage for their own farms, but most was leased to locals to farm in return for their help in times of war, and contributions of money and food. Most of the workers on the land would have had a small area of property on which they could grow food for themselves, but they mainly worked on the ground held by their lords.

Trade Networks

The movement of agricultural and trade goods across medieval England was absolutely essential to the economic well-being and development of everyone in medieval England. Goods moved not only from coastal ports to inland villages, but between inland population centres and seaside towns as well. All manner of goods were traded, including fish, grain, salt, coal, charcoal, and tin, lead, and iron ores. Trade goods were carried the length and breadth of England on the backs of packhorses and mules in trains of up to 20 beasts at a time, each with a load of between one and two hundredweight (112 pounds except in Devon, where it was 120 pounds). Local Lords would encourage

A 15th-century packhorse train crossing a stone bridge

such trade so that they could make money from taxation and tolls (pontage). This meant that market towns often developed and flourished near fords, bridges, monasteries, and the strongholds of leading nobles. Many of these trade networks, rivers, and towns are shown on the Gough Map of the mid-14th century (see pages 296–297)

Community

The form of villages and towns varied widely across the country. In many areas, especially the south, Norman raids had destroyed earlier Anglo-Saxon villages. This meant that completely new settlements were built that usually had two rows of houses arranged either side of a central road, while some larger villages grew up around a central village green. In upland areas medieval villages were not always so well organised and may have been nothing more than a scatter of houses and farms.

Most people's houses would have been simple, wooden structures. These small buildings were easy to build from local materials, which was important as they were often destroyed by raids. Surrounding the village would have been two or three large fields, divided up into strips, and shared by the villagers. Horses or oxen ploughed these fields and this work left large banks and hollows, known as ridge and furrow. The remains of such fields can be seen in many places across the countryside even today *(Lacey & Danzinger, 1999)*.

A Time of Change

During the 14th century, life in the country had been badly affected by the Black Death, which reached England in June of 1348 and killed 40–60% of the population. There were also changes in the climate. The weather became wetter and colder, which made farming more difficult. There were also changes in the organisation of farming. Instead of farming small strips of land scattered across several large fields, these strips were increasingly lumped together into larger blocks making ploughing and harvesting easier. While this was a positive development, in some places powerful families and monasteries were able to manipulate this reorganisation of the fields for their own advantage.

By the end of the medieval period a thousand years had passed and life in 15th-century England was very different from life in the 5th century. Although for most people life was still dominated by agriculture, there were an increasing number of towns concentrating on trade, and specialised industries that would dominate the country from the 15th century onward *(Lacey & Danzinger, 1999)*.

As well as the great noble families, the church had become one of the most important landowners, although its power would have mostly disappeared by the end of the 16th century. However, these changes were as nothing compared with those that were about to begin in the post-medieval period.

Eltham Palace North Bridge – southeast face

Medieval Timeline

What else was happening during this time?

750 BC–AD 43	Iron Age Britain. Roman general Julius Caesar raids south east England 55 BC. Romans arrive in AD 43.
400–499 = 5th century	Romans leave England around AD 410. (The coverage of this book begins). Rome falls in 476. Dark Ages (early medieval period) begin.
500–599 = 6th century	Saxons are settled in southern England by this time.
600–699 = 7th century	Edwin of Northumbria is the first Christian king in the north of England.
700–799 = 8th century	Offa becomes King of Mercia. He orders the construction of a defensive earthwork between Mercia and Powys, now known as Offa's Dyke; it still more or less defines the border between England and Wales.
800–899 = 9th century	The Danes capture York. The reign of Alfred the Great, King of Wessex.
900–999 = 10th century	Aethelstan is crowned King of Wessex. He is generally accepted as the first king of all England.
1000–1099 = 11th century	Middle Ages begin. Norman invasion. Domesday Book.
1100–1199 = 12th century	Henry I is crowned in Westminster Abbey. Population of London exceeds 30,000 for the first time. Richard I dies and is succeeded by his brother John.
1200–1299 = 13th century	John I signs the Magna Carta. Work starts on Salisbury Cathedral. Edward I invades Scotland and takes the Stone of Destiny from Scone to Westminster.
1300–1399 = 14th century	Battle of Bannockburn. The Hundred Years War begins. The Black Death arrives in England. The Peasants Revolt begins.
1400–1499 = 15th century	Battle of Agincourt. The Wars of the Roses begin. William Caxton publishes the first printed book in England. The Renaissance begins in England. Christopher Columbus sails for the 'New World' in 1492.
1500–1536 = 16th century	Dissolution of the monasteries. (The coverage of this book ends).

MEDIEVAL BRIDGES

Criteria for Inclusion

There are many hundreds of bridges in England that could lay claim to the title of medieval. Most villages, towns, and counties are justifiably proud of their 'medieval' bridge but have a quite soft definition of the term. It was therefore necessary to establish a set of criteria by which a structure was included in this book. Those criteria are:

1. The original structure's build date falls between AD 410 and AD 1536.
2. The bridge has some historical significance.
3. It is architecturally and visually interesting.
4. Its position is within, or forms the border of, England.
5. An identifiable and significant portion of the medieval bridge remains intact.
6. The structure (or its remains) is still standing and is publicly accessible.
7. The bridge spans a river, riverbed, moat, or stream.

Chronology and Dating

Establishing a chronology and assigning an accurate build date to English medieval bridges is particularly problematic. The essential function and great cost of bridges ensured that they were periodically widened and occasionally completely rebuilt for the needs of the day. Most medieval bridges that we see today have been altered several times and, in many cases, have only parts that are medieval. The medieval bridges in this book are rarely the work of a single architectural period and it is not uncommon to find bridges exhibiting building styles that span hundreds of years, all of which can make dating them difficult. Thus, bridges or constituent parts of them can be hard to assign even to a particular century, let alone to a specific point within that century. Most late 16th- and 17th-century bridges tended to carry on with the general architectural style, dimensions and building techniques of medieval bridges, so it is impossible to be precise about whether certain bridges are of before or after the stated coverage of this book. A few bridges that are regarded by some as early 16th century have been included, unless there is a specific reason for assuming that nothing of the present fabric is likely to predate 1536.

Some bridges, such as the major urban ones, have documents concerning them in which a bridge may be mentioned as existing as of a certain date. These might be ecclesiastical records, repair costs accounts, chronicles of royal visits, flood histories, or property inheritance proceedings. All sources will be at least secondary if not tertiary or even further removed and at a certain point become historical 'hearsay'. However frustrating or helpful these are for a few bridges, most have little in the way of historical documentation and even when there are trustworthy credentials, any dates discovered require interpreting.

As historical researchers know, dating conventions in English texts can be problematic and these problems can become quite complicated in the case of medieval documents. For example, medieval charters are commonly dated by specifying the weekday, a nearby religious feast day, and the year of the monarch's reign – a convention that clearly has little in common with the modern system of day, month, and calendar year. There were at least six methodologies for dating documents during the medieval period:

1. The civil year versus the historical year
   In England, from about the late 12th century until 1751 the civil, ecclesiastical, and legal year began on 25 March, nearly three months later than the historical year.

2. Regnal years
   From the late 12th century, it became standard practice to date civil documents by the regnal year, that is, the year of the monarch's reign. (The use of anno domini persisted in ecclesiastical documents, and in some private charters.)

3. Exchequer dating
   To complicate regnal dating further, the medieval Exchequer used a different system of regnal years.

4. Religious festivals
   From the 13th century, rather than specifying a day of the month, medieval documents were often dated relative to a nearby saint's day or other religious festival.

5. Moveable feasts
   A further complication arises when the document is dated by reference to Easter or one of the associated feasts, which fall on a different date each year.

6. Roman-style dating
   And finally, a system sometimes used was the Roman one of specifying days of the month as so many days before the following Kalends, Nones, or Ides.

It should also be noted that in early medieval times documents were rarely dated at all. Thus, private charters are commonly dated only from the time of Edward I, and even royal charters are often undated in the 12th century and before. In these cases, or with the absence of any documentation at all, dating becomes a matter of detective work, based on a bridge's architectural stylistic features and knowledge from other sources.

Bridges and Medieval Road Networks

After the period of Roman occupation, the road system of England developed rapidly and organically, growing routes to meet the economic needs of smaller communities and towns *(Taylor, 1979)*. During this period, a new road system developed which built upon, but was significantly different from, its Roman predecessor and which survived fairly intact until the 20th century. Trade routes expanded inland from seaports and grew internally between population centres. They crossed great distances and connected people both economically and culturally and, for the first time, included smaller villages. Minor trade routes sprouted from earlier Roman roads, like smaller branches from a tree limb. As they developed, the challenges of a road system in an environment as wet as England became apparent. The trials presented by the water features of the landscape were addressed by fords, bridges, long causeways, and ferry points. These became a key characteristic of the experience of medieval travel *(Harrison, 2004)*.

Whether Roman or English, the great bulk of medieval bridge-sites and fording points in England had been established by the middle of the 13th century. The previous 200 years had witnessed enormous economic growth and an unprecedented increase in the population, requiring ever greater movement of goods and improved road networks. The focus of effort thereafter became the creation of reliable ways of crossing obstacles, such as rivers and low wetland. To address this need, many large stone and small packhorse bridges had been built by 1530 and efforts to increase the capacity of the road transport infrastructure concentrated on the improvement of existing river crossings with limited new bridge locations. After this time, although bridges were rebuilt and widened, few new bridges were built at new locations. In aggregate those 14th- and 15th-century developments constitute the most substantial investment made to the road network between the Roman period and the turnpikes of the 17th century *(Albert, 1972)*.

Bridges and river crossings fixed the English road network in the landscape, and once established it proved remarkably durable (see the Gough Map on page 296). The medieval bridge network appears to have been able to meet the trade and movement requirements of the country up to the eve of the Industrial Revolution; thus the number of bridges in the mid-18th century was approximately the same as in the Middle Ages.

As towns and territories developed economically, the building of bridges, in particular monumental stone bridges, was an economic and political statement. Bridges may have been built in response to ongoing needs but once in place they exerted a lasting influence on the shape and character of the local and regional transport network. Medieval bridges and river crossings were therefore a key long-term influence on the fundamental underpinnings of the urban, commercial, and social development of the country *(Sheldon, 1928)*.

Basic Components of a Medieval Bridge

There is a glossary at the back of this book that will help you understand the terminology of bridge construction. Like every subject, bridges have their own vocabulary and some of it has been used in the information provided about each bridge.

Whether medieval or modern, the components of all bridges, however complex or simple, fall into two large categories: superstructure (those elements above the deck/roadway) and substructure (those below the deck/roadway).

The superstructure is comprised of the slab (carriageway), parapets, and structures on the bridge such as a chapel or toll house. The superstructure bears the load passing over the span and transmits the weight caused by the vehicle or pedestrian to the substructure *(Burke, 1950)*.

The substructure is comprised of foundations, piers, abutments, and wing walls, which are provided to transmit the load of the superstructure to the earth. These are known as bearings and are part of the substructure.

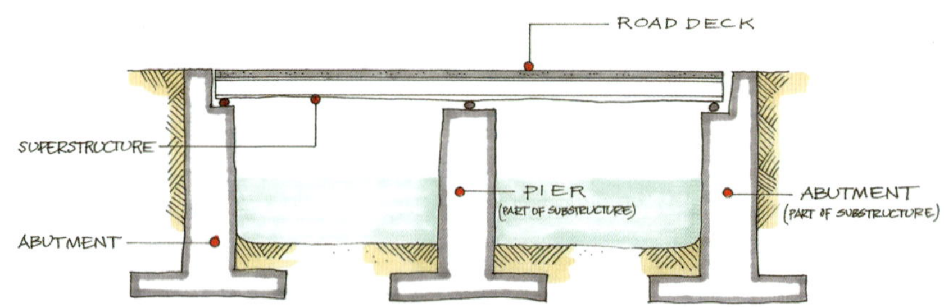

SUPERSTRUCTURE & SUBSTRUCTURE

The substructure is comprised of foundations, piers, abutments, and wing walls which are provided to transmit the load of the superstructure to the earth. These are known as bearings and are part of the substructure.

The abutments of a bridge alone may not have enough strength to take the load the superstructure places directly on them. This is especially true if the load requirement is high, or the span is long. To support these loads, additional bearings such as piers need to be constructed to help carry the load from the deck downward and distribute it evenly over the substructure material such as earth or stone *(History of Bridges, 2020)*.

Medieval Bridges and the Church

It would be impossible to understand the evolution of bridge building in England without at least a cursory study of the influence that monasteries had on life in post-Roman times. Monasticism, particularly in the five centuries after the Norman conquest in 1066, had a huge effect on all aspects of medieval life, including agriculture, economics, civil structure, and not least, the transport infrastructure. The commonly held picture of monks devoted only to prayer and worship couldn't be further from the reality of daily life. While devotion was certainly a major part of their belief, so was farming, community service, manual labour, and construction.

The two monastic orders that dominated medieval life in England were the Cistercians and the Benedictines. Benedict gave his name to the first great order of monks whose original abbey in England was established in Canterbury by the first Archbishop of Canterbury in 597. They became known as the 'Black Monks' because of their dark habits. Five hundred years later, in 1098, the Cistercians broke from the Benedictines and established their first order in Citeaux just south of Dijon in France. They felt that the worldly excesses and loss of morality by their Benedictine brethren could no longer be tolerated. They abandoned the black garments of the Benedictines in favour of undyed woollen habits bleached in the sun and became known as the 'whitefriars'. The first Cistercian abbey in England was formed in Waverley in 1128, followed within a decade by Tintern in Wales and then the great northern abbeys of Rievaulx (1132) in Yorkshire, and Fountains (1132) in North Yorkshire.

The Norman conquest had changed everything about religion in England and the decades following 1066 signalled a boom time for monasticism in the country. Between 'The Conquest' in 1066 and 'The Dissolution' in 1536, the number of monasteries in England went from 40 Benedictine and 10 Cistercian, to over 500. It is no coincidence that during this 470-year period bridge building also boomed. The medieval period was the golden age of both church and bridge building since monasteries were not only centres of religious worship, but they were also important commercial enterprises, selling their surplus and purchasing needed raw goods. Many were strategically located on or nearby important trade routes. Often, they were the largest employers in the area with close links to the economic life of nearby towns. In other words, they had an economic imperative to ensure that trade flourished and the trade networks and transport infrastructure that supported it was developed and maintained. Bridge building thrived and the correlation of passage to another kind of 'other side' wasn't lost on the medieval church.

Even after the reformation, the church was involved in the financing, design, maintenance, and occasionally the physical construction of roads and bridges. In Durham, for example, bridge building was the express responsibility of the bishop, and this was only one of many medieval cities where bridges had an open connection with the cathedral.

The connection between the church and the building and maintenance of bridges, and the provision of chapels on or beside them, was so strong during the whole of the medieval period, up to the time of the dissolution, that studying them together allows an insight into their design and cultural role as well as their economic impact.

Bridge Chapels

Chapels were occasionally built on bridges to be available for the spiritual needs of travellers, who would give thanks for safe arrival in a town after a long and perilous journey. Travel during the medieval period was a dangerous endeavour and many lives were lost in the process. During the Middle Ages, bridge chapels were not uncommon and could be found at such places as Leeds, Bristol, and, of course, there was the chapel dedicated to St Thomas Becket on the Old London Bridge. Today, however, there are only four such chapels remaining in England. These are at Bradford-on-Avon, St Ives (Cambridgeshire), Rotherham, and Wakefield. All of these are included in these books.

In addition to the spiritual needs fulfilled by bridge chapels, some (such as the bridge at Wakefield) also performed a more practical role, strengthening the structure of the bridge itself. Before the Reformation, bridge chapels were known as chantry chapels, so-called because each chapel was served by its own priest, or priests, whose duty was to chant masses or dirges for the souls of the dead. According to George Henry Cook, in *Mediaeval Chantries and Chantry Chapels*, 'masses were sung for the well-being of travellers and for the souls of the victims of highway violence' *(Cook, 1947)*. The chantry priests also assisted the parish priest in services and other work when called upon. Many cathedrals and large parish churches also contained a chantry chapel.

The 1547 Act of Dissolution of the Colleges and Chantries pensioned off the priests and left the chapels redundant. Many chantry chapels rapidly fell into decay, and most were eventually lost to the need for building materials or widening projects. Some bridge chapels survived, however, purely for pragmatic reasons; they may have ensured stability as a structural part of their bridges, and many took on a variety of secular uses. It is the industrial part of Yorkshire that is fortunate enough to have two of the surviving bridge chapels: one at Rotherham, the other at Wakefield on a bridge over the River Calder, both of whom took on purely practical functions *(Green, 2002)*. After the dissolution of the monasteries in 1536, many bridge chapels were converted to other purposes, such as lockups or warehouses, which, ironically, prolonged their survival.

The Economics of Medieval Bridges

In the Middle Ages the cost of a stone bridge was roughly equivalent to the cost of a substantial parish church. Bridges are, and always have been, painfully expensive to build and maintain, but thankfully for us, this did not deter the medieval bridge builders, because throughout the Middle Ages, bridges were vital to support trade route-based commerce and the economics of England. A huge amount of finance and effort was invested by the medieval monasteries and nobles in constructing and maintaining the necessary transport infrastructure for trade. The construction of bridges was central to that challenging task, requiring the provision of suitable materials, engineering expertise, and physical labour.

To build a stone bridge required generous patrons, either political figures or wealthy merchants, and bridges were generally built by boroughs, manorial Lords, or monasteries, though some were paid for by wealthy and public-spirited individuals. Because building a bridge was seen as a public service, their maintenance was often considered a charitable act, like repairing or maintaining a church, and philanthropic citizens often contributed to their upkeep, sometimes via their wills.

Although much of the labour was provided by local communities, a significant part of the material costs came from gifts or bequests from merchants who stood to profit most from reliable bridges. Such gifts might go to a guild, a bridge trust, or some other body that maintained the bridge. Because bridges were of such strategic importance, an economic value could be placed on them, and people wishing to cross a bridge, or take goods across, often had to pay a toll to do so. This was known as 'pontage'. In some respects, medieval bridges were the equivalent of customs points at airports today.

After construction, who was then responsible for their upkeep? The answer to that question changes over the centuries, and the way in which it changes reveals much about law and power in medieval England. Royal grants of land could include a stipulation to do bridgework in return. The Statute of Bridges (1530) decreed that: 'in the absence of any traditional duty upon an individual, parish, hundred, corporation or other body to keep a particular bridge in repair, it should be maintained by the county' *(Naoum, 2012)*.

Medieval Bridge Types

There are many ways of classifying bridges into certain types based on criteria such as materials, function, level of crossing, flood level, permanence, etc. However, unless you are an engineer, types of bridges are usually determined by the substructure. In this book nearly all the bridges are arch type with a few beam bridges in the form of clappers. Some bridges may be combinations of types.

One thing England is not short of is rivers, streams, and brooks, which, when travelling, all need crossing by one means or another. In medieval England there were basically three ways to cross such water courses.

1. a ford
2. stepping-stones (often known as 'Steps')
3. wooden or masonry bridges

The medieval wooden bridge structures (many Roman) are, of course, long gone but numerous masonry medieval bridges remain for our study and enjoyment. These are further broken into three categories:

1. clapper bridges
2. packhorse bridges
3. masonry arch bridges

Each of these methods for crossing a water course are briefly discussed below.

Ford

A ford is simply a shallow spot in the river or stream where people and beasts are able to wade across. These were undoubtably the earliest river crossings and many are still in use today, used by tractors, cars, and children in the summer. The Romans introduced the practice of paving important fords with large flat stones to ensure their ability to cross without affecting the participants or the riverbed.

Most often, fords are naturally occurring rather than man made and as such can be said to have influenced the choice of location for many of England's towns and villages. Indeed, the suffix 'ford' appears in the names of a great number of English settlements, of which Oxford (the place where oxen crossed the river) is perhaps the most well-known. However, many far smaller settlements appear to have developed because of their proximity to a point in which a river was naturally fordable.

Although fords are the cheapest and simplest form of river crossing, they are unreliable and can become impassable when a river is in spate, during times of flood, or even after a period of heavy rain. Fords on estuarine rivers were also subject to the tides and thus also regularly impassable. Although largely replaced by bridges in the middle and later medieval periods, fords still exist in great number in rural areas such as Exmoor, as the means of crossing small water courses. Several bridges in this book have been built adjacent to an ancient ford: the bridge for pedestrian and animal use and the ford for horses and carts (modern cars).

Stepping-Stone Bridges

Smaller crossings may be achieved by strategically placing large stones in the river that allow people and animals to 'step' from stone to stone. These were some of the earliest and simplest forms of constructed crossings. There were severe depth limitations to these crossings and flood water often washed away the entire enterprise. Stepping-stone bridges are often confused with clapper bridges (below), but they are not the same. Officially stepping-stone bridges have open spaces between each of the stones or piers.

A 'cart clapper bridge' at Chalfont St Giles, Buckinghamshire

Clapper Bridges

Tarr Steps stamp of 1968 (Public Domain)

To overcome deeper and wider rivers, 'clapper' bridges were employed. This ancient form of bridge is found mostly in the upland moors regions of England like Dartmoor, Exmoor, and the Yorkshire moors. Formed by large, flat slabs of undressed stone supported on stone piers, these bridges, such as Kebles Clapper Bridge in Gloucestershire, are often thought to be prehistoric in date, but most were erected in the medieval period. Gravity alone holds everything in place without the benefit of mortar. The name 'clapper bridge' comes from the medieval Latin *claperius*, which means 'pile of stones'. They are the earliest type of 'beam' bridge and some smaller clapper bridges, may have the slabs laid directly on the bank of the stream and are known as 'cart clappers'.

In some cases, there are two slabs lying side-by-side, thus forming a much wider span, which allowed bigger carts to cross.

Probably the most famous and biggest clapper bridge is the one in Exmoor National Park called the Tarr Steps, across the River Barle, which is purported to date back to prehistoric times, but others put construction of 'The Steps' at around AD 1400. The Tarr Steps have been commemorated in a stamp issue of 1968.

A TYPICAL PACKHORSE BRIDGE Mark Cowie

Medieval packhorse and donkey, from Hortus Deliciarum. *Illustration by Herrad of Landsberg 1167–1185, 12th century, when packing was a major means of transport of goods (Public Domain)*

According to local legend, the Devil himself built the Tarr Steps so that he could sunbathe on the slabs.

Packhorse Bridges

Packhorse bridges are ones that were built so that packhorses and their loads could cross an obstruction, which was almost always a river or fast flowing stream. Packhorse bridges had certain characteristics that separated them from other bridges. A genuine packhorse bridge is defined as being 1.8 metres wide or less, usually built of undressed or roughly dressed stone, having no or very low parapets to allow unhindered passage by animals with pannier packs, and to have known packhorse associations.

The use of packhorses to carry goods goes back to the transport of salt, which was a very important product from early times. The peak period for packhorses was from 1350 to 1500 when all manner of goods were carried, including fish, as well as corn, coal, charcoal and lead, tin, and iron ores. These were all carried in panniers, which were slung on wooden pack frames on the side of the horse. To ensure that there was adequate clearance, the parapets on packhorse bridges were very low or entirely absent. When the trade ceased, parapets were often added to the bridge for the safety of pedestrians. Over the years many routes have either disappeared or been upgraded to roads and in the latter case this normally meant that the bridge disappeared. Whilst they are still commonly found across southern England, particularly in places like Exmoor and Dartmoor, they were also constructed in the far north of England in the Yorkshire Moors.

Masonry Arch Bridges

A masonry arch bridge is the most technically advanced of the earliest types of bridges and was by far the most common type of advanced bridging for major river crossings in medieval England. The word masonry, within this context, is used as a verb referring to the construction process using stone.

Arch bridges came into use over 3,000 years ago, with the earliest examples found in China, and they remained common until the Industrial Revolution and the invention of advanced materials. They are very strong structures, because the weight of structure and load does not push straight down on the bridge, but instead the thrust is carried outward along the curve of the arch to the supports at both ends. The ends, which are known as abutments, carry the load and keep the arch and the roadway above it in place.

This traditional method of constructing bridges (as we would recognise them today) dates back to early medieval times and involved building an arch, or a series of arches from wedge-shaped pieces of stone (voussoirs), around a wooden frame (false work or centring), which was removed once the keystone of the arch was put in place. The arches were built onto piers or abutments on either side, allowing a relatively wide river to be crossed using several arches or spans. The 14th-century bridge across the River Medway at Aylesford in Kent is a good example of this traditional method of bridge construction.

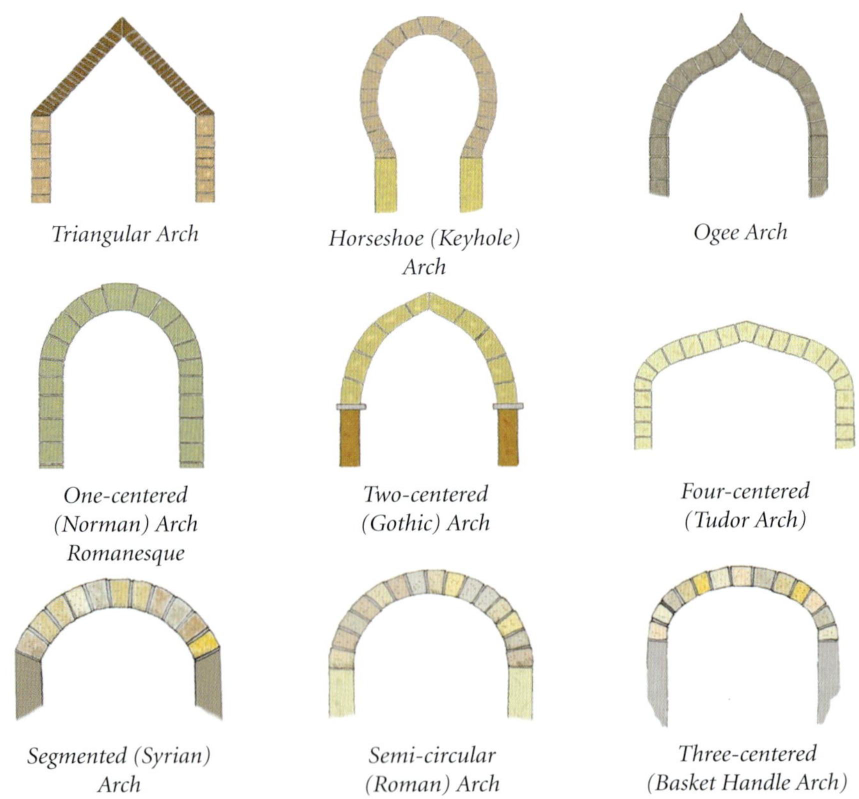

There are many types and styles of masonry arches and their architectural style changed throughout the medieval period. Those changing styles have enabled architectural historians to place bridges with uncertain build dates into broad historic periods. For example, early medieval bridges are often characterised by Gothic pointed or ogival style arches while later Norman-inspired bridges preferred a simpler semi-circular round arch, also known as a Roman arch. Many earlier medieval bridge arches utilised rib supports in the vaulting.

The arch types illustrated above are explained throughout this book as they occur in the bridge photos.

Medieval Bridge Builders

One of the fascinations of looking at and travelling across older bridges, is imagining the story of who built them and how. The complexity of medieval bridges varied greatly and ranged from quite simple clapper bridges and small packhorse bridges to ornate masonry wonders of the urban multi-span stone bridge. Often broad and flat flood plains were dissected by multiple river arms

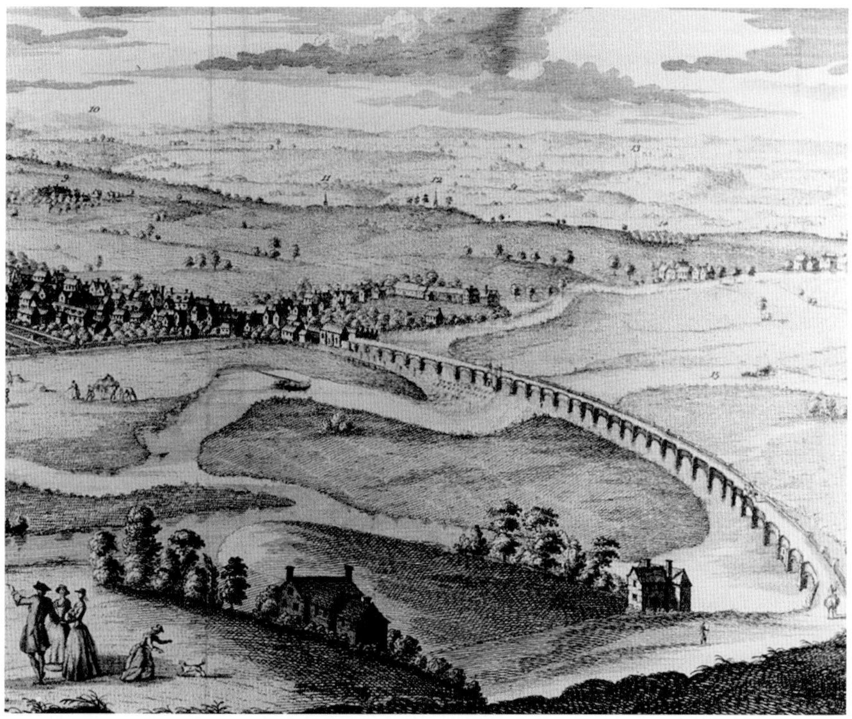

Old Trent Bridge soon after building in 1170, a print produced by Samuel and Nathaniel Buck in 1732, held in the Burton Library (Public Domain)

A view of part of the intended bridge at Blackfriars London, 1902, George Ellis-Modern Practical Joinery (Public Domain)

and required multiple bridges connected by causeways, or bridges of great length. Differences in bridge design were necessitated by the great dissimilarities in the landscape, and the bridging point was often dictated by the location of solid bedrock in the riverbed, or an island between the branches capable of bearing supporting piers. Such was the case at Burton-on-Trent whose 'Great Bridge' was 471 metres long and contained extensive flood arches and causeways *(Simpson, 2020).*

The environment within which bridges were built was very demanding, requiring expertise in hydrology, geology, surveying, and fundraising, as well as the construction arts themselves. In addition to masons, there were quarrymen, boatmen, carpenters, pile drivers, excavators, and overseers. Hundreds of unskilled labourers, usually hired locally, were needed to keep the supply of rubble, stone, and timber to hand.

Carpenters

Even a simple semi-circular voussoir arch could not be built without faux-works known as centring, because the structure would not stand up until the keystone was in place at the top. Temporary centring structures were made of wood, and the carpenters often erected, dismantled, and re-erected the same centring on different ribs of the arch, across the barrel, until each arch rib was completed.

Timber centring was a significant part of the cost, and the same profile could only be used if all the arches were the same size. Hence differently sized arches were rare, expensive, and often the result of another factor such as unstable foundation stone or a different build date to the other arches.

Pile Drivers

The starlings and piers on which multiple arch bridges sat were constructed using cofferdams; a watertight enclosure built within the river, from which water is pumped to expose the riverbed and permit the dry construction of supporting piers.

DRIVING A PILE WITH A MAUL

A HAND RAM

This process was made possible with piles, usually tree trunks, driven into the riverbed. The Romans often made use of timber piles for their bridge construction and many remnants have been found still embedded below modern bridge structures. A specialised team of workers performed this function using a variety of rigs, a technology brought to England by the Romans. The type of rig depended on the geological strata at the build site.

These piles (vertical beams) were typically driven into the ground primarily by hand operated machines until the limits of the driving mechanism were reached and the timber could not be driven any further.

Abutments to support the bridge on each side of the river had to be constructed on solid foundations with anchored masonry, and often short wooden piles were driven into the foundation layer in advance of the masonry.

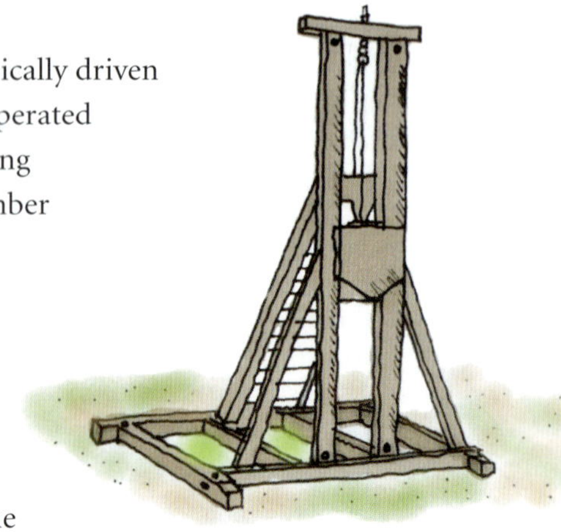

PRINCIPLE TYPE OF HAND-POWER PILEDRIVER

Masons

The early mason was a builder, architect, and engineer, rolled into one. Master masons were the high paid consultants of the period: prosperous middle-class professionals in charge of other craftsmen with support from qualified journeymen (day-wage or *journée*) and apprentices. The master mason was both the architect and Master of Works. Well-known names were in great demand, even internationally.

Their journeymen colleagues were divided into bankers, carvers, and fixers

- Bankers mainly worked on site, dressing and shaping the stone. Some bankers also worked at the quarry.
- Carvers applied art and design; they were effectively sculptors, and usually employed for more ornate bridgework.
- Fixers were occupied raising the stones and putting them in place. Sandstone and granite blocks were extracted from a local quarry in dimensions that matched the natural geologic layers.

Quarrymen

Quarrymen were also very skilled craftsmen. They worked in groups called 'marrows', assisted by unskilled workmen, in the process of extracting ('winning') the stone. Bonfires were applied to expand the rock. Crowbars, feathers, and wedges were then used. The finer ashlar blocks were then cut with saws sprinkled with a mixture of iron filings and sand. These were 'sounded' or lightly struck with a hammer; if a stone rang like a bell it was good; if it had a dull thud, it was rejected. The cost of transporting the stone

Ashlar Masonry

In ashlar masonry, all the stones are cut and dressed, or worked, so they have the same shape, size, and surface texture. When stone is first hewn out of a quarry it is rough and random. Stoneworkers must use chisels and other tools to refine the stone to a more finished appearance. The stone blocks used in ashlar masonry are very different than random uncut stones, which are referred to as rubble. In fact, ashlar masonry is sometimes referred to as 'dressed stone'.

When building a bridge, the ashlar blocks are laid in horizontal courses, or used as voussoirs. The stones have smooth, parallel faces, and they fit together tightly with very little mortar. Because ashlar masonry stones fit so tightly, the resulting structures are strong and sturdy. But it takes a long time to prepare the stones and build with them, and the process is expensive.

Scholars don't know where and when ashlar masonry was developed, but it's been used for thousands of years. Examples of ashlar masonry have been found on pyramids in ancient Egypt and on structures in classical Greece. Ashlar blocks made of local limestone and sandstone form part of the Knossos Palace in Crete, built by the Minoan civilisation between 2000 and 1500 BC. Later, the Mycenaeans used ashlar masonry in citadel and wall construction. Ashlar masonry wasn't only found in the Near East and Asia. In 15th-century South America, expert builders for the Incan civilisation used ashlar masonry for structures at Macchu Pichu and Cusco. These walls were so carefully constructed that despite time and earthquakes, they are still standing.

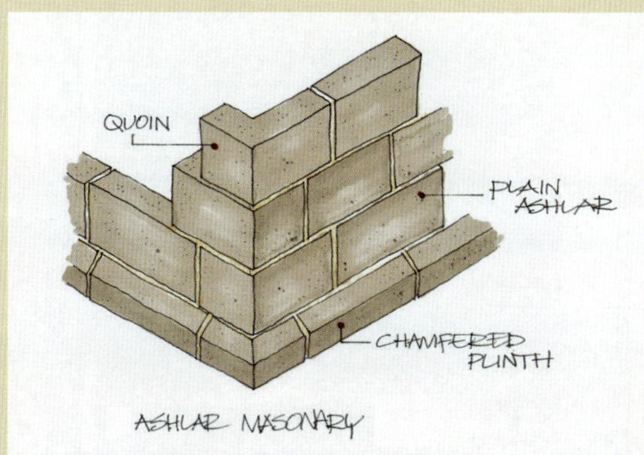

could be almost as much as quarrying it, so local quarries were always preferred. One third of extracted stone might be good for ashlar, with two thirds being allocated to rubble or waste. Rubble blocks were roughly dressed by hammer and often squared. Ashlar was usually reserved for the voussoirs, whereas rubble was used for the spandrels and abutments, though this was not always the case.

Mortar was made from quicklime or slaked lime and sand, which took some time to set as it slowly turned back into calcium carbonate. The speed at which it would 'go off', or set, was determined by the amount of impurity; a faster set was needed in the cold northern climate, particularly for pointing. However, with ashlar, lime putty (very pure hydrated lime) was mixed with whitening (chalk), linseed oil and sometimes horsehair *(Simpson, 2020).*

Islands in the Stream

Multi-span bridges always presented the extra challenge of constructing piers and starlings in mid-stream. Their construction was carried out in a difficult physical environment and, of course, with the engineering challenge of creating a substantial footing underwater. Four techniques were employed.

Cofferdams

As mentioned above, many major bridging projects used 'cofferdams', temporary enclosures erected in the river that could be sealed off and drained, to allow the creation of a dry working space for laying foundations. When possible, a solid rock foundation in the riverbed was chosen and a site without substantial tidal range was preferred. A small tidal range in shallow water might permit the Roman approach of constructing a wooden cofferdam on the riverbed. In this case, a pile driving ram was employed to drive a double set of piles into the mud, tightly adjacent to each other, until a full semi-watertight pointed ovoid was completed, perhaps 15 metres in diameter; then the central pool was emptied by chains of men with ladders and scoops.

Starlings (Islands)

Starlings (sometimes called plinths) are the artificial islands created through the building of a cofferdam. Rubble was poured into the chamber of the cofferdam on each receding tide and finally filled with a crude concrete mix. The stone bridge piers were built on top of the starling created by the cofferdam. This arrangement is commonly seen below English bridges and was clearly recorded at Barnstaple and Exeter.

Branders

A more common approach, and useful for a significant tidal height, was to sink a large prefabricated wooden frame or 'brander' made up of horizontally connected planks. This frame would be filled directly with rubble and sunk on the required spot. In this way, a different form of starling was created that had no vertical piles. There are reliable records describing a variation of this where a 'wooden boat' on which the pier was already partially constructed in ashlar, was sunk when it reached low-tide level height.

Diversion

One further approach was that of diverting the whole river while foundations were being built. This may have been less of a last resort than one might think. Jervoise describes a variation suitable for a meandering river on a lowland basin: the bridge would be built on dry land in advance of a permanent diversion of the river *(Jervoise, 1930)*.

Cutwaters

In all of the above cases, protection against scouring (the undercutting of the foundations by the force of the current) was needed in the form of something that could split the river flow, diverting it to either side of the starling's foundations. These were known as 'cutwaters' and they took a variety of forms but usually were pointed triangular or rounded.

Most multi-span bridges were built with cutwaters on every pier facing the current, to provide the best protection against the destructive scouring effect of the river flow. In the 15th century it was realised that these were just as important on the downstream side and that rounded cutwaters on the downstream side prevented 'eddying', another cause of scouring. The single most important element of maintenance was the constant attention to the risk of scouring.

Longevity

Most major medieval bridges in England were built by skilled masons, and over 200 of them are still standing. Many of the medieval structures in this book have remained upright for more than 600 years. Many more were destroyed in the 19th century, not because they were an engineering risk, but only because they were too narrow for two wagons to pass. Rochester's 171-metres-long medieval stone bridge on the Medway remained so solid that it had to be blown up multiple times in 1856 in order to be dismantled. These old bridges frequently spanned wide, deep, fast-flowing rivers with frequent flooding, and yet stood their ground. Their longevity was largely a function of repair to the foundations: constant attention to starlings or branders, to avoid scouring, and regular inspection of abutments, which are always at risk of vehicular damage.

Today these old masonry arch bridges are often expected to carry modern traffic. Indeed, even considering packhorse bridges, of the 100 bridges in this book 72 of these pre-1500 bridges remain on the English road network of southern England. In all cases, the implied live loads are far beyond the expectations of the original builders.

Bideford Long Bridge

Major Rivers in England by Length

#	River	Miles	Km	Country
1	River Severn	220	354	Wales & England
2	River Thames	215	346	England
3	River Trent	185	297	England
4	River Great Ouse	143	230	England
5	River Wye	135	215	Wales & England
6	River Ure/River Ouse, Yorkshire	129	208	England
7	River Nene	100	161	England
8	River Tweed	96	155	England & Scotland
9	River Avon, Warwickshire	96	154	England
10	River Eden, Cumbria	90	145	England
11	River Witham	82	132	England
12	River Teme	81	130	Wales & England
13	River Ribble	75	120	England
14	River Avon, Bristol	75	120	England
15	River Tyne	73	118	England
16	River Derwent, Yorkshire	72	115	England
17	River Aire	71	114	England
18	River Tees	70	113	England
19	River Medway	70	113	England
20	River Mersey	70	113	England
21	River Dee, Wales	70	112	Wales & England
22	River Don, South Yorkshire	70	112	England

Barnstaple Long Bridge

Number of Medieval Bridges in Southern England by Region and County

SOUTHEAST

Buckinghamshire (2)

- Leckhampstead Bridge
- Thornborough Bridge

Oxfordshire (9)

- Abingdon Bridge
- Burford Bridge
- Culham Bridge
- Godstow Bridge
- Lower Heyford Bridge
- New Bridge
- Ock Bridge
- Radcot Bridge
- Wallingford Bridge

London (3)

- Clattern Bridge
- Eltham Palace North Bridge
- Hanwell Bridge

Kent (7)

- Aylesford Bridge
- East Farleigh Bridge
- Hertsfield Bridges
- Laddingford Bridge
- Teston Bridge
- Twyford Bridge
- Yalding Town Bridge

Surrey (6)

- Eashing Bridges (Upper & Lower)
- Elstead Bridge
- Somerset Bridge
- Tilford East Bridge
- Tilford West Bridge
- Unstead Bridge

Hampshire (3)

- Fordingbridge Bridge
- New Arlesford Bridge
- Stony Bridge, Titchfield

West Sussex (3)

- Stopham Bridge
- Trotton Bridge
- Woolbeding Bridge

SOUTHWEST

Gloucestershire (2)

- Keble's Bridge
- King John's Bridge

Wiltshire (8)

- Barton Bridge
- Bradford-on-Avon Town Bridge
- Coombe Bissett Packhorse Bridge
- Gumstool Bridge
- Lacock Bridge
- Salisbury Crane Bridge
- Salisbury Harnham Bridge
- Salisbury Milford Bridge

Somerset (16)

- Barle Bridge
- Bow Bridge
- Bradford-on-Tone Town Bridge
- Buckland Dinham Packhorse Bridge
- Bury Bridge
- Gallox Bridge
- Haselbury Old Bridge
- Hele Bridge
- Horner Packhorse Bridge
- Ilford Bridge
- Landacre Bridge
- Stanton Drew Bridge
- Tarr Steps Bridge
- Tun Bridge
- West Luccombe Packhorse Bridge
- Wyke Champflower Bridge

Dorset (8)

- Cornford Bridge
- Crawford Bridge
- Fifehead Neville Footbridge
- Holme Bridge
- Holwell Bridge
- Place Mill Bridge
- Wareham North Bridge
- Wool Bridge

Devon (21)

- Austin's Bridge
- Aveton Gifford Bridge
- Barnstaple Long Bridge
- Bideford Long Bridge
- Clyst St Mary Bridge
- Culmstock Bridge
- Dart Bridge
- Ellerhayes Bridge
- Exe Bridge
- Harford Tavy Bridge
- Holne New Bridge
- Holne Old Bridge
- Horrabridge Bridge
- Huckworthy Bridge
- Lydford Bridge
- Plym Bridge
- Postbridge Bridge
- Rothern Bridge
- Staverton Bridge
- Stoke Canon Bridge
- Taddiport Bridge

Cornwall (12)

- Greystone Bridge
- Helland Bridge
- Horse Bridge
- Lostwithiel Bridge
- Panters Bridge
- Respryn Bridge
- Ruthern Bridge
- St Austell West Bridge
- St Thomas Packhorse Bridge
- Treverbyn Old Bridge
- Wadebridge Bridge
- Yeolm Bridge

Total = 100 medieval bridges in southern England

Historic England Listed Bridges and Structures

Listing is the term given to the practice of placing buildings, structures, monuments, parklands, gardens, battlefields, and shipwrecks on the list of protected sites in the UK. Listing carries with it a specific set of rules safeguarding certain aspects of a site or structure. There are four levels of protection afforded to these structures.

Grade II (lowest)

Grade II*

Grade I

Monument (as identified in the 'schedule' of monuments).

The final decision about listing is taken by the Secretary of State for Digital, Culture, Media, and Sport, but the process, promotion and enforcement of rules is managed by Historic England, officially entitled the Historic Buildings and Monuments Commission for England. It is an executive body of the British Government.

Historic bridges are commonly split into two categories – Grade I and Grade II listed structures. If a bridge is labelled as a listed structure, you will immediately know that historical value and some form of interest surrounds the structure. There are a number of reasons why a bridge can become listed, but as a general rule, the older a structure is, the more likely it is to be listed. The age and history of the river crossing will play a significant role in whether it is listed, as this can understandably relate to its importance *(Concrete Renovations, 2019)*.

Listed bridges will be those that are of special historical, cultural, or architectural interest, or those that are of national importance and have been deemed to be worth protecting. Similarly, every bridge built before 1700, surviving in its original condition, is automatically listed, alongside most bridges built between 1700 and 1840.

What is a Grade I Listed Bridge?

If a bridge is listed as Grade I, this is because the site is of exceptional national, architectural, or historical importance. It is rare to find a Grade I listed bridge compared to a Grade II listed site, simply because of the significance that is placed on such sites. Only 2.5% of all listed bridges in the UK fall into the Grade I category.

What is a Grade II Listed Bridge?

Grade II listed bridges are split into two categories – the majority of which are simply labelled as Grade II, while a small percentage are labelled Grade II*, as they are judged to be of particular national importance or special interest. Just under 6% of all Grade II listed bridges in the UK are listed as Grade II*, with 92% simply labelled as Grade II, as they are of special architectural interest. Any bridge or structure erected prior to 1 July 1948 can be listed.

What Does a Listed Bridge Mean?

Listing a bridge is important as it recognises the structure's historical and cultural significance. It also means that in order to make a change to the bridge that could affect its appearance, structure, or historical design, the local authority or bridge owner (if it is privately owned) must apply for listed bridge consent prior to completing any work.

Therefore, it's essential to remember that listed bridges should be celebrated for the rich history and heritage that they represent, and that they should be treated with the utmost care and respect, but this doesn't mean that they can't be changed, extended or repaired.

Scheduled Monuments

A Scheduled Monument is a historic building or site (in this case a bridge) that is included in the Schedule of Monuments kept by the Secretary of State for Digital, Culture, Media, and Sport. The procedure for scheduling is set out in the Ancient Monuments and Archaeological Areas Act, 1979. It is possible for a bridge to be both 'listed' and 'scheduled'.

Applications to schedule or de-schedule a monument are administered by Historic England, who carry out an assessment and make a recommendation to the Secretary of State. The Schedule of Monuments has over 200,000 entries (as of 2021) and includes sites such as Roman remains, burial mounds, castles, bridges, earthworks, the remains of deserted villages, and industrial sites. Monuments are not graded, but all are, by definition, considered to be of national importance. The protected site of a monument may also include any land adjoining it essential for its support and preservation.

Once a monument is scheduled, any works to it that might affect it, with few exceptions, require scheduled monument consent directly from the Secretary of State (not the local planning authority). Historic England manages the process of scheduled monument consent on behalf of the Secretary of State. Metal detecting on a Scheduled Monument is also illegal without a licence from Historic England.

National Grid Reference Numbers

The National Grid provides a unique reference system that can be applied to all Ordnance Survey (OS) maps of Great Britain, at all scales. Great Britain is covered by grid squares measuring 100 kilometres across and each grid square is identified by two capital letters, i.e., SP, TQ. The two-letter codes can be found printed within the squares in faint blue capitals on Ordnance Survey maps and can also be found in the map key. The first letter, for example 'S', denotes 500 kilometres by 500 kilometres squares and this is subdivided into 25 squares that are 100 kilometres by 100 kilometres within it, making 'ST', 'SU', 'SO' and so on.

There are four main first letters: 'S', 'T', 'N', and 'H' covering Great Britain, plus an 'O' square covering a tiny part of North Yorkshire that is usually below high tide level.

A unique National Grid reference should have this two-letter descriptor followed by the grid reference numbers within that square

A series of faint blue lines on every OS map makes up a numbered grid that is used to create the National Grid reference. This is a simple way of finding points and places on a map. You may find a variety of terms used to describe National Grid references, such as 'OS grid ref', 'grid reference', 'OS map ref', or simply just 'map reference'. While the correct term for these is 'National Grid reference', these terms all mean the same thing, and grid references can be given in a number of different formats.

The numbers going across the map from left to right are called eastings, and go up in value eastwards, and the numbers going up the map from bottom to top are called northings, because they go up in a northward direction.

There are four main types of grid reference:

1) four-figure grid reference, such as '19 45', indicates a 1 kilometre by 1 kilometre square on the map;
2) six-figure grid reference, such as '192 454', indicates a 100 metres by 100 metres square on the map;
3) eight-figure grid reference, such as '1926 4548', indicates a 10 metres by 10 metres square on the map; and
4) ten-figure grid reference, such as '19267 45487', indicates a 1 metre by 1 metre square on the map.

In practice, it's the six-digit grid reference number that is most commonly used, although the more digits used the more precise the location. GPS devices often specify at least eight-digit grid reference numbers. In this work I have tried to use the ten-digit reference numbers for each bridge wherever they are available.

To use this number with ease, go to **https://gridreferencefinder.com/os.php** and copy & paste the grid reference into their search engine, and the location will pop up on the map.

The Bridge Tours

One of the purposes of this book is to encourage people to go and have a look at these historic and often beautiful bridges. Nothing fosters ongoing appreciation like a visit. To that end, I have organised the medieval bridges of southern England into 21 separate tours roughly by county, although a few cross borders. I have driven all these tours myself and believe that each can be done in a day from the starting point of the tour. Directions are given that connect the bridges in sequence, but certainly each can be visited individually. Not only are the National Grid reference numbers given, but the postcodes for satnav guidance to each bridge are provided. Points of interest and local amenities are also included to make each stop an enjoyable and relaxing day out.

The Star Rating System

One of the most frequent questions I am asked is, 'Which is the best bridge?'. It is a bit of an impossible question to answer since everyone will have differing ideas on defining the word 'best'. Some people will be interested in the architectural aspects of a bridge while others will value the historical record. Nonetheless, I have put together a five-star system of evaluating a bridge based on the following criteria, in no particular order of priority:

- **Architectural interest**
  What were the engineering and design challenges faced?
  Are there unusual and interesting responses to those challenges?
  What materials were used and why?
  Is the bridge architecturally representative of its build date?
- **Amount of original fabric remaining.** Every bridge in this work has been, to a lesser or greater extent, altered, maintained, and had bits replaced over the centuries.
  How extensive are the non-original parts?
  Has maintenance of the bridge been sympathetic to its history and original materials?

Is the original bridge entombed inside modern widening facades?
How much of the original structure is still visible?

- **Historical significance**
  Has the bridge played a significant role in the history of the country, town, or county?
  Were battles fought nearby?
  What effect did it have on the everyday life of those around it?
  Does the local authority celebrate the bridge as a historical asset?
- **Accessibility**
  How easy is it for a visitor to get to the bridge?
  – Is it now on private land or surrounded by it?
  – Is it on a busy main highway with no possibility of visiting it?
  Has it been incorporated into modern activities or places that allow people to appreciate it, such as a footpath, river walk, or green space?
- **Current condition of the structure**
  Does it appear on the Historic England 'At Risk' register?
  Is it still being maintained?
  Is it still in good shape?
- **Setting**
  Unfortunately, several of the bridges in this book have been swallowed up by rampant urban development and treated poorly by their changing environment. Others have been allowed to disappear into a wilderness of overgrowth and deficient river management.
  The reverse of that is that many still sit in an open setting surrounded by beautiful scenery.
- **Beauty**
  I struggled with whether to include this as an evaluation category because it is just so nebulous to apply – 'in the eye of the beholder' and all. However, I just could not escape that some bridges are simply beautiful to behold because of their engineering marvel, design and style, and the setting within which they exist. With many it is obvious that design considerations were not completely functional, the engineers were also concerned with how it looked and sat in the landscape. They wanted to create a thing of beauty.

I also wanted to create a system of allowing the users of these tours to evaluate which bridges were important to them. To provide a way of making informed decisions about which bridges to visit. Of course, with any rating system, there will be discussions and arguments about the accuracy of the assigned stars and the basis on which they were dispensed.

Elstead Bridge – south face

Medieval Bridges of Southern England

(Arranged Alphabetically in Tours)

We build too many walls and not enough bridges

Joseph Fort Newton (1880–1950)

1 BUCKINGHAMSHIRE & NORTH OXFORDSHIRE TOUR

Using Buckingham as the starting point, these bridges are arranged from east to west and include Leckhampstead Bridge, Thornborough Bridge, and Lower Heyford Bridge.

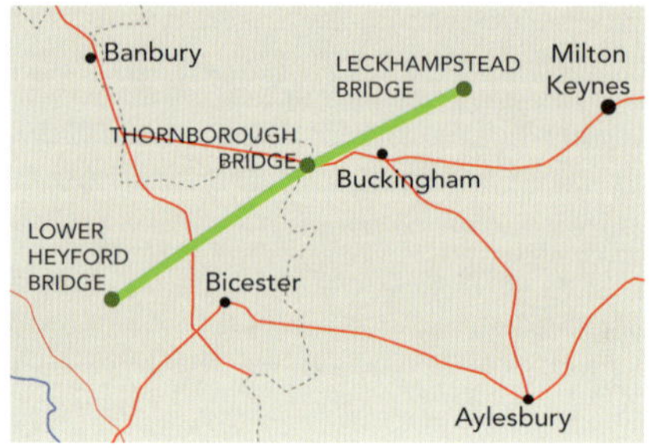

1 Leckhampstead Bridge ★★

Bridge Name: Leckhampstead Bridge

Location: Thornborough – about 3 miles northeast of Buckingham.
Use postcode MK18 5EZ for your satnav.

Setting: Rural / Countryside

OS Ref: SP 73841 35493

Crosses: River Great Ouse

Orientation: North / South

County: Buckinghamshire

Length: 12 metres

Bridge Type: Multiple Arch

Materials: Brick (one of the few brick bridges in this book)

Traffic: Pedestrian and Road

Build Date: 16th century (Reconstructed in the 1950s)

Authority: Transport for Buckinghamshire

Designation: Grade II Listed (at risk)

Directions: From Buckingham

- Follow the A422 east out of Buckingham towards Milton Keynes for a couple of miles northeast to the second road on right signposted Thornborough.
- Turn right and follow for ¾ mile towards Thornborough, past Leckhampstead Wharf House to the bridge.

Driving Time: From Buckingham – 15 minutes.

Information: Although the name would place this bridge in the village of Leckhampstead, it is actually closer to Thornborough. This is an unassuming low-profile, early 16th-century bridge of older rubble fill cased in English bond brick. There are four arches, the three 2.5 metre central arches carrying the primary river flow and an outer arch on the north side acting as a flood arch. Unusually, the four arches are pointed rather than circular and sit on three piers with concrete foundations.

There is a very low parapet, the result of a modern widening effort with concrete coping and later wood posts and railings added. Photographs from the 1950s show different wooden railings without the concrete coping, indicating that there may never have been higher parapets. At only just over 4 metres wide the carriageway can carry only one vehicle at a time. The west face has two large brick cutwaters. The southern two arches have, for uncertain reasons, off-set 'stepped' brickwork on both sides. However, the evidence of two styles of brickwork and, in the central arch, an asymmetric

Leckhampstead Bridge – the carriageway

Leckhampstead Bridge

Leckhampstead Bridge – detail of the 'arch over an arch' reconstruction

Detail of the unusual pointed arches

upper arch reinforcing a lower arch is an indication that perhaps these sections had been rebuilt. On the east side of the bridge there are stepped corbels below the parapet.

At the Bridge: This bridge is rural and surrounded by pasture and farmland. There is no formal parking at the bridge, but a couple of field entrances may allow a temporary pullover. The best views are from the west face. There are no facilities near the bridge.

Detail of the concrete foundations of the central piers

Detail of the stepped brickwork on the southern arches

2 Thornborough Bridge ★★★★

Bridge Name:	Thornborough Bridge
Location:	Thornborough Village, Thornborough Bridge is located on the original Bletchley to Buckingham, A421, road, now bypassed by a modern bridge in 1974 for the A421. Use postcode MK18 7DX for your satnav.
Setting:	Rural / Countryside
OS Ref:	SP 72925 33199
Crosses:	Padbury Brook
Orientation:	East / West
County:	Buckinghamshire
Length:	30 metres
Bridge Type:	Multiple Arch
Materials:	Sandstone
Traffic:	Pedestrian (Bypassed)
Build Date:	14th century
Authority:	Transport for Buckinghamshire
Designation:	Grade I Listed
Directions:	From Leckhampstead Bridge • Continue south on the same road. • At the triangular intersection bear right, signposted Thornborough and follow into the village. • At the first road to the right turn right (southwest), signposted Buckingham, and follow for ¼ mile to the A421 T junction. • Turn right (west) and follow for ¼ mile to the little layby on the right and the bridge.
Driving Time:	From Leckhampstead Bridge – 10 minutes.

Thornborough Bridge

Information: Thornborough was an important place in Roman times, marking the intersection of five major roads. This east to west river crossing is at least 1,200 years old and dates back to Roman times. This position on Padbury Brook was originally a Roman ford, made from limestone blocks held in place with wooden stakes. These were found during excavations in the 1970s.

There are two large burial mounds in fields to the north of the bridge that date to around AD 200, and when excavated in 1839 by the Duke of Buckingham, produced a wealth of treasures; bronze and gold ornaments, pottery and glass. A glass urn containing human remains also survived, indicating that the mounds resulted from a lavish funeral ceremony.

The bridge itself dates to 1400 and is one of only two surviving medieval bridges in Buckinghamshire and is the oldest bridge in the county. It is made of stone with six stone arches, the centre two accommodating the main flow of the river. These centre arches are more ornate with ribbed vaults, hood moulds, and carved voussoirs. Both arches are divided into three bays over the channels by two hollow-chamfered ribs and have hoodmoulds to the south side. The four remaining arches, two on each side, are less ornate and intended for spring flooding overflows. There are three cutwaters on the south side central piers which are carried up through the parapet as passing pedestrian places. The north side has one square passing place with an inscription tablet and shields carved onto the pier below.

The bridge straddles the parish boundaries of Thornborough and Buckingham. The parish boundary follows the line of Padbury Brook or 'The Twins', a tributary of the River Great Ouse. The parish division is marked by a boundary stone in the middle of the bridge. The stone bridge is around 30 metres long and 4 metres wide.

There is evidence of multiple repairs carried out over the centuries, extensively in 1661 with other late 19th and 20th century repairs. There are fragments of an inscription on the north side of the bridge mentioning the 1661 repairs:

THIS BRIDGE WAS REPAIRED BY CHARGE OF THE COUNTY ANO DOMINI 1661 ACCORDING TO A SESSION ORDER: SR R-HARD F MP SR TOBY TYREL BARRON TS … AND THOMAS STAFFORD ESQUIRE BEING APPOINTED TO TAKE ORDER FOR THE BOOKING FOR THE DOING OF THE SAME AND WILL … HEAD OF THORNBOROUYE …OF THE SAID WORK THOMAS … C…SSAN

The parapets show 20th-century damage by modern vehicles struggling with such a narrow road width.

Thornborough Bridge – the 1661 repair inscription (© Buckinghamshire County Council, 2020)

At the Bridge: The bridge is accessible to walkers from an adjacent lay-by with parking. Limited picnic area, no facilities.

Thornborough Bridge in winter

Early 20th-century damage to the parapets

The carriageway

Thornborough Bridge – the north face showing recent repair

Detail of the western flood arch showing the vaulting

The cutwaters

The carriageway looking west showing the pedestrian passing niches

19th-century repairs

Repairs on the north side

Detail of the eastern arch

3 Lower Heyford Bridge ★★

Bridge Name: Lower Heyford Bridge
Other Names: Heyford Bridge
Location: Lower Heyford Bridge carries the B4030 (Station Road) across the River Cherwell, at Lower Heyford village 9 miles north of Oxford and northwest of Bicester. Use postcode OX25 5PB for your satnav.
Setting: Rural / Countryside
OS Ref: SP 47859 24764
Crosses: River Cherwell
Orientation: East / West
County: Oxfordshire
Length: 190 metres
Bridge Type: Multiple Arch
Materials: Oolitic Limestone
Traffic: Road
Build Date: 14th century
Authority: Cherwell (District Authority)
Designation: Grade II Listed
Directions: From Lower Heyford Village

- Follow the B4030 to Lower Heyford.
- In Lower Heyford the B4030 turns west but stay on it for ¾ mile, past the village and to the bridge on the west side past the rail station.

Driving Time: From Thornborough Bridge – 45 minutes.

Information: The River Cherwell splits to the north of this bridge and runs in two arms through this part of the Cherwell Valley. This bridge crosses the western arm of the river. Although there has been a bridge over the River Cherwell since at least 1255, the present Lower Heyford Bridge is thought to date from the 14th century, although it was altered in the 17th century and widened in the 19th century.

Lower Heyford Bridge

The fabric is coursed squared limestone rubble with some ashlar dressings and some brick repairs. The western end of the bridge, spanning the main branch of the river, has four arches, two of which retain chamfered ribs and have added brick linings. The westernmost river arch is segmental, has no ribs and has a single arch ring. The next arch was reduced to half its original span in the 17th century for reasons unknown. The other two arches are pointed Gothic with double flush, chamfered arch rings and an unknown number of

ribs. Between the arches are piers carrying shallow buttresses *(Robertson, 2020).*

At the widened 19th-century face upstream, as a result of widening work the look is very different with segmental arch shapes and single arch rings, while the piers carry low cutwaters. Even after widening in the 17th century the carriageway is less than 4 metres wide and traffic is one-way. The bridge extends for about 190 metres across the river valley and includes a causeway that crosses the low-lying land between the bridge and the village. This lengthy structure constructed from the same stone is pierced by six additional

Segmental (Syrian) Arch

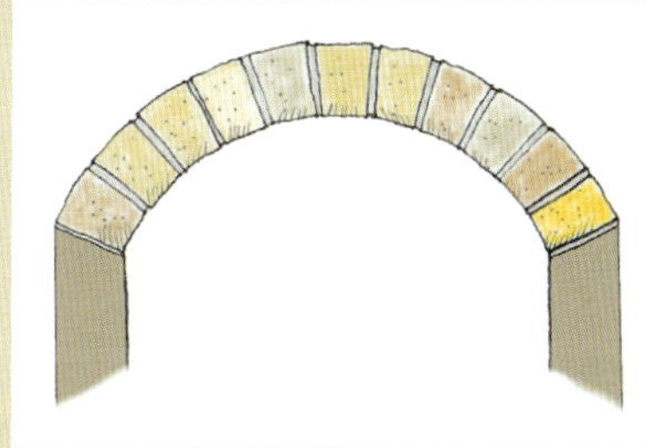

A segmental arch, which is also known as a Syrian arch, forms a partial curve of less than 180 degrees. It has a small rise in the centre and is semi-elliptical across the top. It is shorter in height than the semi-circular arch.

This is considered a basic type of arch, and it is used for bridges where the centre of the arch lies below the springing line. In a segmental arch, the thrust transfers in an inclined direction all the way to the abutment. A segmental arch is considered one of the strongest arches available because it is better able to resist thrust. This form had great value in medieval bridge engineering because they permitted mutual support by a row of arches, carrying the lateral thrust to the abutments at either end of a bridge. There are variations of this form such as the pointed segmental arch (not the same as a gothic arch). The advantages of the segmental arch bridge were that it allowed great amounts of flood water to pass under it, which would prevent the bridge from being swept away during floods and the bridge itself could be more lightweight.

Chamfered support ribs in the east arch vault

Stone copings on Lower Heyford Bridge

Lower Heyford Bridge south side (© Motacilla and licensed for reuse under Creative Commons License 2.0)

The westernmost flood arch

The narrow roadway looking west

flood arches, two of which are medieval with chamfered ribs. There are narrow pedestrian walkways and both sides have plain parapets with flat stone copings.

Part of the bridge, notably the chamfered vaulting-ribs of the arches at the eastern end, probably dates from the late 13th century; there are 19th century additions on the north side.

Records of numerous bequests for its upkeep in the 16th century have survived. In 1544, for instance, William Carter gave two bushels of malt towards its 'mending and reparation' *(British History Online – Lower Heyford, 1959).*

The bridge forms an important feature in the landscape designed around 1740 by William Kent for Rousham Park which runs southwards from the B4030 and encompasses the river and land south of the bridge.

Lower Heyford Bridge – detail of the bridge's spandrel and parapet wall

At the Bridge: There is a busy intersection on the west end of the bridge and the long causeway running east does not allow parking or stopping. Access is difficult and requires substantial walking and climbing, especially to view the medieval downstream face. There is much vegetation in the way. There are facilities and amenities in Lower Heyford.

Lower Heyford Bridge – the two original medieval arches

2 NORTHEAST CORNWALL TOUR

Using Launceston as a starting point these bridges are ordered from north to south and include Yeolm Bridge, St Thomas Packhorse Bridge, Greystone Bridge, and Horsebridge Bridge.

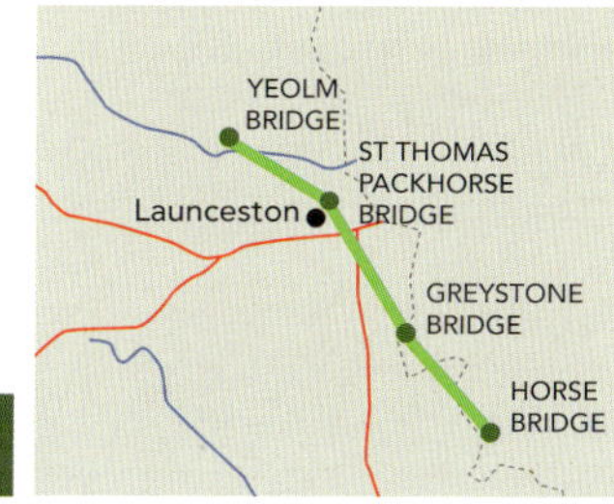

1 Yeolm Bridge ★★★

Bridge Name:	Yeolm Bridge
Location:	On the B2354 through the village of Yeolmbridge located a few miles north of Launceston. Use postcode PL15 8NH for your satnav.
Setting:	Village / Suburban / Countryside
OS Ref:	SX 31800 87400
Crosses:	River Ottery (Attery)
Orientation:	North / South
County:	Cornwall
Length:	15 metres (not including the southern causeway)
Bridge Type:	Multiple Arch
Materials:	Stone
Traffic:	Road
Build Date:	1350
Authority:	Cornwall (Unitary Authority)
Designation:	Grade II* Listed
Directions:	From Launceston • Follow the B3254 north to the bridge in the village of Yeolmbridge. • The bridge is on the southern approach to the town.
Driving Time:	From Launceston – 10 minutes.

Information: Yeolm Bridge crosses the River Ottery, a Tamar tributary, and a broad floodplain. It is located a few miles north of Launceston and is thought

Yeolm Bridge – east face

The squinch in the northeast corner

The date stone in the western parapet

to be the oldest bridge in Cornwall, dating to the middle of the 14th century. Henderson calls it the most perfectly finished bridge in Cornwall *(Henderson & Coates, 1928)*.

No other Cornish bridge has ribs in the arch vaults, but there are three chamfered ribs below each of the two-pointed arches over the river, together with chamfered arch rings. There are two four-centred Tudor style arches over the main river channel which each span 5.4 metres, and the bridge carriageway was originally 3.5 metres wide. The fabric is coursed local freestone rubble. In the late 19th century, the bridge was widened on the downstream (east) side by fractionally over 1 metre, but the exact detail cannot really be seen *(Henderson & Coates, 1928)*.

The bridge has rebuilt stone rubble parapets capped with rounded granite coping on the east side and upturned stone throughout the remainder. On the west side, two ashlar stone cutwaters are carried upwards to provide pedestrian refuges.

There are three flood arches in the long causeway on the south side that were rebuilt in the 19th and 20th centuries. The first with a segmental dressed stone arch, the second with a reinforced steel joist and the third a granite lintel. Recent earth works by the local authority have widened and deepened the riverbed and improved the function of the flood arches to the south by removing built up silt and vegetation *(Robertson, 2020)*.

At the Bridge: The bridge has been well maintained. There is a public green space at the northwest end of the bridge with parking available.

The northern arch – west face

The cutwater and refuge

Three ribs in the vault

The central pier and spandrel – eastern face

The western pedestrian refuge

The flood arch with unusual cattle gate hinged at the top

Yeolm Bridge in the 1940s (© R. Pyke, used with permission of the author)

2 St Thomas Packhorse Bridge ★★

Bridge Name:	St Thomas Packhorse Bridge
Other Names:	Priors Bridge
Location:	In Launceston, off the A388. Use postcode PL15 8HS for your satnav.
Setting:	Village / Suburban
OS Ref:	SX 32789 85095
Crosses:	River Kensey, a small tributary of the River Tamar
Orientation:	North / South
County:	Cornwall
Length:	14 metres (including the approaches)
Bridge Type:	Multiple Arch
Materials:	Slatestone
Traffic:	Pedestrian
Build Date:	15th century
Authority:	Cornwall (Unitary Authority)
Designation:	Grade II* Listed
Directions:	From Yeolm Bridge:

- Turn around and follow the B3254 back into and through Launceston. This intersects with the A388
- Turn right and follow into the town centre.
- At the White Horse Inn roundabout follow straight across to West Bridge Road and follow to bridge.
- Connects West Bridge Road and Riverside Street.

Driving Time: From Yeolm Bridge – 20 minutes.

Information: This small and low packhorse bridge has been dated to the late 15th century and has a total of five arches comprised of four four-centred Tudor style arches (though at least one looks pointed) and the fifth one at the south end is square. There is also a unique drainage port hole at the south end.

St Thomas Packhorse Bridge – east face

Thought originally to have given access to and from Launceston Priory (now Saint Thomas Church) immediately to its south, there has probably been a bridge of some form at the present location since the founding of the priory in the 12th century *(Polsue, 1965)*.

The fabric is slatestone and rubble, the width 2.5 metres, and it has a more modern U-shaped exit ramp at its north end.

There are two large cutwaters on the upstream side, one hosting a lamp post, but only one downstream. Only the arch heads of the bridge are now

The footpath looking south

visible since the starlings and most of the piers are obscured by the riverbed, which has silted up.

The iron railings and a central cast iron lamp probably date to the late 19th century.

At the Bridge: The bridge is by no means robust and it is easy to imagine it experiencing damage during floods. Parking is in a residential area so park whenever you see a spot. Facilities and amenities are in the village.

St Thomas Packhorse Bridge – west face

The central cutwater – east side

St Thomas Priors Bridge *by George Ellis, 1957 (with permission from George Ellis Collection)*

3 Greystone Bridge ★★★

Bridge Name:	Greystone Bridge
Location:	On the B3362 (Old Greystone Road) 5½ miles southeast of Launceston and 8½ miles northwest of Tavistock where the River Tamar forms the Devon / Cornwall border. Use postcode PL15 9PD for your satnav.
Setting:	Rural / Countryside
OS Ref:	SX 36839 80344
Crosses:	River Tamar
Orientation:	East / West
County:	Cornwall
Length:	68 metres
Bridge Type:	Multiple Arch
Materials:	Slatestone
Traffic:	Road
Build Date:	1439
Authority:	West Devon (District Authority) and Cornwall (Unitary Authority)
Designation:	Grade I Listed and Scheduled Monument
Directions:	From St Thomas Packhorse Bridge and Launceston: • Make your way back to the roundabout and turn right (south) onto the A388. • Follow the A388 all the way south over the A30 bypass and 1 mile out of town. • The B3362 splits to the left signposted to Lawhitton & Tavistock. • Follow the B3362 for 3 miles and do not turn off. You will eventually see the River Tamar on your left. • A set of stoplights will signal your arrival at the bridge.
Driving Time:	From St Thomas Packhorse Bridge – 20 minutes.

Information: Named because of the adjacent Greystone Manor house and dating back to 1439, Greystone Bridge was built with money raised by Bishop Lacey and documentation survives from 1439 offering indulgences for contributions. It is the furthest upstream of three ancient crossing points on the River Tamar. The other two ancient crossings are those at Horsebridge and Gunnislake. It is likely that Greystone Bridge and Horsebridge, which is 7 miles downstream, were the work of the same architect, a Mister John Palmar, merchant and MP of Launceston. The patron of these bridges may have been one of the Abbots of Tavistock, whose estate at Endsleigh stretched along the river between the two *(Beacham, 2014)*.

The bridge is constructed of roughly coursed snecked slatestone and ashlar with freestone dressings. The roadway is 3 metres wide, and the bridge's cutwaters extend up to 8.2 metres up from the riverbed.

Roman Arch (Semi-circular Arch)

A Roman arch, which is also known as a semi-circular arch, forms a semi-circle and is made of stone or brick masonry.

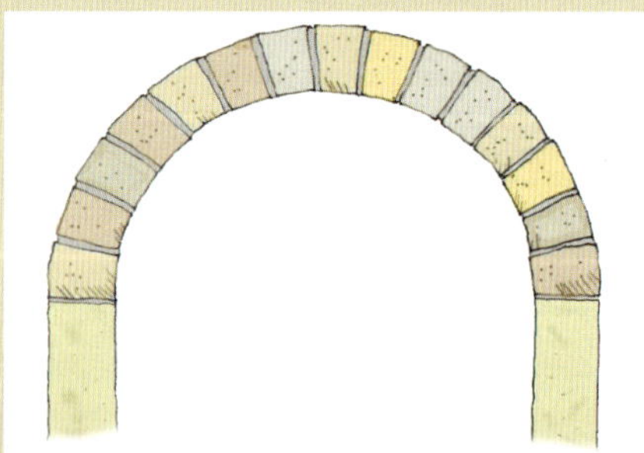

Developmentally, this style of arch followed the horseshoe arch. The Romans learned the arch from the Etruscans and were the first builders who, in the first centuries BC, discovered how to use arches in the construction of bridges and aqueducts. The Roman arch is largely responsible for the expansion of infrastructure across the Roman Empire. The Roman arch became a foundational aspect of Western architecture and generated new systems of building across Europe.

In this type of arch, the shape looks much like a semi-circle, and the thrust is transferred to the abutments in an exact vertical direction. Falling in the category of rounded arches, the Roman arch forms a half-circle, and is a major feature of many bridges built for hundreds of years after the Roman departure from Britain.

It is a strong structure that is frequently found in aqueducts and bridges, and it is simple to construct because each voussoir is identical in taper to the one next to it. It is sometimes called a round arch.

Greystone Bridge – south face

The bridge consists of seven stone arches. There are five semi-circular arches over the river itself springing from high imposts 3 metres above normal water level, each spanning 6.9 metres. Plus, there are two smaller segmental flood arches, one on each bank of the river with spans of 3 metres and 4.2 metres. All arches have very unusual double arch rings separated by hoodmoulds, and there is a string course above each archway, upstream and downstream *(Robertson, 2020)*.

The parapets are of stone rubble with rounded granite coping stones and are splayed on both the east and west ends. Approaches to the bridge were

Arch rings with hood mould

The cutwater and pedestrian refuge

formerly considerably steeper and were altered for the stagecoach between Tavistock and Launceston. Long vehicles often damaged its parapet and repair work was carried out in November 2007, which also widened its entry approach on the Cornwall end, and traffic signals were installed.

The condition of the bridge, which is approaching 600 years old, is marvellous and it has clearly been kept in good repair.

Greystone Bridge is the site of a large aggregate quarry operated by Bardon Aggregates.

Greystone Bridge featured in the 1942 film *The Foreman Went to France* in which a model of the bridge was blown up to create one scene in the film, causing half of Plymouth to visit the site to see if it was still there.

At the Bridge: Access is quite good, though trees obscure the structure to a considerable extent, and this presumably explains why different authorities quote different numbers of arches making up the bridge.

Traffic is light controlled, single lane. There are no formal parking arrangements but country lanes on both ends may afford a temporary pullover. Access to river level is difficult, across private land, but possible. There are no facilities or amenities near the bridge.

The roadway

Greystone Bridge – north face

Greystone Bridge in the 1950s (with permission from George Ellis Collection)

4 Horsebridge Bridge ★★★

Bridge Name: Horsebridge Bridge
Other Names: Hautes Bridge, Hawte Bridge
Location: In Horsebridge between Launceston and Tavistock. Use postcode PL19 8PJ for your satnav.
Setting: Rural / Countryside
OS Ref: SX 40006 74874
Crosses: River Tamar
Orientation: East / West
County: Cornwall
Length: 75 metres (including the causeway at the western end)
Bridge Type: Multiple Arch
Materials: Slatestone
Traffic: Road
Build Date: 1437
Authority: Cornwall (Unitary Authority)
Designation: Grade I Listed and Scheduled Monument
Directions: From Greystone Bridge:

- Reverse directions and make your way back to the A388, about 3 miles.
- Turn left (south) and follow for 4½ miles to the intersection with Stoke Road, signposted Stoke & Horsebridge.
- Turn left (east) and follow for 3 miles to the bridge.

Driving Time: From Greystone Bridge – 15 minutes.

Information: Horsebridge Bridge crosses the River Tamar, where it forms the Cornwall and Devon boundary, at a point 4 miles northeast of Callington in eastern Cornwall. It was built in 1437, by

Horsebridge Bridge – south face

The cutwaters and vaulting

the same architect as Greystone Bridge, a mister John Palmar, merchant and MP of Launceston and paid for by French Benedictine monks with money from an indulgence of 40 days granted to all penitents. It is the middle of three ancient crossing points on the River Tamar. The others are at Greystone and Gunnislake.

Both bridges are constructed from local stone with freestone dressings. The patron of these bridges may have been Bishop Lacey, one of the Abbots of Tavistock, who in 1439 owned large estates between the two bridges and granted another Indulgence for the construction of the slightly smaller Greystone Bridge, surviving 7 miles upstream along the River Tamar. From numerous detailed points of similarity, Horsebridge and Greystone Bridge are considered to be the work of the same medieval architect *(Henderson & Coates, 1928)*.

Horsebridge Bridge has six two-order semi-circular main arches of 6.1 metres span and one flood arch of 4.7 metres giving a total length of 60 metres to which is added a 15-metre causeway at the western end. The height of the central piers from riverbed to parapet is 9.1 metres. The western main arch is very slightly pointed but the others are rounded. The floodwater arch in the western causeway is pointed with a span of 4.7 metres.

The fabric is roughly coursed slatestone with mainly granite coping and dressings. The parapets are finished with chamfered coping slabs, mostly of granite and many with their iron securing cramps *(Robertson, 2020)*.

The five triangular cutwaters on each face rise to pedestrian refuges, which have projecting brackets on the upstream side. The roadway is 3.6 metres wide, the same '12 feet' width as recorded in 1809 indicating that the bridge has not been widened.

Towards the upper end of each pier's upstream cutwater apex is a stone bracket: a lozenge-shaped slab projecting roughly level with the top of the arch vaults. Each with a rounded tip and slightly hollowed underside, these slabs are believed to have held poles to support nets in the late

Horsebridge Bridge – north face showing the stone 'net poles holders'

The easternmost arch – south face

The smooth soffits – no ribs

Horsebridge Bridge (© Derek Harper and licensed for reuse under Creative Commons License 2.0)

medieval Tavistock Abbey's fishery along the River Tamar.

During the English Civil War, on 26 July 1644, the Earl of Essex crossed the Tamar at Horsebridge with a Parliamentarian force of 10,000 men and advanced into Cornwall.

The bridge is still used by the largest of vehicles and unfortunately has been damaged by lorries on several occasions, but otherwise this fine bridge has been kept in good repair, though the details are unrecorded.

At the Bridge: Access is good downstream, less so upstream, but as far as can be determined there is no substantial difference between the two faces. The bridge is directly at the entrance to the village of Horsebridge (officially in Devon). The Royal Inn pub is in the village. Parking may require a short walk back to the bridge.

3 CENTRAL CORNWALL NORTH TOUR

Using Bodmin as the central point, these bridges are arranged from north to south. As in most of Cornwall these bridges are on rural roads and lanes. This tour includes Wadebridge Bridge, Helland Bridge, Panters Bridge, and Treverbyn Bridge.

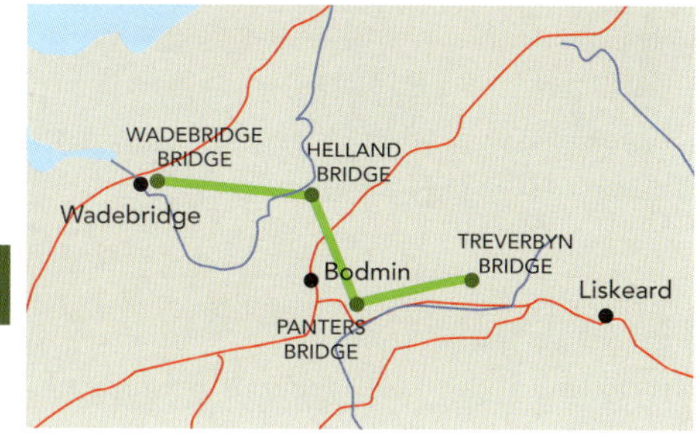

1 Wadebridge Bridge ★★★

Bridge Name: Wadebridge Bridge

Other Names: Known locally as 'The Bridge on Wool' or just 'Old Bridge'

Location: Off the A39 in central Wadebridge, Molesworth Street. Use postcode PL27 7AH for your satnav.

Setting: Town Centre

OS Ref: SW 99131 72464

Crosses: River Camel

Orientation: Northeast / Southwest

County: Cornwall

Length: 98 metres

Bridge Type: Multiple Arch

Materials: Slate and Brick

Traffic: Road (Local)

Build Date: 1468

Authority: Cornwall (Unitary Authority)

Designation: Grade II* Listed

Directions: From Bodmin:

- Take the A389 northwest out of town and follow 9 miles all the way to the northside of Wadebridge at the junction with the A39.
- At the roundabout turn southwest onto the B3315 (Gonvena Hill) into Wadebridge.
- Stay on this road as it descends into town and follow to the bridge.

Driving Time: From Bodmin – 20 minutes.

Wadebridge Bridge – northwest face

Wadebridge Bridge – southeast face

Information: The town now known as Wadebridge was once just Wade, or Wyeth-ford, until a bridge was built on the site of an old tidal ford that was considered very dangerous.

The bridge united the parishes of Egloshayle and St Breock, on either side of the River Camel. Chapels, licensed in the later 14th century, had been built at each end of the ford: 'St Michael's Chapel' at the southwest end and the 'King's Chapel' at the northeast. It was customary for travellers to pray for a safe crossing at one chapel, then, once they had crossed the river safely, to stop and give thanks at the other chapel. The chapels at each end were seized by the Crown after the Dissolution, to be sold off in 1591 for secular use. No remains of either chapel are now known to survive *(Henderson & Coates, 1928)*.

Bridge construction was begun in 1460 on the instructions of John Lovybond, vicar of Egloshayle, with John de Harlyn as the contractor. The Vicar was disturbed by the number of animals and people who died crossing the river and was determined to build a bridge to make the crossing safe. In 1468 he was permitted to obtain stone from St Minver, further down the estuary.

The bridge was completed by 1478, in which year it is mentioned in William of Worcester's itinerary. It is likely that the bridge was paid for by the profits from the wool trade, although local legend has it that the bridge was founded on bales of wool, sunk to create stable bases for the foundations. The story relates how Reverend Lovybond had a dream about sheep shearing and dictated that bales of wool were laid on the riverbed, which apparently swelled up and bound the shifting mud, giving a solid base. Similar stories have been told about many bridges and generally they are believed to be a myth derived from the medieval wealth of the town due to the wool trade. However, when the bridge was widened in 1963, wool was allegedly found in the riverbed, exactly where the legend said it should be.

As built, the masonry bridge was 3 metres wide and consisted of 17 pointed arches, including two smaller spans at each end, and covered a length of some 98 metres. All arches still survive, but with progressive reduction in the estuary width over the centuries, only 13 remain as open and visible arches separated by 12 piers. The three original south western arches, their piers and the medieval riverside abutment are known to survive beneath the modern Molesworth Street. Although 13 of the old, pointed arches remain, they can be seen in their entirety only from the river.

The bridge's medieval arches are pointed, 5.71 metres in span, with vaults 3.68 metres across with single arch rings of local slate voussoirs, visible beneath the later widened arches. The arches spring from the sides of piers 3.42 metres wide that each have pointed cutwaters on both faces and which are also built of local slate. The

The coping stones on the northern parapet

The northwestern cutwaters

The roadway and northern parapet

The bridge plaque

The 1962 soffit next to the ancient ones

cutwaters rise to form 12 refuges in the parapets on each side. Today, there are generous pedestrian walkways on each side and several of the refuges have been given over to modern lighting poles. The bridge's parapets can be no older than the bridge-widening on their respective sides: of 1853 on the downstream side and of 1963 or a later date on the upstream side.

In 1543, the Star Chamber court proceedings of the Old Palace of Westminister, tell of an armed duel on horseback on Wadebridge between John Tredinick, Squire of St Breoke, and George Wolcock, a substantial yeoman of that parish. The bridge was so important that Oliver Cromwell and 1,500 dragoon soldiers commandeered it during the Civil War.

In 1853, the downstream side of the bridge was widened under the direction of William Pease, then Surveyor of Bridges for the eastern division of Cornwall. Extra width was found by adding 1 metre wide segmental arches out from the existing cutwaters.

By 1962, the bridge carried the A39 trunk road and again major widening works were required. The upstream side was widened by more than 6 metres and was comprised of precast reinforced concrete ribs, with piers and spandrel walls, masonry faced to Ancient Monument standards. The new arch work is supported on six 600 millimetre diameter bored piles per pier.

Further works were carried out in 1974 and 1994. The bridge is now 11 metres wide.

In 1993 both the bridge and Wadebridge town were by-passed altogether by an entirely new bridge carrying the A39 trunk road over the Camel Estuary less than a kilometre downstream.

At the Bridge: Access to the bridge at road level is good but getting views from river level is difficult. There is a cycleway along the southeast bank. Parking is available in the town. Several local residents independently told me the story of the swan that returns each year to nest on a man-made raised bed on the island. Apparently, this has been the case for generations, and it now seems to have been adopted by the town as 'their' swan.

The swan on the man-made raised nest on the sedimentary island

2 Helland Bridge ★★★

Bridge Name:	Helland Bridge
Location:	Tredethy Road in the village of Hellandbridge, 3.5 miles north of Bodmin and 4 miles east of Wadebridge, in mid-Cornwall. Use postcode PL30 4QR for your satnav.
Setting:	Rural / Hamlet
OS Ref:	SX 06515 71512
Crosses:	River Camel
Orientation:	North / South
County:	Cornwall
Length:	23 metres
Bridge Type:	Multiple Arch
Materials:	Slatestone
Traffic:	Road (restricted weight and width)
Build Date:	15th century
Authority:	Cornwall (Unitary Authority)
Designation:	Grade I and Scheduled Monument (Heritage At Risk Register)
Directions:	From Wadebridge Bridge: • Turn around and retrace your route back north to the A39 and A389 junction at the roundabout. Then turn back towards Bodmin on the A389. • Follow through Sladebridge. After less than a mile through Sladebridge, turn left (east) onto the road signposted Camelford & St Mabyn (Old School Lane). • Follow ¼ mile to its junction with the B3266. • Turn north and follow for 1¼ miles to the first road on the right, signposted Helland. • Turn right (east) and follow this narrow country road ¼ mile to its T junction with Tredethy Road. • Turn right and follow ½ mile as it descends to the bridge.
Driving Time:	From Wadebridge – 35 minutes.

Helland Bridge – west face

Helland Bridge – the corbelling

The roadway

The east face

The central triangular arch

Information: Helland Bridge carries a minor road over the River Camel, a few miles north of Bodmin, and is thought to date from the early 15th century. The name 'Camel' comes from the river's Cornish name, Dowr Kammel', which means 'crooked river'. The bridge appears on several early post-medieval large-scale maps as being associated with a corn mill at the north end and there is a mill race stream crossed by the bridge. The old mill building is now a private residence at the north end on the right *(Henderson & Coates, 1928)*.

Because it provides a handy short-cut, the road and bridge are still used by a very high volume of traffic, from locals to commercial and tourist traffic. As a result, there are many traffic incidents on the narrow bridge. Indeed, on the day I visited a large commercial lorry became stuck at the north end.

It is comprised of four very irregular pointed arches springing from the normal water level, each 4.5 metres in span; the carriageway is 2.8 metres wide only. There are double arch rings, the inner recessed on some arches, but others are single.

The parapets are a 19th or 20th century rebuild, in slate masonry, some non-local. The parapets are finished with granite coping slabs mostly with a curved upper profile, some retaining their iron securing cramps. Along the narrowest sector, the inner faces of the parapets are lined at intervals by low granite slabs set on end, called 'kickstones', further restricting the carriageway's usable width.

At the north end of the bridge, a short masonry-faced causeway extends from the apron walls and carries the road over adjacent flood ground. The northern causeway was modified to add a fifth, round arch, 3¼ metres across, over the mill leat. In the centre of the bridge is an unusual asymmetrical arch, almost triangular with a double row of slate voussoirs, the inner row slightly recessed. Detail of the masonry around the arch and in the adjacent piers shows this arch is a later rebuild, probably to repair flood damage. On 16 July 1847, a flash flood swept down the River Camel, damaging Helland Bridge and rising over its parapets, but not causing the same complete destruction that it wrought on most of the other local bridges along the valley. The bridge's rebuilt central arch is believed to be part of the repaired damage from that episode *(Robertson, 2020)*.

The fabric is slate rubble with dressed slate voussoirs. The large triangular cutwaters vary in size but rise to road level to provide refuges.

There is a curious ledge cum lintel on another arch, which may also indicate a rebuild. Over the medieval northern abutment and arch, the realigned downstream parapet has been underlain by three stepped granite slabs supported by granite corbels bonded into the bridge.

At the Bridge: Access to view each face of the bridge is easy enough, but only from upstream is it possible to photograph a substantial part of the bridge. From downstream the concealment by trees is almost total, at least in summer. Parking near the bridge is difficult.

Helland Bridge – the roadway looking north

3 Panters Bridge ★★★

Bridge Name:	Panters Bridge
Other Names:	Pontwise Bridge
Location:	East of Bodmin just off a minor road 2 ¾ miles west of St Neot. Use postcode PL30 4DP for your satnav. Near Treverbyn Bridge
Setting:	Rural / Countryside
OS Ref:	SX 15892 68020
Crosses:	River Bedalder (or) Warleggan River
Orientation:	East / West
County:	Cornwall
Length:	12 metres
Bridge Type:	Multiple Arch
Materials:	Slatestone
Traffic:	Road
Build Date:	1415
Authority:	Cornwall (Unitary Authority)
Designation:	Grade II* Listed and Scheduled Monument

Directions: From Helland Bridge:

- Turn around and retrace your route back to the B3266.
- Turn left (south) and follow to the junction with the A389.
- Join heading south and follow through Bodmin. The A389 eventually becomes the A38.
- At the big roundabout follow the A38 east, signposted to Plymouth.
- Follow east to the road marked Mount & Warleggan. Turn left (north) and follow to the first crossroads.
- Turn right (east) and follow 1 mile to the bridge.

Driving Time: From Helland Bridge – 30 minutes.

Information: Panters Bridge lies just off a minor road running west from St Neot to Bodmin and crosses the River Bedalder, a tributary of the River Fowey. Although now a minor road, this was once the main medieval route linking the important market towns of Liskeard and Bodmin. In a document about this route dated 1613, there is a reference to a 'Pontwise' bridge, and this may well be the original name.

The present bridge sits directly adjacent to the new bridge and largely dates to the early 15th century, but its western abutment incorporates material from an earlier phase. The form and construction of the bridge is typical of that date, bearing close similarities to other 15th century bridges elsewhere in southwest England. A similar example can be found at Treverbyn Bridge approximately three miles to the east on the same route and documented as being rebuilt in 1412 to 1413.

The fabric is mainly coursed slatestone rubble with some granite boulders and slabs.

There are two four-centred Tudor arches, with double arch rings of slatestone, the inner slightly recessed, and with spans of 4.2 metres. The western arch is mostly silted up. The arches are slightly pointed and spring from a low level above the riverbed, although some of the abutment and piers may be buried in the silt. The abutment walls continue from the bridge across both riverbanks for several metres.

The broad pier carries a triangular cutwater rising to a refuge on each face.

The parapet walls are 1 metre high and have iron-cramped (some missing) granite coping slabs, some with a slight chamfer along each upper edge. On the downstream side the walls are continued for about 9 metres and splayed outwardly.

The bridge is 2.5 metres wide and its total length is 12 metres. The only alterations to the bridge have been for necessary maintenance.

A new bridge was built adjacent to Panters Bridge in 1968, leaving the medieval structure for pedestrian use only, although there are no bollards to prevent vehicular use.

At the Bridge: The bridge is easily viewed from downstream. The approaches to the bridge provide some space for a temporary pullover.

Panters Bridge – south face

The pedestrian refuge in the north parapet

The western silted up arch on the north side

The roadway looking west

3 Treverbyn Old Bridge ★★★

Bridge Name:	Treverbyn Old Bridge
Location:	Treverbyn Mill to the east of St Neots and north of Liskeard. West of Bodmin. Use postcode PL14 6HG for your satnav.
Setting:	Rural / Countryside
OS Ref:	SX 20639 67444
Crosses:	River Fowey
Orientation:	East / West
County:	Cornwall
Length:	10.5 metres
Bridge Type:	Multiple Arch
Materials:	Slatestone
Traffic:	Pedestrian
Build Date:	1412
Authority:	Cornwall (Unitary Authority)
Designation:	Grade II* Listed
Directions:	From Panters Bridge: • Turn east on Tripp Hill and follow 1½ miles through St Neots past the church. • On the east side of the village the road splits. • Turn left and follow Liskeard Hill 2 miles to the bridge.
Driving Time:	From Panters Bridge – 20 minutes.

Information: Beautiful Treverbyn Old Bridge crosses the River Fowey, at a relatively wide point in its otherwise narrow steep-sided valley, south of Bodmin Moor. The old bridge is now bypassed and disused but still sits beside the new A38 road, 1½ miles to the east of St Neots. It is directly alongside the bridge built to replace it in 1929, and now entertains pedestrians only. The bridge is dated to around 1412 when Bishop Stafford, the Bishop of Exeter, granted indulgences to build it *(Collcut, 1929)*.

The two slightly pointed main arches, each about 4.25 metres across, are separated by a pier about 2.5 metres wide with pointed cutwaters on both faces. This pier marks the highest point of the bridge's carriageway. The small

Old and new mill stream arches at Treverbyn Old Bridge

Treverbyn Old Bridge – south face

arch is thought to include parts of an even earlier bridge.

The single arch furthest to the west, which is over a small mill stream branch of the river, has a squinch at the top, then a lintel below, and lower still and behind, an arch ring belonging to the main vault. The span is 2.7 metres and is known to be a later strengthening addition *(Robertson, 2020)*.

The fabric of the bridge is slatestone and granite rubble, with some granite boulders and slabs. The single arch rings are very slightly recessed. From upstream, the arches look segmental, and the recessing of the arch rings is more pronounced *(Henderson & Coates, 1928)*.

The parapets are low, 0.5 metres high, enclosing a roadway 2.6 metres wide and there are refuges above the cutwaters, both upstream and downstream. A slate string course marks the parapet base on the cutwaters' outer faces.

The eastern abutment projects slightly from the riverbank, with widely splayed sides rising to the level from which the arch ring springs. The parapet on the north is 25.3 metres long while the southern is 28 metres long. They are mostly of local slatestone with a bit of granite content over the western pier, arch, and abutment where the parapet is partly rebuilt, but they will have reused the dismantled rubble of its predecessor. The parapets are capped by iron cramped granite coping slabs displaying a diversity of lengths and forms, with most dressed to a shallow chamfer along each upper edge *(Robertson, 2020)*.

Henderson described this bridge in the 1920s as 'one of the prettiest and most interesting bridges in Cornwall' *(Henderson & Coates, 1928)*.

At the Bridge: A small cluster of buildings including Treverbyn Mill mark a small farm complex on the west bank of the river. Access is very good downstream but more difficult upstream. There is no formal parking at the bridge but adequate space for a pullover at the eastern end.

Treverbyn Old Bridge – the roadway

The mill stream arch – south side

The south face and roadway looking east

4 CENTRAL CORNWALL SOUTH TOUR

Starting from Bodmin these bridges are arranged from north to south and include Ruthern Bridge, Respryn Bridge, Lostwithiel Bridge, and St Austell West Bridge.

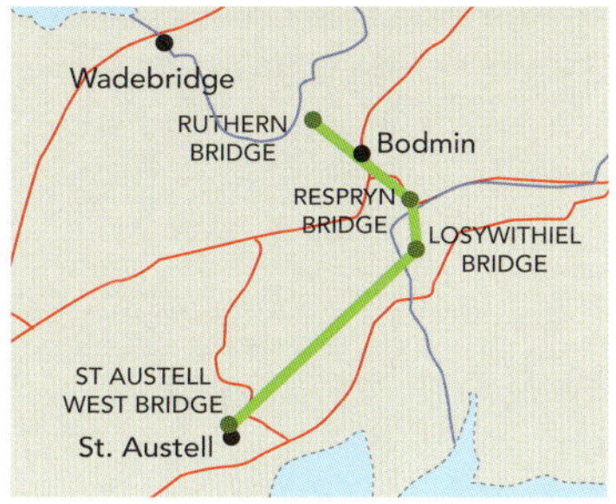

1 Ruthern Bridge ★★

Bridge Name: Ruthern Bridge

Location: In Ruthernbridge on a minor road across the River Ruthern, a tributary of the River Camel, four miles to the west of Bodmin. Use postcode PL30 5LY for your satnav.

Setting: Rural / Countryside

OS Ref: SX 01296 66827

Crosses: River Ruthern

Orientation: East / West

County: Cornwall

Length: 16 metres

Bridge Type: Multiple Arch

Materials: Stone

Traffic: Road

Build Date: Mid-15th century (1450)

Authority: Cornwall (Unitary Authority)

Designation: Grade II* Listed

Directions: From Bodmin:

- Take the A389 westwards out of town for ½ mile.
- Turn to the right (north) onto an unnamed road signposted Nanstallon and Ruthernbridge.
- Follow ½ mile to Nanstallon, at the village entrance turn left (west) signposted to Ruthernbridge.
- Follow 2 miles to the bridge.

Driving Time: From Bodmin Bridge – 15 minutes.

The Ruthern Bridge plaque on the east end

Ruthern Bridge – south face

Information: Ruthern Bridge crosses the River Ruthern, a major tributary of the River Camel, at a hamlet named Ruthernbridge, 3¼ miles west of Bodmin in mid-Cornwall. The River Ruthern takes its name from the redness of waters when tin streaming was in practice since 'ruth' means red in Cornish.

The bridge is largely of a mid-15th century date with some later modification. Although no historical records survive to fix its exact date of construction, a bridge is mentioned here in 1412, perhaps a predecessor to the visible bridge whose earliest surviving record, as 'Rothyn Brygge', is in 1494. The bridge is first documented in 1498, so it can be assigned to the 15th century.

It has two arches separated by a broad pier. The arches are slightly pointed and the western one has a span of 3.66 metres while the span of the eastern is

3.43 metres. Each arch has a single arch ring with slate voussoirs, slightly recessed below a projecting string course.

There are large cutwaters on both faces of the pier which rise to form refuges, and unusually there are two smaller refuges that rise from the abutments at the upstream face outside the arches. The fabric is rubble, some coursed, especially around the cutwaters. The roadway is 2.8 metres wide, and there is no evidence of widening in the soffits *(Robertson, 2020)*.

The parapets are ¾ metre high, finished with granite coping slabs of various profiles, though most are chamfered along each edge. The parapet fabric facing the highway is of random rubble but towards the river it reflects that of the bridge sides below, generally of local random rubble.

There are surviving remains of a ford adjacent to the south side of the bridge, and two cast-iron plaques recording an unusually early weight restriction imposed on the bridge. Dating from the 1890s–1900s, these cast-iron plaques are affixed near the west end of the northern parapet and the east of the southern parapet, advising those 'in charge of locomotives' that the 'bridge is insufficient to carry weights beyond the ordinary traffic of the district'.

At the Bridge: Access to river level is possible but difficult. There are no formal parking arrangements, but a temporary pullover may be possible on the eastern end of the bridge. There are no amenities or facilities at or near the bridge.

Ruthern Bridge – north face

Voussoirs with hood mould

The roadway looking east

2 Respryn Bridge ★★★★

Bridge Name: Respryn Bridge

Location: Southeast of Bodmin on a minor road close to Lanhydrock House, a National Trust property, to the north of Lostwithiel. Use postcode PL30 4AF for your satnav.

Setting: Rural / Countryside

OS Ref: SX 09939 63490

Crosses: River Fowey

Orientation: Northwest / Southeast

County: Cornwall

Length: 41 metres

Bridge Type: Multiple Arch

Materials: Moorstone and Rubble

Traffic: Road (restricted)

Build Date: 15th century

Authority: Cornwall (Unitary Authority)

Designation: Grade II* Listed

Directions: From Ruthern Bridge:

- Reverse your directions and head back to the A389 and back towards Bodmin.
- At the roundabout turn right onto Westheath Road and follow ½ mile south to the next roundabout.
- Turn right, go under the railway bridge, and then immediately left onto Kirland Road.
- Stay on this narrow road for 3 miles and do not veer off at any of the opportunities.
- You will eventually T junction into the B3268. Turn right (south) signposted to Lostwithiel.
- Follow this over the A30 bypass for ½ mile to the first roundabout.
- Turn left (northeast) for ½ mile, at the first opportunity turn right (northeast) onto a minor road and follow ½ mile past the entrance to Lanhydrock House & Gardens.
- At the T junction turn right (south) and follow ¼ mile to the bridge.

Driving Time: From Ruthern Bridge – 25 minutes.

Respryn Bridge – south face

Information: Respryn Bridge, over the River Fowey, carries a minor road close to Lanhydrock House, a National Trust property just to the north of Lostwithiel. The name Respryn means 'ford'. The first records of a bridge here date to 1300, but that bridge was replaced in the early 15th century with the one we see now. The fabric is a mixture of dressed, coursed moorstone and rubble and is about 40 metres long *(Richards, 1984)*.

The bridge has five arches of differing shapes, spans, and ages. The central arch is the oldest dating to the 15th century and is slightly pointed with a single granite arch ring, although it seems to have sagged slightly, and spans 3.9 metres *(Henderson & Coates, 1928)*.

The two eastern arches are thought to survive from a century later. They are segmental and wider, have double arch rings, of which the upper are narrow, the lower wider and recessed; none are chamfered.

The two western arches are four-centred, have single, flush arch rings, and are clearly different in style and are probably a 19th century reconstruction using material salvaged from earlier structures.

There is chamfered granite coping on the parapet walls, which are low and splayed outward at the east end. There are three upstream cutwaters, and two downstream, all in the eastern part of the bridge, and all rising to provide refuges in a narrow roadway only 3.3 metres wide. There is one central pier with the remains of a cutwater at the base.

Documentary evidence indicates there was a pre-dissolution chapel dedicated to St Martin on the southeastern side of the riverbank in the 12th century. This predated the bridge and served as the fording point.

The bridge was the site of skirmishes in August of 1644 during the English Civil War, lying as it did between the two major estates of Lanhydrock and Boconnoc, one side Royalist (King Charles) and the other in Parliamentarian hands. The pass at Respryn Bridge was one of the most important strategic points in Cornwall and was on the old track from Bodmin to Looe. The bridge was eventually secured by the royalists, who were supported by the local people with both provisions and intelligence. King Charles rode over the bridge in 1644 on his way from Boconnoc to Lanhydrock, and after the war the avenue of trees leading up to Lanhydrock House from Respryn Bridge was planted by Lord Robartes to celebrate his party's victory.

At the Bridge: Access to the riverbank is possible downstream though trees restrict the view of an interesting bridge. On the northeast side the riverbanks adjoin the grounds of Lanhydrock House, which is owned by the National Trust.

Respryn Bridge – north face

The easternmost arch of Respryn Bridge. This is dry, unless in flood

The coping with cramp irons

The roadway

The suspended parapet at central cutwater

The bridge has weight and width restrictions with serious bollards. In 2006 a 40-tonne lorry became stuck while trying to cross and caused significant damage to the parapets.

There is a National Trust car park located at the northwest end of the bridge. There are public toilet and refreshment facilities available at Bodmin Parkway station, and within the National Trust property at Lanhydrock.

3 Lostwithiel Bridge ★★★★

Bridge Name:	Lostwithiel Bridge
Location:	Carries the B3268 through central Lostwithiel, on North Street. Use postcode PL22 for your satnav.
Setting:	Town Centre
OS Ref:	SX 10615 59809
Crosses:	River Fowey
Orientation:	East / West
County:	Cornwall
Length:	27 metres
Bridge Type:	Multiple Arch
Materials:	Slatestone
Traffic:	Road
Build Date:	Late 1300s
Authority:	Cornwall (Unitary Authority)
Designation:	Grade I Listed and Scheduled Monument
Directions:	In Lostwithiel: • Follow the A390 south as it curves into the town. • Turn left onto Fore Street (one-way system), which becomes the B2368 again. Follow it as it curves continually left and eventually arrives at the bridge. Park when you get a space.
Driving Time:	From Respryn Bridge – 20 minutes.

Information: Lostwithiel Bridge is situated in the town centre at the lowest crossing of the River Fowey at its tidal limit, and dates from the medieval era when Lostwithiel was the capital of the Duchy of Cornwall, and a busy city for the export of tin. Until the bypass was opened in 1939 this bridge was the main road between Liskeard and St Austell.

Historians have generally dated at least part of the bridge to either the late 13th century or very early 14th century. There are no records of its construction, but it is mentioned in records of 1314 and 1357. In 1437, Bishop Lacy of Exeter granted an Indulgence for its repair.

The people of Lostwithiel are justly proud of their bridge, which is probably the best-known old bridge in Cornwall *(Henderson & Coates, 1928)*. The

Lostwithiel Bridge – south face

The large buttress on the north side

The roadway looking west

The main river arches

The stone coping

bridge is built of slatestone rubble and originally had nine spans. The foundations and arches of the four westernmost arches are buried under North Street and are no longer visible.

The western end is the oldest and has five remaining pointed arches with double arch rings, and cutwaters rising to pedestrian refuges at road level. These arches vary in span from 3.4 to 3.8 metres. Close examination of the four oldest arches, to the west, shows that their faces are nearly identical on both sides, suggesting that this part of the bridge has never been widened. In the 18th century the remains of a long-lost causeway continuing the bridge westwards into the town were discovered beneath North Street and it is now known that there was a medieval chapel at one end. One can only imagine that the further four buried arches must have looked identical.

The middle section of the bridge has a rounded arch of 4.3 metres span which crosses a sedimentary island. When Leland visited Lostwithiel in 1539 he found the bridge was 'nearly choked with sand and sediment to within 4 or 5 feet of the arch heads and this sediment was also blocking the river so that barges could not approach with ½ mile' *(Leland & John, 1549)*.

To remedy this, in the 16th century, a new 'relief' channel was dug in the river to the east of the bridge and at first, a timber structure carried traffic from the stone bridge to the riverbank, but this was soon replaced by stone arches. This noticeably different construction with a large buttress is what we see today after the river channel moved, leaving the western end of the bridge on dry land. The two easternmost relief channel arches, one large and one small, are rounded, the largest is of 3.1 metres span.

The low parapets were added in 1676 and the distance between them varies from 3.5 metres to 4.5 metres. These have chamfered granite coping stones with iron cramps. They are splayed back at the west end and extend overall about 10 metres. Several of the refuges have been used for modern signage and lighting. A stone in the southern bridge parapet dated 1676 must refer to this repair work.

This bridge has been the scene of many notable and emotional occasions, including the arrival of the Black Prince and his retinue to hold Court at Restormel Castle in 1354, and the dispatch of the defeated Parliamentary army by the angry citizens in 1644.

At the Bridge: The bridge remains open to two-way traffic. There is a public green space to the southwest end and parking is available in the village. There are facilities and amenities in the village.

4 St Austell West Bridge ★★

Bridge Name:	St Austell West Bridge
Other Names:	The Old Bridge, West Bridge
Location:	Off the A390 in the town centre of St Austell, on Westhill Road. Use postcode PL25 5FJ for your satnav.
Setting:	Town Centre
OS Ref:	SX 00952 52260
Crosses:	St Austell River
Orientation:	Northeast / Southeast
County:	Cornwall
Length:	13 metres
Bridge Type:	Multiple Arch
Materials:	Stone
Traffic:	Pedestrian and cycle traffic
Build Date:	c. 1500
Authority:	Cornwall (Unitary Authority)
Designation:	Grade II* Listed
Directions:	In St Austell: • Follow the A390 south several miles into and through St Austell. • At the big roundabout follow the A390 signs south towards Truro. The bridge is on the west side of town. • Turn right (northwest) onto the A3058 Edgcumbe Road. • Take the first right onto Ledrah Road and follow to the bridge.
Driving Time:	From Lostwithiel Bridge – 30 minutes.

Information: St Austell West Bridge, also called 'The Old Bridge', crosses the St Austell River on the west side of the town, on Westhill Road. It is now closed to motor vehicles.

It is formed of three segmental, slightly stilted arches of which the central river one spans 3 metres. This central arch

St Austell West Bridge – south face

St Austell West Bridge roadway looking west

Stone lintels under the western arch

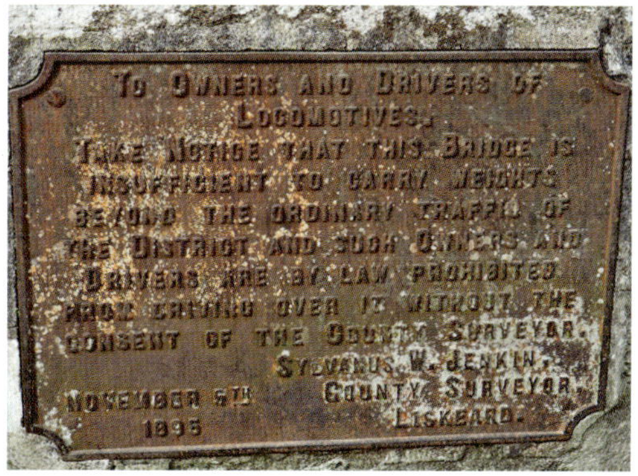

The bridge plaque

The pedestrian refuge with modern plaque

The north face

has double flush arch rings, whereas the others have single flush arch rings, curiously angled in the case of the northeastern arch *(Robertson, 2020)*. Throughout most of the year the central pier is the only one with water.

There are two broad piers with large cutwaters on each face rising to form parapet walls of the same material, with four refuges. The parapets are capped with granite coping with iron cramps. The fabric is uncoursed local brown rubble in varying sizes.

The westernmost arch has entombed at its centre, yet still visible, three lintels forming a beam bridge structure, which obviously supported an earlier bridge.

Henderson records the carriageway width as 2.4 metres, in the 1920s *(Henderson & Coates, 1928)*.

The soffits do not supply conclusive evidence, but a heavy horizontal beam in the northern arch suggests that it changes shape at the downstream face.

The bridge was mentioned in 1538 or thereabouts. John Leland wrote of the bridge: 'the poore toun of St Austelles is nothing notable but for the paroch chirch. And there is a bridge of stone of the same name' *(Leland & John, 1549)*, which implies origins of around 1500, and certainly the overview with broad piers, and proportionately narrow arches supports such dating, though modifications have been made since.

At the Bridge: The roadway of the bridge is easily accessible but getting down to river level is difficult. There is parking in the nearby lanes. Park where you can and walk. Facilities and amenities are available in the town.

5 NORTH DEVON TOUR

Using Barnstaple as a starting point these bridges are arranged north to south and include Barnstaple Long Bridge, Bideford Long Bridge, Rothern Bridge, and Taddiport Bridge.

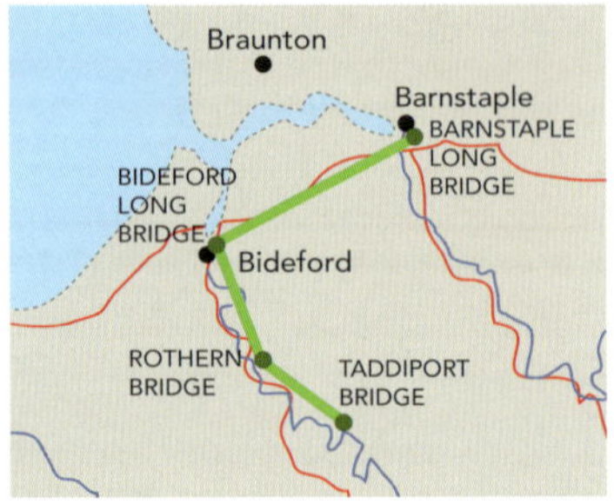

1 Barnstaple Long Bridge ★★★★

Bridge Name: Barnstaple Long Bridge

Other Names: Barnstaple Bridge

Location: Barnstaple town centre only a few miles from Bideford Long Bridge. Use postcode EX32 8LN for your satnav.

Setting: Town Centre / Urban

OS Ref: SS 55778 32921

Crosses: River Taw

Orientation: Northeast / Southwest

County: North Devon

Length: 159 metres

Bridge Type: Multiple Arch

Materials: Stone

Traffic: Road

Build Date: 1280

Authority: North Devon (District Authority)

Designation: Grade I Listed and Scheduled Monument

Directions: To Barnstaple Long Bridge:

- The bridge carries the A3125, also called Long Bridge Street, across the River Taw. It is right in the centre of Barnstaple. Park at the Pay and Display on the north side near the museum.

Information: Barnstaple Long Bridge is a medieval bridge linking Tawstock with Barnstaple in North Devon spanning the River Taw. The river is still tidal at this point causing great fluctuations in river levels twice a day. Barnstaple Long Bridge is one of the largest medieval bridges in Britain and is associated with Bideford Long Bridge over the Torridge, a few miles away.

The fabric of the bridge is of grey rubble. It was constructed around 1280 as the main river crossing and has been widened at least three times. The bridge has 16 pointed, Gothic

Barnstaple Long Bridge – east face

The eastern segmental arches

The bridge plaque

The stone coat of arms at the northeast parapet

The steps leading up to the roadway

Barnstaple Long Bridge – west face

masonry arches, without ribs and with single flush arch rings. The arches vary in span from 5.5 metres to 7.9 metres, with broad piers, making up the total length of 159 metres and approached by two causeways. Triangular cutwaters on each pier are capped at impost level below the parapets *(Robertson, 2020)*.

The date of the first bridge at Barnstaple is imprecise. A will of 1274 left money for its upkeep and it is believed that construction work began around 1280, with further work being undertaken in 1333. Leland mentions that a chapel dedicated to Thomas Becket was located 'Juxta' Barnstaple Bridge's east end *(Leland & John, 1549)*. It is clear from historical records that the 13 arches on the southwest end were originally built of stone and that the three arches on the northern town side were wooden arches (known as 'maiden arches') until their replacement with stone in 1589. The term 'maiden arches' has several suggested meanings, the popular one being that maiden ladies raised some of the necessary money by spinning and teaching. A second meaning is that maidens of the town went down to the river at this point to fetch water. It was even considered by some that 'maiden' is a corruption of 'midden' or sewer, and that the town drainage emptied into the river at this point *(Cruse, 1982)*.

By the early 16th century, records showed that the bridge's original 13 stone arches were 'much dilapidated' and needed repairs *(Cruse, 1982)*.

The original bridge was less than 3 metres in width and widening was carried out first in 1796, by constructing segmental arches between the existing cutwaters on the western face. The medieval, pointed arches, 4.1 metres wide, can be clearly seen beneath the modern arches.

The bridge was widened further between 1832 and 1834, by installing footways, 1.2 metres wide, supported on cantilevered ironwork supplied by the Neath Abbey Iron Company at a cost of £4,000. This modification increased the roadway width to 4.9 metres.

In 1963, the bridge was widened once more, on the upstream (southeast) side of the structure only. The new masonry can be seen in the arch soffits. In the 1960s some of the original stonework of the deck was replaced and masonry parapets constructed above the original stone arches, removing the Victorian ironworks to give the bridge an image identical to how it would have looked between 1796 and 1832. The result of all this was two 1.8-metre-wide footways flanking a 7.3-metre-wide carriageway *(Henderson & Jervoise, 1938)*.

The parapets are also of reddish grey stone rubble with plain stone coping. Generous pedestrian walkways are provided on each side but there are no pedestrian refuges. There are five lighting poles on each side of the bridge, some of which are embedded into the parapet wall. There is no access to the river from the bridge structure but stairs at the northwest corner lead down to a pedestrian walkway. A stone coat of arms is embedded into the north end of the eastern parapet.

Traffic congestion remained considerable on the bridge until May 2007, when the Barnstaple Western Bypass was opened about 1 mile southeast (upstream). Traffic on the A39 heading towards Braunton and Ilfracombe now avoids travelling through the town centre and over the ancient bridge, reducing the traffic load on the old structure.

This bridge is very similar to Bideford Long Bridge in both looks, history and construction.

At the Bridge: Access is good all around the bridge allowing the various stages of its construction to be viewed. There is a pedestrian tunnel running under the bridge across the north end. At the northeast end of the bridge the Museum of Barnstaple and North Devon is on the right and provides some excellent views of the bridges eastern face. Across the street there is some limited Pay and Display parking. Facilities and amenities are available in the town.

2 Bideford Long Bridge ★★★★

Bridge Name:	Bideford Long Bridge
Location:	Bideford on the north Devon Coast southwest of Barnstaple on Bridge Street. Use postcode EX39 for your satnav.
Setting:	Town Centre / Urban
OS Ref:	SS 45569 26427
Crosses:	River Torridge
Orientation:	Northwest / Southeast
County:	North Devon
Length:	206 metres
Bridge Type:	Multiple Arch
Materials:	Stone
Traffic:	Road (with a 3-tonne weight restriction)
Build Date:	1474
Authority:	Torridge (District Authority)
Designation:	Grade I Listed and Scheduled Monument
Directions:	In Bideford: • As you enter the outskirts of Bideford on the A39 from the north, turn right at the only set of lights. This is the B3233. • Follow around the approach ramp, signposted East-the-Water. At the roundabout bear left (south) and follow for 3 miles. This is still the B3233 but it also becomes Barnstaple Street. Continue to the bridge.
Driving Time:	From Barnstaple Long Bridge – 35 minutes.

Bideford Long Bridge – west face

At the southwest corner

The east face

The piers and plinths

Information: Bideford Long Bridge spans the tidal estuary of the River Torridge, connecting the east and west parts of Bideford. A very large fluctuation in water levels occurs twice daily under the bridge. It is just over 206 metres long creating one of the longest medieval bridges in England without a causeway. It was later surpassed by others, such as the almost intact Swarkestone Bridge in Derbyshire.

Bideford Long Bridge was constructed originally from timber around 1286, but between 1460 and 1500, a masonry bridge was built around the wooden one, using the old structure as scaffolding while it remained open to traffic. Tradition states that, like London Bridge, its piers were built on wool bales, an allusion to the great wealth generated by the wool-trade to the economy of England in the Middle Ages. In fact, the foundations are firmly fixed stone sitting on the rock riverbed *(Burton Art Gallery and Museum, 2017).*

In the Middle Ages there was a chapel at each end of the bridge: St Anne's Chapel on the east, and Allhallows Chapel on the west. Each chapel would probably have had a clergyman attached to it who would have been paid by the Bridge Trust or by a wealthy local businessman. Various legends concerning the building of the bridge are given in the 1863 *Transactions of the Devonshire Association* and one is that St Mary and the Devil had differing ideas about where the bridge was to be located *(Henderson & Jervoise, 1938).*

As built, the Long Bridge has 24 pointed arches, varying in span from 3.7 metres to 7.6 metres. Verbal tradition says that the 24 arches of the bridge are different sizes because they were paid for by local businessmen, with the larger arches reflecting the more generous contributions. Of course, no records are available to verify this traditional version of events and more realistically the differing spans reflect the lengths of timber used for arch lintels in the underlying original structure, or the differing spans were the result of the location of solid foundation stone. The fabric of the current bridge is of locally sourced stone rubble with dressed stone voussoirs in single flush arch rings. The granite bridge piers vary from 2.7 metres to 3.7 metres in width *(Robertson, 2020).*

Widening was carried out from 1792 to 1810 by James Green, who also widened Barnstaple Long Bridge in a similar fashion. Semi-circular segmental arches were constructed against both sides of the bridge, springing from the existing triangular cutwaters. The roadway was increased from a width of around 3 metres to almost 4 metres. The original medieval pointed arches can clearly be seen encased within both sides of these facades. In the 1840s the bridge trustees rejected the offers of three separate rail companies to lay a railway track over it, although a temporary track was laid during World War I (1914–18) to help the war effort *(Henderson & Jervoise, 1938).*

In the mid-1860s, footways were added by constructing a framework of steel girders supported on stone corbels built onto the cutwaters. Decorative cast iron parapets were fixed to the girders. The full width of the masonry structure could then be used for traffic, resulting in 1.4-metre-wide footways flanking a 4.5-metre-wide road *(Christie & Whiting, 1986).*

The medieval arches underneath the 1810 widening

The bridge was widened once more in 1925, using reinforced concrete to replace the earlier iron and the parapets were rebuilt on projecting reinforced concrete cantilevers using Penarth Ashlar stone. During the alterations of 1925, some of the original medieval timbers were found encased in the masonry. One of them is preserved in Bideford Public Library and some were used to make a large ornamental chair for the chairperson of the Bridge Trust. For the first time the bridge was lit at night with lamp standards on both sides. Today the superstructure of the bridge overhangs the substructure and covers the tops of the cutwaters, and each parapet wall carries six iron lamp-standards on concrete pedestals; these closely resemble the originals of 1925, although their tops are late 20th century *(Pevsner & Cherry, 1989)*.

In January of 1968, the westernmost arch of the bridge, nearest the Town Wall, collapsed under the pressure of winter flood water. This cut the town in half and extensive repairs were undertaken. Amphibious army vehicles were enlisted to provide a ferry service, a temporary tubular foot bridge from the quay to the undamaged part of the bridge was constructed, and the railway line between Barnstaple and Torrington was reopened, but motorists still faced a lengthy detour.

In 1987, a new high-level trunk road bridge was constructed over the River Torridge, north of Long Bridge, at Northam, which relieved excess traffic pressure on the old structure. A 3 tonne weight restriction on the old bridge was introduced in 2002.

An ancient New Year's Eve tradition was to try to run across the Long Bridge during the time taken for the bells of St Mary's parish church, near the west end, to chime midnight. A sight enjoyed by many in the winter months is of the starlings at dusk, as they come in large flocks to roost underneath the bridge. A large-scale model of the Long Bridge in all its stages from 1280 to 1925 is displayed at the Burton at Bideford museum in the town (*Bideford Bridge Trust, 2019*).

At the Bridge: Access is good around a spectacular bridge. There is parking at the west end of the bridge. The Royal Hotel is on the corner.

3 Rothern Bridge ★★★

Bridge Name:	Rothern Bridge
Location:	Just west of Great Torrington on the north side of the A386 on a bypassed section of road on the river's east side. Use postcode EX38 8JD for your satnav.
Setting:	Rural / Countryside
OS Ref:	SS 47910 19742
Crosses:	River Torridge
Orientation:	Northeast / Southwest
County:	Devon
Length:	41 metres
Bridge Type:	Multiple Arch
Materials:	Stone

Rothern Bridge southern arches – west side

Traffic: Bypassed and disused

Build Date: Early 15th century

Authority: Torridge (District Authority)

Designation: Grade II Listed

Directions: From Bideford Bridge:

- At the west end of the bridge take the A386 south towards Great Torrington for 5½ miles.
- You will eventually cross over the River Torridge on the new bridge.
- Immediately after crossing turn left (north) into a little commercial space cum diner.
- Bear left past that and follow the road 200 metres to the end. The bridge is on the left obscured by trees.

Driving Time: From Bideford – 30 minutes.

Rothern Bridge under refurbishment in 2021

Information: Rothern Bridge is a multi-span bridge of four arches that once carried the A386 across the River Torridge, between Great Torrington to the east and Frithelstock to the west, though it has now been bypassed and is disused.

The original four arches have single flush arch rings and are thought to date back to the early 15th century. They are pointed and have a span of 5.7 metres and together with broad piers give an overall bridge length of 40.5 metres. Above the arches there is a projecting string course and above this the parapets *(Muckley, 2004)*.

The bridge was widened on both sides in a similar fashion to those at Bideford and Barnstaple by adding segmental arches alongside, springing from the triangular cutwaters. The original arches can still be clearly seen encased in the newer facings. It is suggested that this had been done by the early 19th century. The width now is 4.7 metres while before widening it was only 2.8 metres.

The central cutwater

Otherwise, the bridge is rubble built with ashlar dressings and a prominent string course, and with cutwaters of different sizes which now are cut off below the top of the parapets. At the points where the cutwaters rise, these continue above the stringcourse as pilasters. The parapets are very low and have flat but chamfered ashlar copings.

In 1928 the bridge was rendered redundant when the adjacent Rolle Bridge, 100 metres downstream, was constructed and the road diverted over the new bridge. In 2021 the bridge parapets underwent a refurbishment and repointing.

At the Bridge: When the river level is low the banks of gravel provide access and there is a walkway down to river level on the west end. There is ample pullover space at the east end. Access is possible only from downstream, but there is no doubt that this bridge in its location is a particularly fine sight.

4 Taddiport Bridge ★★★

Bridge Name:	Taddiport Bridge
Other Names:	Originally known as Town Bridge
Location:	In Taddiport immediately to the south of Great Torrington, carrying the B3227. Use postcode EX38 8AT for your satnav. Only about 4.5 miles south from Rothern Bridge
Setting:	Rural / Countryside
OS Ref:	SS 48815 18728
Crosses:	River Torridge
Orientation:	North / South
County:	Devon
Length:	33 metres
Bridge Type:	Multiple Arch
Materials:	Stone
Traffic:	Road
Build Date:	14th century
Authority:	Torridge (District Authority)
Designation:	Grade II Listed
Directions:	From Rothern Bridge: • Continue eastward on the A386 for 2 miles towards Great Torrington. • Just as you are coming into the town, turn right (south) onto the B3227, also called Limer's Hill, signposted Langtree. • Follow ½ mile south around many curves to the bridge on the approach to Taddiport.
Driving Time:	From Rothern Bridge – 10 minutes.

Information: Taddiport Bridge crosses the River Torridge immediately to the south of Great Torrington about 6 miles south of Bideford. The bridge carries the B3227.

The bridge has three deep segmental arches, the northern one with the greater span, the central one spanning 9 metres. The arches sit on the abutments and two broad piers with cutwaters capped below the level of the parapets, giving a total bridge length of 33 metres.

Taddiport Bridge – east face

Taddiport Bridge – west face

Victorian iron reinforcement

The bridge has been substantially widened on the downstream side in 1879, according to Jervoise, to just less than 4.5 metres, from 2.7 metres, by abutting shallower segmental arches, supported on extended cutwaters. Visual inspection confirms this, and the original arches can be seen hiding behind the newer ones on this western face *(Henderson & Jervoise, 1938)*.

The cutwaters are ashlar, like much of the extension work. Very unusually, the faces of the extensions carry no separate arch rings, but rather near vertically arrayed thin blocks continue to the top of the parapets.

The mainly rubble upstream face must be, at least in part, original, and certainly the southern arch with its rough voussoirs in a single arch ring looks the part. The radial blocks here are also carried up towards the top of the parapet. The rough rubble parapets have coping of vertical stone arranged in castellations as a result of the repairs in 1879. Iron plates that secure tie rods are dated 1911 *(Robertson, 2020)*.

The other eastern arches have dressed arch rings and may have been rebuilt to a greater or lesser extent. They also have some radial stonework in the parapets.

There was once a chapel adjoining the southern end of the bridge, for mention is made in church records of the 'Chantry of St Mary Magdalene juxta Pontem de Chepyngtoritone' and by the mid-1500s it was known as the 'Chantry of Tadyport' *(Henderson & Jervoise, 1938)*.

As regards dating the bridge, there is some disagreement. Taddiport bridge is said to be medieval (13th century) but has also been attributed to the 16th century. However, the critical clues are the width, less than 3 metres before widening, and the very heavy piers. Jervoise, and the Historic England listing, ignored these facts and each favoured a late 16th century date. There is documentation of repairs in the early 15th century, so the bridge may date in part to around 1400, albeit that it has been much repaired since then *(Pevsner & Cherry, 1989)*.

At the Bridge: The narrow old toll house for the bridge (also Grade II listed) sits within the causeway wall on the right side of the north end. Joseph Mallord William Turner painted this bridge in 1814. Access is good on the north side with a public footpath and green space near this especially interesting bridge. There are no facilities or amenities in Taddiport.

The central cutwaters and piers

The old toll house

The arch vault of the northern arch

6 SOUTHEAST DEVON TOUR

Using Paignton as the starting point these bridges are arranged south to north and include Staverton Bridge, Austin's Bridge, Dart Bridge, Holne Old Bridge, Holne New Bridge, and Postbridge Clapper Bridge.

1 Staverton Bridge ★★★

Bridge Name:	Staverton Bridge
Location:	Southwest of Staverton, 5 miles north of Totnes. Use postcode TQ9 6FE for your satnav.
Setting:	Rural / Countryside
OS Ref:	SX 78473 63722
Crosses:	River Dart
Orientation:	Northwest / Southeast
County:	Devon
Length:	62 metres
Bridge Type:	Multiple Arch
Materials:	Stone
Traffic:	Road (with weight and width restrictions)
Build Date:	1413
Authority:	South Hams (District Authority)
Designation:	Grade I Listed
Directions:	From Paignton: • Take the A385 4½ miles west through Totnes to the village of Shinner's Bridge. • At the roundabout turn right (north) onto the A384, signposted Exeter A384. • Follow the A384 for 1 mile to a road on the right signposted Staverton Bridge. Follow less than a mile to the bridge.
Driving Time:	From Paignton – 20 minutes.

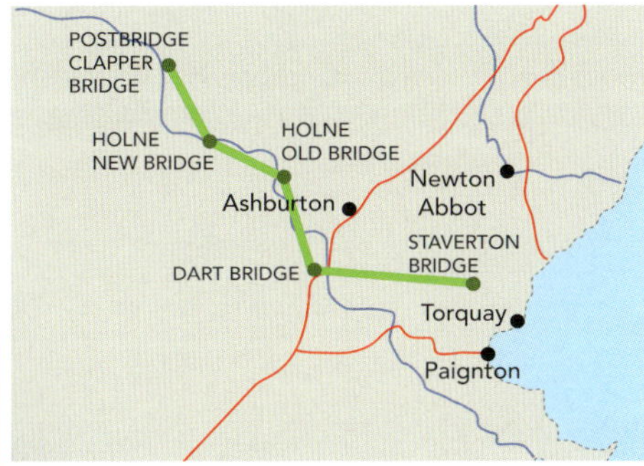

Staverton Bridge – north face

Staverton Bridge – south face

Information: Staverton Bridge carries a minor road over the River Dart at the west end of the village of Staverton. It is one of the oldest bridges in Devon. Indulgences for the building of Staverton Bridge were issued in 1413 by Bishop Stafford and it appears to have been little altered since.

The River Dart

Bridges in this book: Dart Bridge
Holne New Bridge
Holne Old Bridge
Postbridge Bridge
Staverton Bridge
Austin's Bridge

Main Tributaries: East Dart
West Dart

The River Dart is approximately 45 miles in length and begins high on Dartmoor National Park from two different sources. The East Dart and West Dart, together with 15 smaller tributaries, effectively act as a mechanism to drain a vast area of upland Dartmoor where annual rainfall can approach 100 inches. It is interesting to note that the East Dart, which drains southwards, rises south of Cranmere Pool, only 500 metres from the source of the River Taw, which drains north to Barnstaple.

On Dartmoor, the East Dart and West Dart meet at Dartmeet (hence its name), a point where the Dart heads south towards Buckfastleigh. The Dart's entire catchment area covers 183 square miles and takes in a population of 31,000 people.

As the Dart crosses Dartmoor you can see some lovely old stone bridges. All bridges on the Dart are located above Totnes as the river is tidal from Totnes, and there are no bridges between the town and the mouth of the Dart. The River Dart flows in a southeasterly direction until it leaves the moor at Buckfastleigh and continues in a southerly direction through Totnes until filtering into the sea at Dartmouth.

Dartmoor, Dartmouth, Dartington, Dartmeet; the River Dart lends its name to many of the places it meanders through en route 36 miles from the moors down to the sea.

Like Dartmouth, Totnes thrived as a result of overseas trade. Merchants made fortunes thanks to the river location, and mills were built along the banks of the Dart. It was the same story for towns further up the Dart – including Buckfastleigh, where woolen mills, paper mills and tannery works were all built. Even the monks at Buckfast Abbey made the most of their riverside position.

The Dart has played an instrumental role in powering industry and transporting goods, allowing the growth of the towns and villages that lie along the river. With its stunning National Park setting, plethora of wildlife and host of activities on offer, it is no wonder the Dart is such a well-loved feature of the West Country.

The rubble-built bridge has seven slightly pointed arches with flush single arch rings, five of which span 6.3 metres, and two span 4.8 metres, which, with the broad piers, account for a bridge length of 62 metres. Documentary records declared it to be in a state of decay in the 17th century, which would have required repair or even some rebuilding.

The width is just 3 metres and only allows single lane traffic. There are low parapets with chamfered granite coping. There are no pedestrian walkways but the V-shaped cutwaters, both upstream and downstream, all rise to give five refuges at roadway level on each side. The refuge at the northwest extremity of the bridge is brought outwards to an enlarged rectangular shape.

Henderson relates the following story about Staverton Bridge. In 1436 Sir Laa Lage, a priest, was walking home from a friend's house in Dartington when he was assailed by John Gayne and his wife who had also been entertained at the mutual friend's house. During the course of the evening, Gayne's wife Isabella took insult from something the priest said. As they all took to return home and reached the very high and narrow bridge, Gayne and his wife assaulted the priest with a stick and proceeded to hold and beat him. Finding himself cornered in one of the pedestrian refuges the priest drew his dagger and stabbed his assailant. John Gayne was carried dying to his house and confessed it was his fault *(Henderson & Coates, 1928)*.

Staverton Bridge – north face

Staverton Bridge – looking northwest

The bridge's name was adopted for a folk group formed in the 1970s.

There is another Staverton Bridge in Wiltshire, which is Grade II listed but not medieval and not included here.

The southern parapet and pedestrian refuges

At the Bridge: Access to the bridge below the carriageway is not good with private property occupying the land at each end. Staverton railway station on the South Devon Heritage Railway line is next to Staverton Bridge and railway passengers often make a visit to the bridge. There is some limited parking at the railway station.

Coping stones with iron cramps

The northwestern river arch on the southern side

Staverton Bridge roadway looking northwest

2 Austin's Bridge ★★★

Bridge Name:	Austin's Bridge
Location:	South of Buckfastleigh on Totnes Road immediately as it joins the A384, one mile south of Dart Bridge. Use postcode TQ11 0LN for your satnav.
Setting:	Rural / Countryside
OS Ref:	SX 75010 65959
Crosses:	River Dart
Orientation:	Northeast / Southwest
County:	Devon
Length:	62 metres
Bridge Type:	Multiple Arch
Materials:	Dark grey limestone rubble
Traffic:	Road (restricted width and weight)
Build Date:	16th century
Authority:	Teignbridge (District Authority)
Designation:	Grade II Listed
Directions:	From Staverton Bridge: • Make your way back to the A384 and turn right (west). • Follow for 5 miles towards Buckfastleigh. The bridge is on the left (west) side of the road.
Driving Time:	From Staverton Bridge – 15 minutes.

Austin's Bridge – southeast face

Information: Austin's Bridge crosses the River Dart below Buckfastleigh about 1 mile from Dart Bridge within the sound of the A38. The bridge is thought to date from the early 16th century, though a bridge is recorded here as early as the 13th century, and the corn milling family of William Austyn from Kilbury is given responsibility for its building. The name 'Buckfast' means 'stronghold' – traditionally a place where deer and buck were held, and 'Leigh' would have been the pasture belonging to Buckfast. A tollhouse once stood at the junction of the old Totnes Road at the end of the bridge and the newer present-day A384 *(Jenkinson, 2009)*.

The old medieval arch under the widenings

The bridge encompasses five arches four of which are segmental with single flush arch rings without ribs. Very unusually the second arch from the east is only a 'half arch' and

does not show the same signs of widening; perhaps as the result of a later rebuild. The easternmost arch is obviously a flood arch but is used today primarily to carry a pedestrian footpath and provides good views of its vault soffit.

The road surface is quite narrow at only 2.7 metres, but examination of the vaults reveals evidence of at least three widenings, the latest in the 19th century. There is a sharp bend on the west end of the bridge and the east end directly T junctions into the A384.

There are cutwaters on all piers on both faces but only the central river cutwater is carried upward from a triangular shape to form a circular pedestrian refuge on both sides. The others change from triangular to circular buttresses at the parapet level. Turner painted this bridge in 1814.

At the Bridge: Parking is very difficult but there is a narrow pullover on the A384. Traffic is quite fast, so caution is advised. Access to river level is possible if the water level is not too high. There are no facilities or amenities at the bridge.

The central cutwater on the south side

Austin's Bridge roadway looking south

3 Dart Bridge ★★★

Bridge Name:	Dart Bridge
Location:	Northeast of Plymouth on the B3380 (Dartbridge Road) just to the northeast of Buckfastleigh. Use postcode TQ11 0PR for your satnav.
Setting:	Countryside / Rural
OS Ref:	SX 74445 66724
Crosses:	River Dart
Orientation:	Northeast / Southwest
County:	Devon
Length:	45 metres
Bridge Type:	Multiple Arch
Materials:	Local Stone
Traffic:	Road
Build Date:	14th century
Authority:	Teignbridge (District Authority)
Designation:	Grade II Listed
Directions:	From Austin's Bridge: • Proceed north on the A384 and follow for 1 mile to Buckfastliegh. As you approach the village the road passes over the A38. • Stay on the A384, which at this point has changed name to Dartbridge Road. • The bridge is ¼ mile ahead.
Driving Time:	From Austin's Bridge – 10 minutes.

Information: Dart Bridge carries the B3380 over the River Dart, just to the northeast of Buckfastleigh. It has the distinction of being the last crossing place of the river Dart before it leaves the boundary of Dartmoor National Park. It is not surprising that there has been a bridge here for

Dart Bridge – northwest face

The arch vault showing widening

The cutwaters on the northwest side

centuries due to the proximity of Buckfast Abbey (Sandles, 2016). It is thought that a significant part of the bridge structure may date from the 14th century when it is first mentioned in local documents.

The original 14th century bridge had four slightly pointed arches with flush double arch rings. These can still be seen set-back from the modern face. That bridge was of 45 metres in length, with individual arch spans of 8 metres each, and broad piers. It had a very narrow carriageway width of 2.25 metres only, and whether it had refuges is unknown.

The narrowness of the bridge in the early 1800s is reflected in the following report that appeared in *The Times* on Saturday, 23 June 1827.

> *On Saturday morning last, as the mail coach from Exeter to Plymouth was crossing Dart Bridge, about three miles from Ashburton, the leaders* [leading horses] *took fright at a heap of stones which had been laid down for repairing the road, and suddenly crossed to the opposite side. In consequence of which, the coach received so great a jerk, that the driver was thrown from the box and fell among the horses. A man, the only outside passenger, was also thrown off, but he received no other injury than a few slight bruises. The coachman was, however, not so fortunate, for the vehicle passed over his body from the groin to the shoulder, and bruised him severely, but without breaking any bones. The guard at the moment of the accident got down to assist the coachman, who was, after a few minutes, enabled to rise and follow the coach.*
>
> *In the meantime, the horses proceeded at a rapid pace, and in going through Buckfastleigh, they passed so close to the houses that the lamp and handle of the* [coach] *door were torn off, and the splinter bar and one of the traces were broken. Upon this a gentleman, who was the only inside passenger, became alarmed, and looked out to ascertain what was the matter. Seeing that the coachman was not in the box, he got out of the coach, and having succeeded in reaching the ground safely, he laid hold of the reins and stopped the horses without further mischief being done.*
>
> *On reaching Buckfastleigh the coachman was put to bed, and medical aid being procured, the necessary remedies were applied, and we have much satisfaction in adding, that it is expected he will be able to resume his duties in a few days. His escape was indeed miraculous.*
>
> *We understand that he is a steady driver, and that no blame can attach to him on this occasion. The splinter bar and trace having been replaced; the guard drove the coach to Plymouth.*

Dart Bridge – southeast face (© Mike Faherty and licensed for reuse under Creative Commons License 2.0)

Who says you can only find the 'Wild West' in America? The west of England can also have heroes that save stagecoaches *(Sandles, 2016).*

The first widening took place in the early 19th century and increased the width to 5.7 metres. This widening extended the cutwaters to support the new arches, and these followed the original arch shapes quite closely and can be seen in the downstream (southeast) extensions to the vault soffits.

Dart Bridge roadway looking south

Around 1930, a further widening took place at the downstream face, whereby flush segmental arches were added alongside giving the present overall width of close to 12 metres. There are a pair of date plaques in the middle of the southern parapet. The upper one is mostly indecipherable but reads:

Widen?? ??27
J Gree Esq??rch
J Brown Builder

The lower plaque reads:

County of Devon
DART BRIDGE
Reconstructed and widened 1929
Br?an Viller??? & crew Warren
Clerk ??-?? County Surveyor

Henderson and Jervoise describe how the bridge is built of local stone, which is unusual, for Dartmoor bridges are normally constructed with granite. They also note how the earliest bridge consisted of four arches and how in 1809 the roadway was just over 2.5 metres wide and described as being, 'narrow and inconvenient' *(Henderson & Jervoise, 1938).*

The 1930 extension in limestone rubble dominates the downstream aspect, with semi-circular buttresses above the cutwaters rising to parapet level as a notable feature. There is a protruding string course at road deck level and the parapets are similarly constructed of local stone with a flat top coping of stone. There are no pedestrian refuges, but these may have existed once.

At the Bridge: Public access is practically non-existent below the roadway. However, there is a steep (with a rope) kayaker's access hidden at the southeast corner of the bridge. There are generous pedestrian walkways on both sides of the roadway. There is a café and antiques business to the north end of the bridge.

The parapet of the causeway leading north

4 Holne Old Bridge ★★★

Bridge Name:	Holne Old Bridge
Location:	In Dartmoor, on the B3357 road between Ashburton and Poundsgate, about 4½ miles from Ashburton. Easiest access is via Ashburton off the A38. Use postcode TQ13 7NP for your satnav.
Setting:	Rural / Countryside
OS Ref:	SX 73016 70585
Crosses:	River Dart
Orientation:	North / South
County:	Devon
Length:	31 metres
Bridge Type:	Multiple Arch
Materials:	Granite Stone
Traffic:	Road (restricted width and weight)
Build Date:	1413
Authority:	Teignbridge (District Authority)
Designation:	Grade II* Listed
Directions:	From Dart Bridge: • Make your way back to the A38 and take it left (north). • At the next exit, signposted Dart Country Park, follow the exit around to join the B3352. • At the T junction turn right (northwest) and follow for 3½ miles to the bridge.
Driving Time:	From Dart Bridge – 20 minutes.

Information: The bridge is constructed of local granite rubble. This bridge was built after an earlier bridge was destroyed by a flood in 1413. It was rebuilt in 1413, at the same time as the building of the nearby New Bridge.

Holne Old Bridge – east face

Bishop Stafford offered indulgences to those who contributed to its rebuilding. It was repaired by the adjoining hundreds in 1558 *(Henderson & Jervoise, 1938)*.

The bridge itself consists of three near-semi-circular arches across the river, although only the central one spans the channel when the river is low. There is also an additional, much smaller and presumed later flood arch on the south bank. The central arch is the largest of all, spanning 8.1 metres, but architecturally like the other arches, with a slightly recessed arch ring rising from a string course around the pier and some moulded corbels at the base of the arch. The decoration on the western, upstream side is slightly different as some widening works were carried out in the 19th century *(Henderson & Jervoise, 1938)*.

Between the arches, triangular cutwaters of the same stone rise into four pedestrian refuges, which look newer than the main structure, on both sides of the narrow roadway, and there are a couple of small, corbelled sections between the parapets and refuges. There are no

Dartmoor National Park

I have never before, in my long and eclectic career, been gifted with such an abundance of natural beauty as I experienced filming War Horse on Dartmoor.

(Steven Spielberg)

Portion of a stone wall on Dartmoor

Dartmoor National Park is a thriving heather-covered moorland in Devon on the southwest tip of England between the cities of Exeter and Plymouth, that houses rocky granite tors and stone circles. It legally came into being on 30 October 1951 and today it receives between 11 and 12 million visitors each year. This vast wilderness covers an area of some 368 square miles with a tiny local population of approximately 47,000 inhabitants.

Its medieval villages, which hold traditional events, grant visitors the opportunity to engage with its special community whilst enjoying the park's historic archeology and brilliant wildlife. The Dartmoor National Park Authority owns a small proportion of the moorland with landowners and farmers making up the rest, working together to ensure that the area's natural beauty, wildlife, and cultural heritage remain conserved.

The park also encourages the public to understand and enjoy these qualities by exploring Dartmoor's dramatic landscapes via the area's many walking and cycling routes through its steep wooded river valleys, as well as its cozy hamlets. The granite tors are perfect for climbing and bouldering, and the River Dart is excellent for salmon and trout fishing. There are many interesting archaeological sites to explore, including medieval villages and Bronze Age settlements.

Wild ponies on Dartmoor

Dramatic Dartmoor is home to rare wildlife including red grouse and roe deer. Because Dartmoor is the only national park in England to allow wild camping, visitors sometimes encounter its stunning wildlife one-on-one. They often come across the semi-wild moorland ponies, one of the most iconic sights on Dartmoor, which are native to the region. These animals have been associated with the Moor throughout the centuries, but the first written evidence is documented in a manorial record of 1012. It refers to the 'wild horses of Ashburton' belonging to the Bishop of Crediton.

The expansive Dartmoor horizon

During the Middle Ages, the ponies were crucial in transporting the tin being mined on the moor to the stannary towns. The ponies were used as packhorses to transport goods over the rough Moorland and across the clapper bridges. There are over 200 of these medieval bridges remaining on Dartmoor, some believed to date back as far as the 12th/13th century. The most famous of these is in Postbridge.

Dartmoor's many vistas have inspired films, books, and music and include:

- *The Hound of the Baskervilles*, Sir Arthur Conan Doyle
- *Silver Blaze*, Sir Arthur Conan Doyle
- *War Horse* (Film), Michael Morpurgo and Stephen Spielberg
- *The Sittaford Mystery*, Agatha Christie

Holne Old Bridge – the corbelled squinch at the northeast corner

The west face

dedicated pedestrian walkways. The parapets are remarkably low, just three or four courses of rubble stone below the granite coping stones *(Robertson, 2020)*.

The 3-metre narrowness of both this bridge and nearby New Bridge means that the length and width of vehicles on this road are restricted. The road across the bridge is now unclassified, but still busy allowing only one-way traffic. The approaches on both ends contain hard 90-degree angles with the road.

At the Bridge: Access to the riverbank is obtained easily enough but foliage interferes with general views of this impressive bridge. There are no facilities and there is no formal parking.

The roadway looking north

The river bedrock on which the bridge sits

The vault of the central river arch

5 Holne New Bridge ★★★

Bridge Name:	Holne New Bridge
Other Names:	Newbridge
Location:	East of Poundsgate on the same Newbridge Hill Road as Holne Old Bridge, which crosses the River Dart about 2½ miles further west. Easiest access is via Ashburton off the A38. The bridge is situated at the eastern end of the glorious Dart Gorge. Use postcode TQ13 7NT for your satnav.
Setting:	Rural / Countryside
OS Ref:	SX 71143 70884
Crosses:	River Dart
Orientation:	East / West
County:	Devon
Length:	18.5 metres
Bridge Type:	Multiple Arch
Materials:	Granite Stone
Traffic:	Road (restricted width and weight)
Build Date:	1413
Authority:	South Hams (District Authority) and Teignbridge (District Authority)
Designation:	Grade II* Listed
Directions:	From Holne Old Bridge: • Continue west on the B3352 and follow for 2½ miles to the bridge.
Driving Time:	From Holne Old Bridge – 10 minutes.

Information: It is unclear why this bridge is called 'new' bridge when its sister bridge just up the road has the same build date. The bridge consists of two large arches crossing the river with a smaller third arch crossing the west side of Widecombe bank, all springing from high imposts. The fabric is coursed granite rubble, and there are single

Holne New Bridge – south face

Holne New Bridge – north face

The roadway looking west

The northern pedestrian refuge

recessed arch rings beneath hood moulds. They have well-cut dressed voussoirs, the masonry above resting on slightly chamfered corbels.

The two piers are of the same squared and coursed rubble up to springing level of the arches. Upstream and downstream sharply pointed cutwaters are carried upwards to provide four pedestrian refuges in the roadway which is only 2.7 metres wide.

The parapets may be a later addition, but they blend in reasonably well with the rest of the structure. Those on the Holne (east) side are of ashlar as far as the first cutwater, sweeping outwards at the end to finish in low, oblong-section piers; the rounded granite coping extends to one half of the first cutwater. On the west side the parapets are of rubble, also sweeping outwards at the end, but here dying away into the ground *(Robertson, 2020)*.

The bridge was constructed by the Abbots of Tavistock and is thought to date, without significant alteration, from the 15th century, though it was refurbished and reinforced in the 19th century, and its exceptional condition perhaps owes much to that operation. In 1645 Sir Thomas Hare and some fellow judges surveyed the bridge and recorded that they had; 'viewed the decayes of the Bridge called Holne New Bridge and ordered the sum of £13 to be raised for necessary repairs' *(Jervoise, 1930)*.

Newbridge features in Eden Phillpotts' story of *Orphan Dinah* and it was here that she finally came to the decision to tell her foster brother John Bamsley, the water bailiff, that she could not marry him. After the deed was done, 'Dinah leant upon the parapet of the bridge and dropped big tears into the crystal Dart beneath her' *(Phillpotts, 1921)*.

At the Bridge: The Tavistock Inn is just up the road to the north. Holne's Church House Inn and Scoriton's The Tradesman's Arms are just south. Access to riverbank level is easily gained. There is ample parking to both the east and west ends of the bridge. There are public toilets and, usually, an ice cream van in the summer.

6 Postbridge Clapper Bridge ★★

Bridge Name:	Postbridge Clapper Bridge
Location:	In the heart of Dartmoor National Park. On the B3212 Moretonhampstead to Princetown about 3 miles east of Two Bridges. Use postcode PL20 6TJ for your satnav.
Setting:	Rural / National Park
OS Ref:	SX 64829 78901
Crosses:	East Dart River
Orientation:	Northeast / Southwest
County:	Devon
Length:	13 metres
Bridge Type:	Clapper
Materials:	Granite Stone
Traffic:	Pedestrian
Build Date:	12th century
Authority:	West Devon (District Authority)
Designation:	Grade II* Listed
Directions:	From Holne New Bridge: • Continue northwest on the B3352, which at this point is called Newbridge Road, northward through Poundsgate village. About 1 mile north of Poundsgate the road curves sharply to the left (west) and becomes the B3357. • Follow this road for 13½ miles through Dartsmeet (which has a beautiful bridge of its own, but not medieval) and continue towards Two Bridges. • Just outside Two Bridges the road intersects with the B3212. Turn right (north) and follow for 5½ miles to the bridge.
Driving Time:	From Holne New Bridge – 35 minutes.

Postbridge Clapper Bridge – south face

Information: Just a short walk from Dartmoor National Park Visitor Centre, Postbridge Clapper Bridge is one of the finest examples of a clapper bridge in the country. It is believed to date back to medieval times and would probably have replaced stepping-stones to help packhorses cross the river. It is thought to have been constructed to allow cart and packhorses to carry tin to the stannary market in Tavistock. The first documentary record of a clapper bridge here dates from a lease dated 1655. The bridge then appears on John Ogilby's Exeter to Truro road map of 1675 where it is marked as 'a Stone bridge, 3 Arches Called Post bridge'.

The central piers

John Ogilby: The first Atlas

John Ogilby, engraving by William Camden Edwards, 1820, after a drawing by J. Thurston, The Mansell Collection/ Art Resource, New York (Public Domain)

John Ogilby was a cartographer born in November 1600, near Edinburgh. He died 4 September 1676, in London. He became a British pioneer in the making of road atlases. His 'opus majus' was *Britannia . . .a Geographical and Historical Description of the Principal Roads thereof . . .*, published in 1675, just before he died.

This work contained the antique 'strip maps' of 'Britannia' and has the distinction of being the first ever road atlas of England and Wales, although hardly small enough to be taken on any trip. The format he chose for his atlas was highly original – a system of scrolled parchment taking the reader from one destination, often London's outskirts – to a designated town looking only straight ahead. The 100 maps contained within were also the first to work by the principle of one inch to the mile and to use the statute mile of 1,760 yards. The rules of reading are made very clear and sensible in the preamble. Each road map depicts a route in the form of six or seven vertical strips with a compass rose to register changes of orientation. Additionally, miles, furlongs, towns, churches, windmills, rivers, hills, and even gallows are depicted. The peripheral information is eccentric and often perverse – but always fascinating.

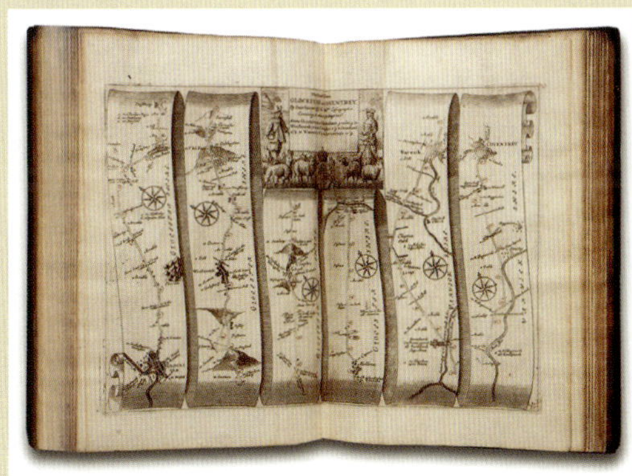

Ogilby's Gloucester to Coventry 'strip' map (from Altea Antique Maps (London, United Kingdom), used with permission)

This book contains two bridges marked on Ogilby's maps: Iford Bridge in Hampshire and Postbridge Clapper Bridge in Somerset in his Exeter to Truro road map where it is marked as 'a Stone bridge, 3 Arches Called Post bridge'.

Bellever Bridge – south face

The bridge sits beside a replacement three-arch bridge built in 1792, interesting in its own right, called Bellever Bridge. They both cross the East Dart River, before it joins with the West Dart to form the River Dart.

Postbridge Clapper Bridge has four roughly shaped granite slabs (clappers) acting as lintels, calculated to weigh 8 tonnes each. A single slab of granite extends from substantial stone abutments on each bank made of piled stones, and two smaller slabs in the middle are supported on two piers made up of seven stacked granite blocks.

The clappers

The slabs were probably brought from Bellever, 1½ miles away, or possibly from Lower White Tor, 2 miles distant. The actual geological make-up of the slabs is different from one another as the feldspar content of the two central slabs differ from that of the side ones, possibly suggesting two separate sources. The large stone slabs are locally called pawsts or posts, and this is how the village of Postbridge got its name. Steps leading up onto these abutments provide pedestrian access to the bridge. In 1979 repair work to the riverbanks was carried out by the Dartmoor National Park Authority, it was during this operation that the steps leading up to the bridge were built. It is worth noting that the depth under the bridge is around 2 metres *(Bellamy, 1998)*.

The three spans thus formed, are each of length 4.5 metres. The path across is 1.8 metres wide and sits more than 2 metres above the water surface in normal flow. The eastern pier is the one that experiences the largest force of the flowing river and so has a pointed cutwater to help deflect the scouring effect of the water *(Robertson, 2020)*.

There seems to be a consensus that the bridge originated in the 13th century. There are build dates offered as early as the 11th century, though evidence for this can only be tenuous. It is known that repair work to the piers, and the provision of steps up to the bridge are of a recent date *(Greeves, 2019)*.

The clapper bridge at Postbridge is just one of about 30 across Dartmoor. Nonetheless, it is the finest example of its type.

At the Bridge: Access is good, though obtaining photographs that don't include other visitors may be difficult. The bridge is one of the most photographed on Dartmoor. There is a large car park and visitor centre with facilities on the south side of the bridge. There is a hotel and a B&B to the north.

Postbridge Clapper Bridge – the steps at the west end

7 SOUTHWEST DEVON TOUR

Using Plymouth as a starting point these bridges are arranged north to south and include Lydford Gorge Bridge, Harford Tavy Bridge, Horrabridge Bridge, Huckworthy Bridge, Plym Bridge, and Aveton Gifford Bridge.

This long tour could be broken into two days.

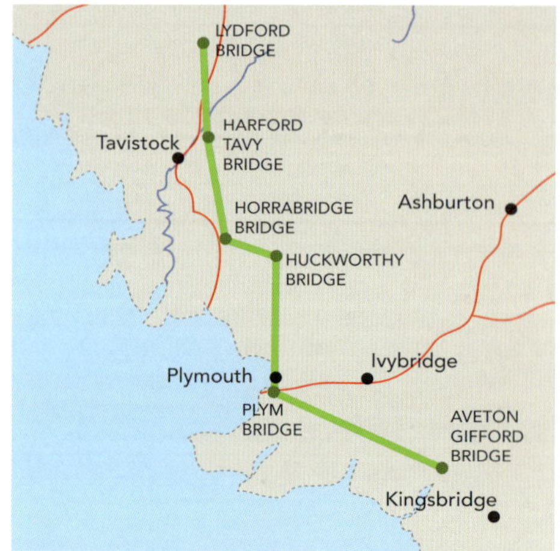

1 Lydford Bridge ★

Bridge Name:	Lydford Bridge
Location:	At the entrance to the Lydford Gorge just south of Lydford Village north of Tavistock. Use Postcode EX20 4BH for your satnav.
Setting:	Rural / Countryside
OS Ref:	SX 50925 84561
Crosses:	River Lyd
Orientation:	North / South
County:	Devon
Length:	5 metres
Bridge Type:	Multiple Arch
Materials:	Stone
Traffic:	Road (restricted width)
Build Date:	1478
Authority:	West Devon (District Authority)
Designation:	Grade II Listed
Directions:	From Plymouth: • From the north side of Plymouth take the A386 north 17 miles, through Tavistock, to the crossroads of Downton. • Opposite the Dartmoor Inn at Lydford turn left (west) onto School Road and follow it as it curves for 1¼ miles through the village of Lydford to the bridge.
Driving Time:	From north Plymouth – 1 hour and 15 minutes.

Lydford Bridge from the walkway

Information: Lydford Bridge over the River Lyd (30 metres below), a tributary of the River Tamar, gives access to the village of Lydford from the south. The earliest documentation of the bridge dates to 1478, and its form supports this date, though the fabric, which is visible after widening, is much later.

The bridge has a single slightly pointed arch with double flush arch rings of fairly regular voussoirs. The fabric is rubble, with recent concrete reinforcement at lower levels, surmounted by dressed and rusticated blocks of granite.

The dimensions are modest with a span of only 4.8 metres, but the gorge below is the main feature of this bridge. In 1666 the bridge was reported as being in decay, which, for the time, was about the same condition as many of the roads *(Henderson & Jervoise, 1938)*.

The bridge was recorded as being 3.3 metres wide in the pre-modern era but is now 6.6 metres wide. There are clear signs of widening in the soffits, though the extent suggests that either it was a second phase or at least must have taken place at the other face *(Robertson, 2020)*.

Jervoise refers to widening in the early 20th century, and the all too obvious concrete could well have been added then, but the stonework looks older. The setting is what matters most about this bridge, and there are many legends linked to it regarding suicides and lost love.

At the Bridge: The bridge can be viewed from the top but a real appreciation of it comes with the walk along the valley floor. Lydford Gorge is managed by the National Trust, but they are not responsible for the bridge itself. There is no parking or even pulling over at the bridge itself. Go past the bridge about 50 metres to the entrance of the Lydford Gorge National Trust Visitors Centre entrance and walk back. While you're here it is worth taking the time to walk the beautiful gorge floor to the base of the bridge.

https://www.nationaltrust.org.uk/lydford-gorge

Lydford Bridge over the Gorge – the roadway

The concrete reinforcement of the northern impost

Lydford Bridge

The west face

The east face

2 Harford Tavy Bridge ★★★

Bridge Name:	Harford Tavy Bridge
Other Names:	Tavy Bridge
Location:	Just to the east of the A386, north of Tavistock. It gives access to the village of Peter Tavy. Use postcode PL19 9LS for your satnav.
Setting:	Rural / Countryside
OS Ref:	SX 50571 76757
Crosses:	River Tavy
Orientation:	East / West
County:	Devon
Length:	21 metres
Bridge Type:	Multiple Arch
Materials:	Granite Stone
Traffic:	Road
Build Date:	1500
Authority:	West Devon (District Authority)
Designation:	Grade II Listed
Directions:	From Lydford Bridge: • Go back through Lydford and return to the A386. (Perhaps stop at the ruined castle. The Castle pub is next door.) • Turn right (south) and head back down the A386 for 5¼ miles to an unnamed road on the left signposted Peter Tavy along with signs for camping. • Turn left (east) and follow 500 metres to the bridge.
Driving Time:	From Lydford Bridge – 20 minutes.

Information: Harford Tavy Bridge over the River Tavy is just to the east of the A386, north of Tavistock, and gives access to the village of Peter Tavy.

This substantial bridge has three arches, with the one in the centre segmental and of significantly greater span than each of

Harford Tavy Bridge – south face

Harford Tavy Bridge – north face

Harford Tavy Bridge – the roadway

The eastern arch on the south side

the other two which are pointed, the one to the east more so. The arches have double arch rings in two orders, with light chamfering.

The triangular cutwaters at each face rise to provide four refuges at roadway level; otherwise, the road is 3 metres wide with no accommodation for pedestrians. The parapet walls are about 1 metre high, splayed outwardly at each end with one square granite pier to the southwest.

The fabric is roughly coursed granite rubble except that the slightly higher eastern arch is built of metamorphic stone, which is coursed, and the voussoirs of the central and eastern arches are finely dressed.

Jervoise accepts that there was a bridge of some kind on the site in the 16th century but dismisses the likelihood that what we see now is of that period, because the spans of the present arches seem incompatible with measurements presented in the early 19th century *(Henderson & Jervoise, 1938)*.

The Historic England listing suggests that the eastern, pointed, arch may be early, but that the other two arches were built later with moulding along inner springing of arches. This fits with the account given in local records that the central and western arches were destroyed by flood waters in the 1890s, after which the river changed course, presumably slightly to the west. The larger and newer segmental central arch is explained by the need to lengthen the bridge to accommodate the change in the river's course. The westernmost arch must have been made pointed for aesthetic reasons to preserve symmetry, given that the eastern arch had survived.

It is surprising that an effort was not made at that time to also widen the bridge; nonetheless, it carries a little used road. If this scenario is correct the surviving eastern arch is sensibly dated to around 1500, albeit that it has been restored since.

At the Bridge: Access is good, especially upstream. There is no formal parking nearby. There is a campsite at the western end of the bridge. There are no facilities or amenities at the bridge itself.

③ Horrabridge Bridge★★★

Bridge Name:	Horrabridge Bridge
Other Names:	Harrowbridge Bridge
Location:	In the village centre of Horrabridge, within Dartmoor National Park. Use postcode PL20 7TP for your satnav. This bridge is only 2 kilometres downstream from Huckworthy Bridge.
Setting:	Village / Rural
OS Ref:	SX 51329 69924
Crosses:	River Walkham
Orientation:	Northeast / Southwest
County:	West Devon
Length:	17 metres
Bridge Type:	Multiple Arch
Materials:	Granite Stone
Traffic:	Road (single file with width and weight restrictions)
Build Date:	1396
Authority:	West Devon (District Authority)
Designation:	Grade I Listed and Scheduled Monument
Directions:	From Horrabridge: • As you approach Horrabridge from the north, Gray Bridge Road is on the left, signposted Village Centre. • Turn left and follow to the bridge. At the left curve in the road, its name changes to Station Road.
Driving Time:	From Harford Tavy Bridge – 20 minutes.

Information: The village of Horrabridge grew up around an ancient crossing over the River Walkham, a tributary of the River Tavy. This three-arched, stone bridge was constructed in 1396 using funds released by Bishop Stafford of Exeter.

The footpath down to the river at northeast corner

Horrabridge Bridge – east face

The northern arch – west side

The double arch rings of the southern arch

The roadway

The bridge has three sharply pointed Gothic arches, of slightly different shapes, two with a span of 4.2 metres, the other 3.3 metres to give a total bridge length of 17 metres with the piers. There are double arch rings flush to the bridge faces and two pointed cutwaters on each pier, which rise to create four refuges in the roadway that is 3.3 metres wide. There are no dedicated pedestrian walkways on the road deck *(Robertson, 2020)*.

The fabric is granite rubble, squared and coursed in the piers, but more random masonry above the substructure. The parapet wall is 1½ metres high and splayed at the north end. It runs about 8 metres beyond the bridge. To the south, the causeway wall is continued about 25 metres as a boundary wall to the park *(Henderson & Coates, 1928)*.

The bridge is thought to date back at least to the 14th century, possibly even a century earlier, and apart from minor repairs has not been altered since. It is thought that there was a settlement in the area of the bridge even in prehistoric times. There is evidence of an even older bridge beneath the existing Station Road. The present bridge is one of the oldest in Devon.

The bridge was built to carry the Okehampton to Plymouth Road and continued in this function for centuries. It is listed as such in the Ordnance Survey of 1809, which lists it under the name of Harrowbridge. The main road has since been realigned, and both the bridge and surrounding village are known as Horrabridge.

There is a significant size weir in the upstream river that is viewable both from the bridge and the park.

At the Bridge: Access to view the bridge is excellent and there is parking in the village near the bridge. The village green is on the southeast corner of this bridge. The London Inn pub is further up Station Road. There are good views of the bridge from a public viewing point on the northwest corner of the bridge.

4 Huckworthy Bridge ★★

Bridge Name:	Huckworthy Bridge
Location:	Southeast of Tavistock on a minor road leading north out of Walkhampton, just upstream from Horrabridge. Use postcode PL20 6LP for your satnav.
Setting:	Rural / Countryside
OS Ref:	SX 53143 70538
Crosses:	River Walkham
Orientation:	North / South
County:	Devon
Length:	15 metres
Bridge Type:	Multiple Arch
Materials:	Granite Stone and Slatestone
Traffic:	Road
Build Date:	15th century
Authority:	West Devon (District Authority)
Designation:	Grade II* Listed
Directions:	From Horrabridge Bridge: • Turn around and make your way back up Station Road less than ¼ mile. • At the curve in Station Road turn left (east) onto Walkhampton Road and follow out of Horrabridge. The road becomes Knowle Terrace and after 2 miles leads you into the village of Walkhampton. • At the T junction in the village centre turn left (north) signposted Dousland and follow 1½ miles out of the village to the bridge.
Driving Time:	From Horrabridge Bridge – 10 minutes.

Information: This picturesque bridge in an idyllic setting spans the River Walkham on a minor road leading north out of Walkhampton, just upstream from Horrabridge.

The fabric is granite and slatestone rubble, squared and dressed lower down and for the voussoirs. The masonry becomes more random above.

Huckworthy Bridge – west face

The southern arch – east face

The western pedestrian refuge

The corbelled squinch at the northwest corner

The bridge has two unequally sized, slightly pointed arches, with the smaller to the north, giving a total length of 15 metres. The arches have double arch rings, with the lower ones slightly recessed *(Robertson, 2020)*.

There are off-centre, squared granite cutwaters both upstream and downstream, which rise to provide refuges in the roadway, which is 2.5 metres wide with rounded granite coping to the parapet walls. There is an unusual, corbeled support for the northwest parapet as it passes to the abutment there. The parapet's walls are about 80 centimetres high, splayed outwardly at each end, and diminishing in height to north and south. They extend about 4 metres to the southeast, 20 metres to the southwest, 8 metres to the northeast, and 4 metres to the northwest *(Henderson & Jervoise, 1938)*.

The build date is thought to be around 1500, and although some repairs have been made, the configuration is mainly unchanged.

Huckworthy Bridge has been featured in many artists' work, and in wildlife, travel, and historical television programmes over the years. The bridge is also featured in *Edith Blackwell Holden's Country Diary of an Edwardian Lady (Henderson & Jervoise, 1938)*.

At the Bridge: Access is good, though the upstream aspect is hard to view. At the south approach to the bridge there is room for a single car to pull over near a public green space with a bench. There are no facilities or other services nearby.

Huckworthy Bridge – the northern arch and cutwater – west side

5 Plym Bridge ★★★

Bridge Name:	Plym Bridge
Location:	Carries a track into a woodland recreational area on the eastern outskirts of Plymouth. Use postcode PL6 8AW for your satnav.
Setting:	Rural / Suburban / City Park
OS Ref:	SX5237758709
Crosses:	River Plym
Orientation:	Northwest / Southeast
County:	Devon
Length:	32 metres
Bridge Type:	Multiple Arch
Materials:	Killas Stone
Traffic:	Pedestrian
Build Date:	14th century
Authority:	South Hams (District Authority)
Designation:	Grade II* Listed
Directions:	From Huckworthy Bridge: • Reverse directions and make your way back to the A386 via Walkhampton and Horrabridge. • At the A386 turn left (south) and make your way 5¾ miles into northern Plymouth. • As you get into the built-up area just past the Park & Ride, get in the left lane and turn left, signposted Leigham, Estover, Glenholt. • The road bears left (east) and becomes the B3432. Follow this for a total of 3 miles. Past the first roundabout the road is called Plymbridge Road. • Stay on this road and at the second big roundabout follow straight across. This is still Plymbridge Road, and it gets increasingly narrow, rural, and it curves to the right. • The bridge is on the left, parking is on the right.
Driving Time:	From Huckworthy Bridge – 40 minutes.

Plym Bridge – south face

Information: Plym Bridge over the River Plym now carries a pedestrian footpath into a woodland recreational area on the eastern outskirts of Plymouth but must have once given important access into the city. A bridge has existed at this location from as early as 1238, with the current bridge being rebuilt in the 18th century, but it is seated on earlier piers. The imposts of the earlier arches can be seen just above water level inside the fourth arch *(Pevsner & Cherry, 1989)*.

It is built of Killas rubble and includes five segmental arches of varying proportions with single slightly recessed arch rings. These arches are attributed to the 18th century, but the piers are much older. The riverbed under the arches is paved with cobbles.

There are triangular cutwaters to all piers on both the upstream and downstream sides. The cutwaters are capped at road deck level below the level of the parapets. The parapets are splayed outward at either end over the abutments and have chamfered granite coping stones.

The original bridge was built in the 14th century and it is possible that the piers date from then.

The bridge had a chapel associated with it in pre-reformation times. Papal documents from 1450 refer to the *Chapel of Saint Mary the Virgin Plymbrigge.* The River Plym around Plym Bridge is popular with swimmers.

The total length of the bridge is 32 metres, and its width, a narrow 2.6 metres, which is surprising if it was largely rebuilt in the 18th century.

At the Bridge: Plymbridge Road provides easy access and there are free parking areas at both ends. Access is good, downstream, though it is hard to view the bridge from upstream.

The eastern arch with squinch in the parapet

Plym Bridge – north face

Unusual remnants of earlier arch rib imposts inside the fourth arch

Rubble material of the vault soffits

5 Aveton Gifford Bridge ★★

Bridge Name:	Aveton Gifford Bridge
Location:	Southeast of Plymouth just south of Aveton Gifford on the A379 road heading towards Bridge End and Churchstow. Use postcode TQ7 4NU for your satnav.
Setting:	Village / Suburban
OS Ref:	SX 69278 46969
Crosses:	River Avon (Devon–Tidal portion)
Orientation:	North / South
County:	Devon
Length:	366 metres (including all the causeways)
Bridge Type:	Multiple Arch
Materials:	Stone
Traffic:	Road
Build Date:	1440
Authority:	South Hams (District Authority)
Designation:	Both the bridge and the causeway are Grade II Listed
Directions:	From Aveton Gifford: • Follow the A379 into Aveton Gifford. • Stay on the A379 all the way south of Aveton Gifford to the bridge.
Driving Time:	From Plym Bridge – 1 hour and 40 minutes.

Information: Aveton Gifford Bridge carries the A379 over the upper tidal portion of the Devon River Avon just to the south of the village of the same name, a few kilometres northwest of Kingsbridge. It is named after the river and the family of Giffard who held the manor.

Here the river creates a broad tidal marshland and the original ford across this low-lying basin is said to have been first bridged around 1440. In 1427 the then Rector of Churchstow, Roger Bachiler, left a bequest of 100 shillings in his will for 'ad fabricam pontis de Aveton Giffard' (for the building of Aveton Gifford Bridge) *(Jones, 2019)*. Later in 1442 the Bishop granted indulgences to all those who contributed to its building maintenance and repair.

Aveton Gifford Central Bridge – east face

Aveton Gifford Northern Bridge – west face

The River Avon

Bridges in this book: Aveton Gifford
Barton
Bradford-on-Avon
Coombe Bisset (River Ebble)
Fordingbridge
Harnham
Huntington Warren
King John's
Lacock

Main Tributaries: River Ebble
River Bourne

The name Avon comes from the Brythonic language and stems from the word for river, which is 'abona'. Brythonic was an ancient, insular Celtic language of the British Isles spoken between the Iron Age and the 5th century, by a race of people called Britons. Because of this historic fact, there are no less than seven rivers across England with the name Avon. They are:

1. River Avon, Warwickshire, running from Naseby to Tewkesbury (also known as Shakespeare's Avon)
This is the longest River Avon in the British Isles and travels for 85 miles through the English counties of Leicestershire, Northamptonshire, Worcestershire, Warwickshire, and Gloucestershire, from its source at Naseby in Northamptonshire until it merges with the River Severn at Tewkesbury in Gloucestershire.

This River Avon is also known as the Warwickshire Avon, as it travels through more of that county than any other, or Shakespeare's Avon, as it also travels through William Shakespeare's birthplace of Stratford-upon-Avon. It is here at Stratford-upon-Avon that the river is spanned by the 14-arch masonry bridge known as Clopton Bridge, built in 1480 by former Mayor of London, Hugh Clopton.

2. River Avon, Bristol, running from Acton Turville to Avonmouth
This River Avon, also known as the Lower Avon or Bristol Avon, travels for 70 miles from its source at Acron Turville near Chipping Sodbury in Gloucestershire until it merges with the River Severn at its estuary at Avonmouth near the city of Bristol.

The river is navigable for most of its route and is served by several locks and is also spanned by many bridges including the famous Clifton Suspension Bridge, which spans the 245-feet-high Avon Gorge.

3. Avon Water, Hampshire, running from Holmsley in the New Forest to Keyhaven
Also known as the Hampshire Avon or Salisbury Avon, this River Avon is a 60-mile-long waterway, which rises at two locations, one at Devizes in Wiltshire and the other at Pewsey, also in Wiltshire, then travels through the counties of Wiltshire, Hampshire, and Dorset on England's south coast before draining into the English Channel at Mudeford, in Dorset.

The river has several tributaries, including the Rivers Bourne, Ebble, Nadder, and Wylie.

The river is served by several old bridges, including a three-arch stone bridge in the village of Ibsley in Hampshire and a six-arch masonry bridge situated at Fordingbridge, also in Hampshire.

4. River Avon, Hampshire, running from Pewsey to Christchurch (also known as Salisbury Avon)
The River Avon in Hampshire is also known as Avon Water, to distinguish it from the River Avon described above, which also flows through the county. It is a 9-mile-long stretch of water that rises near Holmsley in the New Forest before flowing in a southeasterly direction towards its mouth on the Solent, situated not far from the shingle bank at Keyhaven, which leads to the 16th-century Hurst Castle.

5. River Avon, Devon, running from Ryder's Hill to Bigbury (also known as River Aune)
England's shortest River Avon is just 7 miles long.

The river rises near Ryder's Hill on the boggy moorlands of the 368 square mile Dartmoor National Park, in the county of Devon, and flows in a southerly direction towards the south Devon coastal town of Bigbury-on-Sea, where it drains out into the English Channel.

Just to confuse things further, there is also:

6. The Little Avon River, running from Wickwar to Berkeley, in Gloucestershire

7. The Tetbury Avon, a tributary of the Bristol Avon (also called Little Avon)

Aveton Gifford Central Bridge – west face

In fact, there are three bridges and a lengthy causeway creating a total length of 366 metres. This bridge was not a simple thing to build; it had to include two raised sections to carry the road above the marshes on either side of the main river as well as the three bridges.

1. At the north end of the structure is a smaller branch of the Avon crossed by a bridge incorporating three 4.9 metre arches.
2. In the centre is a five-arch bridge crossing the main river stream. It once had six slightly pointed, rubble-built arches, each spanning 4.8 metres, and was 3.6 metres wide, probably without parapets; one of the arches is now buried like many of the smaller ones piercing the causeway.
3. At the south end is a single-arch bridge crossing a mill leat.

In all cases the fabric of the bridge is rubble local stone with flush single arch rings, voussoirs, and triangular cutwaters without pedestrian refuges.

The parapet walls are continuous on the east side with only four small access openings for the public footpath crossing the marshland. However, for the bridges themselves, pedestrians must still use the dangerous bridge roadway. On the west side, in the centre causeway, the parapet was removed as the marshland was reclaimed allowing access to several modern businesses and their respective parking. The remaining parapet walls are flat topped without coping and have a series of vertical through stones in regular bays, characteristic of bridges in the area *(Henderson & Jervoise, 1938)*.

The original bridge was narrow; it only had to take pedestrians, packhorses, and carts. In 1817, the bridge was widened by 2 metres on the upstream face by a local mason, Walter Macey. This was accomplished by supporting shallow segmental arches on the cutwaters, and at some stage, something similar but more limited was done again upstream *(Pevsner & Cherry, 1989)*.

The carriageway appears to be 5 metres wide between the parapets. There are no pedestrian footpaths anywhere on the bridges or causeways. Wear a Hi Vis vest.

In 1688, a house was built on the west side of the central bridge, which, by 1842 had become an inn, the Maltman's Arms, later known as the Bridge Inn (now Bridge House). One could assume it did good trade with all the passing traffic! Later, it became a private house and in the 1930s William Damerell set up the first garage and cycle shop there, and thus began the steady increase of businesses by the bridge. Today the back of the house sits on foundations that are in the river halfway across the causeway *(Robertson, 2020)*.

This river crossing is still of great importance and is heavily used as the only A road in the area. There is limited access upstream, though the best view is from the river.

At the Bridge: At the north end of the bridge there is public parking off the roundabout. The Fisherman's Rest Inn is at the north end of the bridge. At the south end of the causeway there is a small access area to the mill leat which may afford a temporary pull over.

Aveton Gifford Central Bridge – east face

A small arch of the southernmost bridge

Soffit of the vaulting showing the old arches and widened arches

8 EAST DEVON TOUR

Using Exeter as the starting point these bridges are arranged north to south and include Culmstock Bridge, Ellerhayes Bridge, Stoke Canon Bridge, Old Exe Bridge, and Clyst St Mary Bridge.

1 Culmstock Bridge ★★★

Bridge Name:	Culmstock Bridge
Location:	In the village of Culmstock, which is 11½ miles east of Tiverton on the B3391. Closest exit off the M5 is exit 27. Use postcode EX15 3JJ for your satnav.
Setting:	Rural / Countryside
OS Ref:	ST 10113 13764
Crosses:	River Culm
Orientation:	North / South
County:	Devon
Length:	23.5 metres
Bridge Type:	Multiple Arch and Beam
Materials:	Calp Limestone
Traffic:	Road
Build Date:	14th century
Authority:	Mid Devon (District Authority)
Designation:	Grade II Listed
Directions:	From Exeter: • Travel up (north) the M5 to junction 27. • Exit onto the A38 heading east, signposted Wellington, across the roundabout and follow 3 miles. You will cross over the M5. • 100 metres after crossing over the M5 the B3391 intersects from the right signposted Culmstock. • Turn right and follow for 2 miles to the bridge.
Driving Time:	From Exeter – 30 minutes.

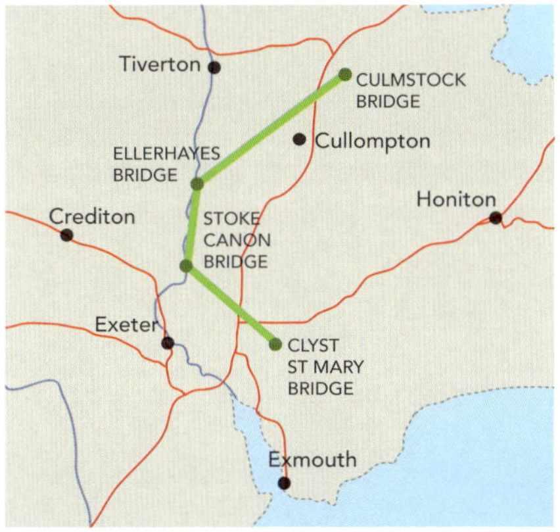

Culmstock Bridge – the large southern cutwater and flat beam arch – west side

Culmstock Bridge – west face

Information: Culmstock Bridge, in a beautiful setting, carries the B3391 over the River Culm, a tributary of the River Exe. The river makes a hard western turn to run under the bridge and under a modern arch.

The limestone rubble bridge, as seen now, results from three phases of building separated by many centuries. First, a bridge of three segmental arches is thought to have been built in the 14th century (repairs in 1412 are documented), but one arch was swept away by severe flooding in 1774 and replaced by two arches. It is tentatively assumed that the original arches are to the north, but they all look similar, so this is in doubt. At the same time, another two arches were added giving presumably six in total (not five as suggested by Jervoise).

Then in the 20th century, sometime after 1938 since Henderson makes no mention of it, the southernmost sixth arch was replaced by flat steel beams with lengthwise brick vaulting and a concrete facade. It may also be that at that time the pier and starling beside it was greatly broadened and the road deck was widened at that point. It appears as a mill leat, but it is not. Instead, it was intended to reduce the water pressure at that point and allow the river's sharp western turn.

There are several Victorian era iron reinforcement ties through the bridge that occasionally are half buried under the cutwater and refuge. This suggests that these were rebuilt and covered, probably in the 20th-century refurbishment.

The other five arches are all segmental and stilted of varying heights and spans. The largest two span 6 metres each, the other three segmental arches each span 4.8 metres. There are single flush arch rings of dressed voussoirs.

The eastern parapet and granite coping stones

The vault and soffit of the central river arch

The bridge over the river itself narrows to only 3 metres wide but the approaches are more generous in width. There are rubble parapets with rounded ashlar coping splayed outward at each end. The eastern parapet wall continues southward for many metres running parallel with the river.

There are cutwaters both upstream and downstream. Three of them upstream (east) and two of them downstream (west) rise to create pedestrian refuges. The remainder are capped below the parapets. There are no dedicated pedestrian walkways on the bridge.

There is a local legend about Culmstock Bridge that relates the story of a local man named Frankan, a 'maltmaster' beer brewer who, because of declining sales due to the popularity of cider, made a deal with the Devil. The story goes that the Devil and Frankan had a fight on Culmstock Bridge, with the victor throwing the other off the bridge into the River Culm. Each year on 21 May, this fight is repeated. If Frankan wins, the Devil kills off the apple blossom with a late frost; if the Devil wins, cider makers will have a good year.

At the Bridge: The bridge is easily viewed from downstream, though the trees obscure some angles. There is street parking at both bridge ends. The Culm Valley Inn sits at the northern end of the bridge.

Culmstock Bridge – southern flat beam arch – west side

2 Ellerhayes Bridge ★★

Bridge Name:	Ellerhayes Bridge
Location:	To the north of Killerton near Killerton House, 8 miles north of Exeter. Use postcode EX5 4PX for your satnav.
Setting:	Rural / Countryside
OS Ref:	SS 97559 01171
Crosses:	River Culm
Orientation:	Northeast / Southwest
County:	Devon
Length:	15 metres
Bridge Type:	Multiple Arch
Materials:	Killerton Stone
Traffic:	Road
Build Date:	15th century
Authority:	Mid Devon (District Authority)
Designation:	Grade II* Listed
Directions:	From Culmstock Bridge: • Reverse direction and make your way back towards the M5. • 1 mile before you reach the M5, there is a crossroads called Waterloo Cross. • At the roundabout turn left (south) onto the B3181, signposted Willand. • Follow this road south for 10 miles, through Willand and Cullompton. In southern Cullompton at a roundabout signposted Broadclyst and Killerton House, bear left and continue to follow the B3181 south to Beare Lane, signposted Silverton Mill. • Turn right and follow this road ¾ mile south to its T junction with an unnamed road (possibly Silverton Road). • Turn right and follow to the bridge.
Driving Time:	From Culmstock Bridge – 40 minutes.

Ellerhayes Bridge roadway looking southwest

Ellerhayes Bridge – northwest face

The central cutwater on the southeast side

Ellerhayes Bridge – southeast face

Information: Ellerhayes Bridge carries a minor road over the River Culm, a tributary of the River Exe, and is found by Killerton House (National Trust) to the southeast of Silverton, a village to the north of Exeter.

The bridge structure is of coursed rubble volcanic trap known as Killerton stone. It has four two-centred, slightly pointed river arches, together with two flood arches, the easternmost one built in brick.

As a result of extensive widening, each face of the bridge is markedly different in appearance. The downstream face, to the northwest, has double chamfered arch rings but the upstream face is much plainer with single arch rings. Unfortunately, the altered upstream face is more easily viewed than the downstream face.

The present bridge is 4.8 metres wide, but this follows an 18th century widening, which added 1.8 metres upstream, though the evidence is not clear in the soffits.

There are cutwaters both upstream and downstream, capped off below the level of the parapets. There are no pedestrian walkways or refuges on the bridge. A string course protrudes at the level of the cutwater caps. Chamfered coping stones top the parapet walls on both sides.

The original build-date is normally estimated as the 15th century with the widening perhaps taking place in the late 18th century.

At the Bridge: There is parking in the National Trust car park on the southern end of the bridge and at the overflow parking to the north of the bridge.

3 Stoke Canon Bridge ★★

Bridge Name: Stoke Canon Bridge

Location: At the south end of the village of Stoke Canon on the A396 over the River Culm just short of its juncture with the River Exe. On the northern outskirts of Exeter. Use postcode EX5 4BG for your satnav.

Setting: Rural / Village

OS Ref: SX 93787 97590

Crosses: River Culm

Orientation: North / South

County: Devon

Length: 270 metres (including the causeway)

Bridge Type: Multiple Arch

Materials: Thorverton Stone

Traffic: Road

Build Date: 15th century

Authority: East Devon (District Authority)

Designation: Grade II* Listed and Scheduled Monument

Directions: From Ellerhayes Bridge:

- Continue across the bridge (north) on Elleyhayes Road for 2 miles into the village of Silverton. The road changes names several times.
- In the village centre, at the only roundabout, follow straight across and continue to the junction with the A396.
- Turn left (south) and follow for 4 miles, through Stoke Cannon, to the bridge.

Driving Time: From Ellerhayes Bridge – 25 minutes.

Information: Stoke Canon Bridge and causeway stretch over two arms of the River Culm. The first documentation of a bridge here dates to 1326, but the medieval bridge we see today is thought to date to the 15th century. Bishop Walter de Stapledon, the 15th Bishop of Exeter, left £4 in his will of 1326 for its upkeep.

Stoke Canon Bridge – east face

Stoke Canon Bridge – west face

The river has two branches and runs across a broad marshy valley, thus much of the bridge takes the form of a long causeway. The bridge is constructed from dressed Thorverton stone with string courses above the arches at road level. The bridge has low parapets with saddle-back coping, repaired with concrete in places. There are no dedicated pedestrian walkways or refuges anywhere on this long and narrow bridge. The causeway contains some old sections but has been much widened to carry the main A396 road.

At the very north of the structure is a single flood arch, which usually holds water under it unless in drought. It is a two-centred flood arch but with double chamfered arch rings on its west 'downstream' face, even though it was apparently widened in the 19th century in the same fashion as the river bridge.

The main river is slightly further south and is spanned by a bridge with three segmental arches of ashlar and dressed stone. On the upstream (east) face, double chamfered arch rings remain, but the bridge was widened downstream in the early 19th century by building additional facades onto the cutwaters, and the arches here have unembellished single arch rings *(Robertson, 2020)*. The bridge was originally 3 metres wide, and even after widening there is still only room for one-way traffic.

In the causeway are two 19th-century flood arches, one dry and one with pooled water.

Further south, towards the bend in the road, is a smaller but still substantial branch of the River Culm which is crossed by a single low-level arch.

Since there are early references to a bridge with nine arches it must be assumed that the causeway has been rebuilt.

At the Bridge: There is no formal parking at the bridge but space at its north end may allow a temporary pull over. There are no facilities or amenities at the bridge, but these are available back in Stoke Canon. The long causeway makes access to the river level very difficult.

The underside vault of the main river arch

The northernmost flood arch – east side

④ Old Exe Bridge ★★★★

Bridge Name:	Old Exe Bridge
Location:	South Devon in central Exeter next to the modern A3015. It now sits high and dry in a park on the north side of the River Exe a few blocks south of Exeter Cathedral. Use postcode EX1 1BR for your satnav.
Setting:	City Centre / Urban
OS Ref:	SX 91656 92164
Crosses:	River Exe
Orientation:	Northeast / Southwest
County:	Devon
Length:	180 metres
Bridge Type:	Multiple Arch
Materials:	Mixed Stone
Traffic:	Pedestrian
Build Date:	c. 1200
Authority:	Exeter (District Authority)
Designation:	Grade II Listed and Scheduled Monument
Directions:	Within Exeter: • Follow the A3015 into the city centre to the river. • The bridge is in a park on the left (north) side of Edmund Street. Find a convenient place to park and walk to it. The nearest car park is the Cathedral and Quay Car Park off Western Way. Allow some time at this bridge.
Driving Time:	From Stoke Canon Bridge – 15 minutes.

Information: A short section of the causeway of Old Exe Bridge is all that remains, and that sits on dry land. Old Exe Bridge no longer crosses water but the surviving arches from the northeastern end are preserved in a basin-shaped open park space hemmed in by roads in the city centre of Exeter. It is the second oldest surviving (remnants) bridge in England. Old

Old Exe Bridge and St Edmunds Church Tower – southeast face

Old Exe Bridge arch

Ancient arch ribs

The River Exe

The River Exe at Topsham (© David Dixon, and licensed for reuse under Creative Commons License 2.0)

Bridges in this Book: Stoke Canon
Landacre (River Barle)
Exe (on dry land today)
Barle (River Barle)
Bury (River Haddeo)
Tarr Steps (River Barle)

Tributaries: Barle
Culm
Clyst
Haddeo
Horner Water

The River Exe is more than 50 miles long and wends its way through the beautiful Exmoor landscape, almost all the way from the Bristol Channel in the north to the English Channel in the south. The catchment area of the Exe is largely underlain by impermeable sandstones, which leads to an elevated and rapid drainage. The very upper catchment of the River Exe on Exmoor is moorland with large amounts of peat.

The source of the Exe is near Simonsbath, on Exmoor, in Somerset at an altitude of 1,400 feet above sea level, and it reaches the sea at Exmouth. On the way it flows across the Devon moorland and passes across the rural Exe valley landscape passing through many communities that take their name from the river including Exford (where the ford has long been replaced by a bridge), Exton, Exbridge, Exmouth, and of course Exeter.

A mile above Exbridge, the Exe is joined by the River Barle. The major tributaries of the Exe are the River Barle and River Haddeo, but there are many smaller rivers in the northern reaches of Exmoor known as the 'waters', which dash to join the Exe. These include Weir Water, Horner Water, and Badgworthy Water to name but a few.

The name 'Exe' is thought to stem from the Latin take on the Brittonic word 'isca'. This translates either as 'water' or 'abounding in fish'. The Exe is known for its salmon population. Back in 1924, a staggering 61-pound salmon was caught in the river.

Many ancient bridges span the River Exe and its tributaries including the structures of Landacre and Tarr Steps. The River Exe also provides water for Wimbleball Reservoir and Lake. Throughout its journey from source to sea, the River Exe forms a central part of the lives and identities of those who live along its banks.

London Bridge was built slightly earlier. It is very likely that there was an even earlier wooden Roman bridge spanning the river at the important civitas of Isca Dumnoniorum *(Brown, 2019)*.

There is a documentary record of a bridge chaplain in 1196, suggesting that the bridge was at least part-built by then. It was built by Nicholas Gervys and his son Walter between 1196 and 1214 across the river from which it takes its name. During that time, they wrote that 'There is no bridge over the River Exe but only clappers of tymbre which men pass over on foote but in the wynter the passage is dangerous, and many people thereby perished and wer carried awaye with the ffloude and drowned'. Nicholas and his son were determined to build a bridge of stone *(Henderson & Jervoise, 1938)*.

That original stone bridge was comprised of 17 or 18 arches, of which nine survive, one partially buried under the bypass. A further length of about 25 metres of bridge lies buried beneath Edmund Street and the modern reclaimed bank of the Exe.

The bridge was built 4.2 metres in width and was never widened. It carried a roadway some 4 metres wide if allowance is made for the parapets that no longer exist. Some medieval paving of the roadway survives above the seventh arch whilst the rest is a modern reconstruction.

The original structure had both semi-circular and Gothic pointed

The foundations of former bridge buildings

arches of ribbed construction, all resting on three or four vault ribs, which can be clearly seen beneath the surviving arches. The pointed arches are constructed differently to the semi-circular ones. The spans of the pointed arches are constructed with five narrow vault ribs. The semi-circular arches have just three much wider ribs. The largest arch spanned 5.7 metres, which added to the broad piers carrying large cutwaters, created a total estimated bridge length of around 180 metres *(Robertson, 2020)*.

The fabric of the bridge was rubble, faced with ashlar, and a mix of mauve volcanic stone quarried locally and known as 'Exeter Trap'. Sandstone from Salcombe Regis in Devon was used for repairs, and patching over the centuries has employed a variety of other materials. The bridge piers were founded on bases of rubble and gravel contained within bays of wooden stakes driven into the riverbed *(see Starlings in the glossary)*. Dendrochronological (tree-ring) dating has documented that some of these oak stakes were felled in the years 1190 to 1200.

There were originally houses on the bridge, along with chapels at each end. The northeast chapel was dedicated to St Edmund and opposite was a chantry chapel dedicated to St Mary. At the southwestern end, across the river, was a chapel to St Thomas. The six arches in the very centre of the river remained clear of buildings and never had any structures on them.

St Edmund's Church at the northwest end, first recorded in 1214, formed an integral part of the bridge's original construction with its tower a structural component of the bridge. The floors of both the nave and chancel were supported above the river by the second and third bridge arches. St Edmund's was destroyed by fire in 1832 and rebuilt in 1833. In 1975 the church was partly demolished (intentionally) with much of the 19th-century masonry removed. All of the ancient walling was retained, and the bell tower stands today, surviving to its full original height *(Henderson & Jervoise, 1938)*.

Almost opposite St Edmunds was a chantry chapel dedicated to St Mary. When Walter Gervase, one of the original fundraisers for the bridge construction, died in 1256 he was allegedly buried at the chantry on the bridge dedicated to St Mary. According to local records, when the chantry chapel was demolished in July 1833 the workmen discovered a tall skeleton under the floor, which was then reinterred on the site *(Brown, 2019)*.

The chapel dedicated to St Thomas that had been established at the southwestern end of the bridge in the mid-13th century, was almost entirely destroyed by fire in the early 1400s, and the parishioners rebuilt the chapel further away from the river. The final remnants of St Thomas's chapel were removed from the bridge in 1778.

Shops also encroached onto the bridge during the medieval period, supported on beams laid precariously across the cutwaters and timbers that sprang from the stone arches of the bridge.

The stereoscopic photograph above was taken in the 1860s and shows surviving late 17th-century timber-framed houses balanced on the remaining arches of the medieval bridge. By this date, over half of the bridge had been demolished but the north eastern half, closer to the city, had retained many of its ancient timber-framed structures. These houses on the north side of the remaining portion of the bridge survived well into the latter-half of the 19th century. The tower of St Edmund's church is to the left in the photograph. It's the only photograph ever taken of these properties, although such was their peculiar antiquarian charm that they appeared in several drawings and watercolours throughout the 19th century. The houses on the south side of the bridge were sketched by JMW Turner in 1811 (Wolfpaw, 2013)

The northern remnants of the bridge and St Edmund's Church

These supported a great horizontal beam, and this beam supported the rear of the houses while allowing the water to flow through the arches unimpeded. The houses were built by the Exe Bridge Trust as part of their mandate to provide money to maintain the bridge.

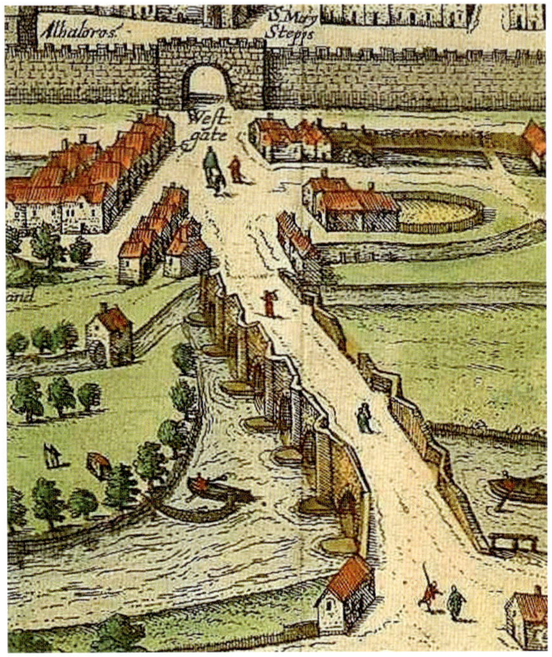

Above is a 1587 drawing by John Hooker, showing the Exe Bridge in some detail. In reality, the bridge had more arches than is shown but St Edmund's church is visible towards the West Gate, as is Frog Street. The plan also shows the refuges in the bridge used by pedestrians to keep out of the way of carts. Various mills and leats can also be seen. The mills were used for weaving cloth, upon which much of Exeter's medieval and early post-medieval wealth was based (Wolfpaw, 2013)

In 1775, a tragedy took place in the public house named The Fortunes of War, which was built on the bridge. A fire broke out that could not be extinguished by the local fire engines, even though they were close to the river. Twenty people died in the conflagration, many of whom were vagrants

The 1727 drawing above is by the antiquarian William Stukeley. It shows the view from the south across the river from the suburb of St Thomas to St Edmund's Church. The church's bell tower is visible at the far end of the bridge

who lodged at a penny per night. The cause of the fire was thought to be some of the occupants melting brimstone over a fire for making matches, to sell during the day *(Henderson & Jervoise, 1938).*

After 600 years the bridge was finally replaced in the 1770s, following the construction of a new bridge, which took a different alignment further upstream. The new three-arch bridge, designed by Joseph Dixon, was erected in 1778, linked by a roadway appropriately named New Bridge Street. As soon as the new bridge was opened the western part of the old one began to be taken down, as far as the houses at the northeastern end. The demolition left only the nine arches that still

Old Exe Bridge and St Edmunds Church Tower – northwest face

Detail of the Tudor House

Old Exe Bridge and St Edmunds Church Tower – remnants of the roadway looking south

survive in the park today, but the bridge continued to be used as Edmund Street with the arches filled in. That 18th-century section was itself replaced in 1905 by an iron structure and the bridge's long history was gradually lost to the public. Then parts of the medieval bridge were exposed by German bombing during the Second World War. Finally, in the late 1960s, a new project was begun to construct two new bridges to improve traffic flow. During that project, the remains of the northeastern end of the medieval bridge were discovered intact.

The bridge and chapel were left as an historic attraction in the centre of the new road complex, in a park area just off Frog Street. Part of the park design incorporates foundations of the medieval stone houses that lined the original riverbanks *(Pevsner & Cherry, 1989)*.

At the Bridge: The Old Exe Bridge is bounded by Edmund Street and Frog Street, near the river. The bridge is viewable at any time. Access is good all around this marvellous survivor, undoubtedly one of the oldest in England. The shelter of the arches attracts some homeless. There is a well-preserved Tudor house on the appropriately named Tudor Street only a few metres north from the bridge that serves as a good example of the structures that might have once been on the bridge itself.

5 Clyst St Mary Bridge ★★

Bridge Name:	Clyst St Mary Bridge
Other Names:	Bishop's Clyst Bridge
Location:	Just off junction 30 of the M5. The bridge sits alongside the A3052 just to the west of the village of Clyst St Mary (formerly Bishop's Clyst) 5 kilometres east of Exeter. Use postcode EX5 1BS for your satnav.
Setting:	Suburban
OS Ref:	SX 97159 91091
Crosses:	River Clyst
Orientation:	East / West
County:	Devon
Length:	250 metres (including the causeway)
Bridge Type:	Multiple Arch
Materials:	Basalt and Sandstone
Traffic:	Pedestrian
Build Date:	13th century
Authority:	East Devon (District Authority)
Designation:	Grade II* Listed
Directions:	From Exe Bridge: • Make your way to the A3015, Western Way heading east. This becomes Topsham Road. • Follow through Exeter to Rydon Lane. • Turn left (north) and follow for only ¼ mile. Bear to the left to exit as it becomes the A379 and approaches the big M5 roundabout. • Follow to the right as it becomes exit 30 for the M5. Follow the roundabout east under the M5 as the road becomes Sidmouth Road. The bridge is on the left. • Follow ¼ mile into Clyst St Mary and at the first roundabout take the first left and then left again to the bridge. The Half Moon pub is on the corner.
Driving Time:	From Exe Bridge – 20 minutes.

Clyst St Mary Bridge – south face

The coping stones of the parapet

Information: Clyst St Mary Bridge and causeway cross two arms of the River Clyst and the broad floodplain in between. It is first recorded in the early decades of the 13th century and is made up of five arches linked by a walled causeway and once carried the road from Sidmouth to Exeter. It now sits directly alongside the A3052 (Sidmouth Road) just to the west of the village of Clyst St Mary, at a crossing point of the river, which may have been in use during the Roman period. The stone-built bridge is thought to be the oldest surviving medieval bridge in Devon outside the city of Exeter, with the earliest documentary reference of 1238 (as 'pontem de Clist') *(Brown, 1982)*.

There were at least four stages of construction. The two low segmental arches spanning the River Clyst itself at the western end of the bridge are thought to be the most ancient part of the structure, presumably that referred to in 1238. These arches are 3.4 metres wide and would have carried a roadway 2.8 metres in width. Each vault rests on four chamfered ribs. This section of the structure sits under the A3015.

The fabric of the bridge is of trap (volcanic basalt) and sandstone ashlar, and the ribs are entirely of sandstone.

The absence of the distinctive red breccia known as Heavitree stone, quarried nearby after the middle of the 14th century, supports the early construction date of these arches. Quarries of volcanic trap lie at a much greater distance and Heavitree stone would almost certainly have been used had it been available to the early bridge builders. The same logic applies for a single arch at the centre of the causeway and the two arches at the eastern end of the bridge, which carry it across a mill leat. These three arches are sufficiently similar in construction to suggest that they were built at the same time, although they are clearly different to the western arches, and may date to a recorded substantial improvement to the bridge, which was made in 1310. They have a chamfered starling at the base and are wider than those at the west thus allowing for an increased road width, 3.94 metres in the case of the central arch, and 3.35 metres over the two eastern arches *(Robertson, 2020)*.

The revetment walls and substantial buttresses of the causeway appear to be noticeably of one build. In this case extensive use has been made of Heavitree stone, which suggests a mid-14th-century or later date for their construction.

An order to undertake major repairs in 1603 is believed to relate to the causeway rather than the arches. All five medieval arches were, however, widened after the mid-19th century by the addition of semi-circular arches of breccia, unfortunately at both the north and south faces.

The bridge was reportedly the site of a minor battle of the Wars of the Roses in 1455.

It also featured in the Western Prayer Book rebellion of 1549 when it was barricaded against the King's forces led by Sir Peter Carew. This followed an incident in which an elderly lady parishioner of the village was upbraided by Sir Walter Raleigh (father of the famous explorer) for openly displaying her Catholic rosary in contravention of the new liturgy. Further acts of rebellion led to an army being dispatched from London and on Sunday 4 August 1549 the village was captured and burnt with the rebels falling back onto the west bank of the River Clyst but continuing to defend the narrow bridge. Unable to cross the bridge, royalist troops forded the river further upstream and attacked the bridge rebels from behind. A battle ensued at Clyst Heath, which led to a victory for the King's army who then marched into Exeter to find that all the surviving insurgents had dispersed.

At the Bridge: Access to land north and south of the bridge is available. There is an information board about the bridge and battle at its western end where it adjoins a public footpath. The Half Moon pub sits at the eastern end of the bridge.

The long causeway parapet

The old mill leat and eastern flood defense arches

The rustic and obviously red sandstone parapets

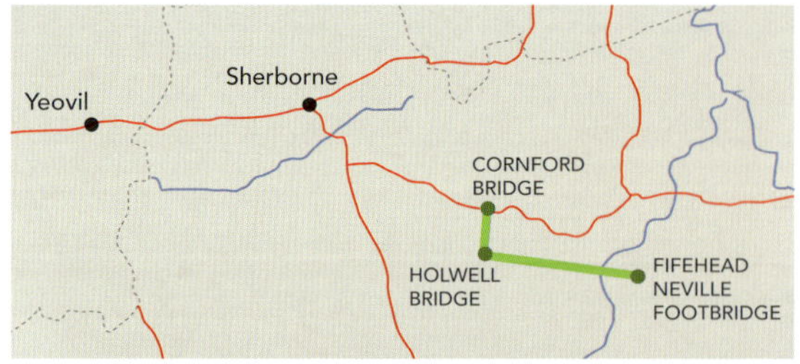

9 NORTH DORSET TOUR

Using Yeovil as a starting point these bridges are arranged from west to east and include Cornford Bridge, Holwell Bridge, and Fifehead Neville Footbridge.

1 Cornford Bridge ★★

Bridge Name: Cornford Bridge

Location: To the southwest of the village of Bishop's Caundle, and a few miles southeast of Sherborne. This bridge is only 1 mile from Holwell Bridge. Use postcode DT9 5JZ for your satnav.

Setting: Rural / Countryside

OS Ref: ST 69161 12044

Crosses: Caundle Brook

Orientation: Northwest / Southeast

County: Dorset

Length: 13.5 metres

Bridge Type: Multiple Arch

Materials: Sandstone

Traffic: Road (but there are serious width restrictors on the road approaches)

Build Date: 1480

Authority: Dorset (Unitary Authority)

Designation: Grade II* Listed

Directions: From Caundle Marsh:

- Just south of Caundle Marsh the road splits with a minor road veering right and signposted Holwell 2½. This is the bridge road, do not turn off. Follow this minor road south to the bridge.

Driving Time: From Yeovil – 25 minutes.

Information: Cornford Bridge is named after the field name closest to it and carries the minor road from Bishop's Caundle to Holwell over the Caundle Brook, a tributary of the River Stour, to the southwest of the village of Bishop's Caundle.

Cornford Bridge – west face

The central cutwater – west face

The fabric is coursed mellow, honey-coloured local stone rubble with ashlar dressings. The bridge comprises three pointed arches, each spanning 3.3 metres with double unchamfered arch rings in two orders on the upstream face.

There are two large triangular cutwaters on the 1.5 metre broad piers, which rise to the level of the parapets, where they are in part capped, and part projected into small rectangular refuges: a very unusual arrangement. Vertical slits incised into the cutwaters appear to be an embellishment rather than having a practical use.

Jervoise refers to some rebuilding of the downstream face, indicating that the central arch only has one ring of voussoirs,

Voussoirs forming double arch rings

The western parapet

and that there is only a single cutwater. Both he and the Historic England listing refer to a 3-stage buttress that replaces the other cutwater, though the listing seems to regard it as part of the original structure.

Both sources confidently attribute the bridge to the 15th century and suggest that work was done on the downstream face in the 18th century. The bridge is 3 metres wide with single direction traffic and the rubble parapets are capped with bevelled coping stones except at one point where a hollow-chamfered medieval coping stone is used *(Robertson, 2020)*.

In 1994 the bridge was subjected to a major repair, strengthening and cleaning project. Further repairs were carried out in the early 21st century after the parapet was seriously damaged by a vehicle strike. The (supposedly temporary) repair used modern dressed stone completely out of character for the bridge.

At the Bridge: Access is fairly good to the west, though foliage prevents the three arches from being viewed together. There is a public footpath nearby. The east face, however, is nearly impossible to view with private gardens and perilously steep riverbanks. There is no formal parking near the bridge, but it is out in the country and wide verges on the approach roads will provide temporary pull over if it is dry. There are no amenities or facilities.

The unusual partly capped pedestrian refuges – western side

2 Holwell Bridge ★

Bridge Name:	Holwell Bridge
Location:	No road utilises this bridge. It sits just behind (60 metres north of) St Lawrence's Church, on a bridle path connecting the villages of Holwell and Bishops Caundle. This bridge is only 1 mile from Cornford Bridge. Use postcode DT9 5LP for your satnav.
OS Ref:	ST 69922 12023
Crosses:	Caundle Brook
Orientation:	North / South
County:	Dorset
Length:	17.5 metres
Bridge Type:	Multiple Arch
Materials:	Stone
Traffic:	Bypassed and disused
Build Date:	15th century
Authority:	Dorset (Unitary Authority)
Designation:	Grade II Listed, At Risk Register
Directions:	From Holwell (Dorset): • The tiny village of Holwell lies at the end of a small road called The Borough off Cornford Hill Road. • At the large triangular intersection at the junction of Crouch Lane and Cornford Hill Road turn northeast onto The Borough and follow to the end at the Church. It may look at times as if this is a private driveway but persevere.
Driving Time:	From Cornford Bridge – 10 minutes.

Holwell Bridge – west face

Information: This poor structure started its life as a packhorse bridge but has had a troubled history, especially in recent decades. Originally it consisted of two shallow three-centred 'basket handle' arches of about 3.6 metre spans and an additional channel that looks like a mill stream race. There are two giant piers between.

Today it is a hybrid structure with only one intact arch to the north end and to the south, a 9-metre wooden footbridge supported on two very large piers, the more northern one with an upstream cutwater rising to the level of the trackway. The only remaining stone arch is a particularly shallow segmental 'basket handle' rubble stone arch, springing from quite high on the pier and abutment.

The southern pier is square and serves a double function as the side of the mill stream at the southern end of the structure. All the piers and abutments are thought to be medieval.

The arch – east face

The 'mill race' – east face

Rubble built parapets and arch ring

Three-Centred (Basket Handle) Arch

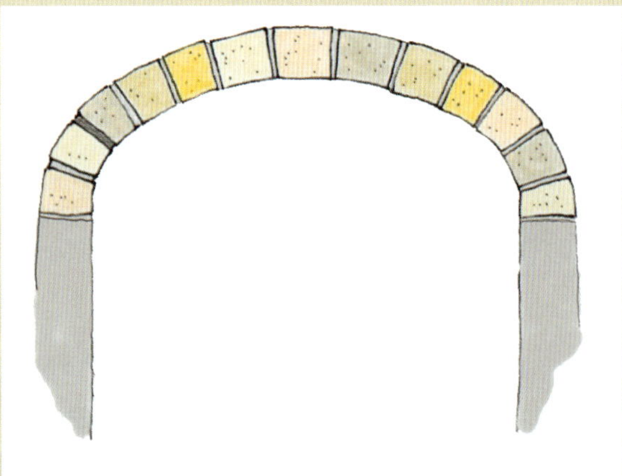

Also known as a depressed (flattened) semi-circular arch and sometimes (in the vernacular) a 'basket handle' arch. The width of this form is wider than its height and is dependent upon a keystone.

This arch style is a strong structure and is often found in bridges and aqueducts that handle large volumes of water. The strength of this design, as with the semi-circle and the segmental arch, comes from the regular consistent shape of the voussoirs, as each is identical in taper to its neighbour.

The Historic England listing explains that until recent times there was a stone slab and a wrought iron structure instead of the current wooden one. The eastern face of the bridge is in particularly poor shape and it is clear that without intervention this bridge will not be with us for long.

The trackway is just over 1.5 metres wide, and above the arch there are parapets just under a metre high above rough string courses, though they look like a relatively modern addition. Perhaps it would be reasonable to assign the piers to the 15th century, the stone arch to the early 18th century, and the rest to the last 100 years *(Robertson, 2020)*.

At the Bridge: The only parking is at the church and the bridge is accessible down a small bridleway. Access to view both faces of the bridge is good but a bit perilous. There are no facilities or amenities at the bridge.

3 Fifehead Neville Footbridge ★★

Bridge Name:	Fifehead Neville Footbridge
Other Names:	Fifehead Neville Packhorse Bridge
Location:	Fifehead Neville, alongside a ford/Irish Bridge on a minor road called Dark Lane at the east side of the village of Fifehead Neville, which is just southwest of Sturminster Newton. Use postcode DT10 2AL for your satnav.
Setting:	Countryside
OS Ref:	ST 77189 11146
Crosses:	River Divelish
Orientation:	Northeast / Southwest
County:	Dorset
Length:	10.5 metres (with abutments)
Bridge Type:	Two Arch
Materials:	Stone
Traffic:	Road
Build Date:	14th century
Authority:	Dorset (Unitary Authority)
Designation:	Grade II* Listed
Directions:	To Fifehead Neville Footbridge: • Fifehead Neville is one of three Fifehead villages including Fifehead St Quintin. There is only one road through the village. • Once you've found Fifehead Neville on the map, follow ¾ mile northwest through Fifehead Neville. The road becomes Dark Lane and has several sharp curves. Follow through the countryside to the bridge.
Driving Time:	From Holwell Bridge – 20 minutes.

Information: Fifehead Neville Footbridge spans the River Divelish, which is a tributary of the River Stour, alongside a paved ford on a minor road called Dark Lane at the east side of the village of Fifehead Neville.

It is of unusual configuration with two stilted, slightly convex sided triangular pointed arches, almost ogee-shaped, which each span 1.8 metres, contributing towards a bridge length of 4.5 metres. It was constructed as a packhorse bridge, without a parapet, to avoid animals' panniers hitting as they crossed the bridge. There are low embankment walls on each side that rise to bridge level.

Triangular Arch

The earliest of all arches, the triangular arch, also called a Mayan arch, is formed with two very large diagonal stones, which mutually support one another in order to span an opening. It may also be constructed of voussoirs stacked in a triangular shape and the triangle can sometimes be suppressed and flattened.

First developed by the Mayans, the triangular arch is seldom seen in larger bridges where spans are too great, and the support of immense weights is crucial. The triangular arch is weak as it tends to buckle under load because the thrust is too horizontal. It is also sometimes called a mitre arch. It occurs in early pre-Roman Anglo-Saxon architecture and only very occasionally in packhorse bridges in England.

The triangular arch detail

Fifehead Neville Footbridge – southeast face

The trackway over the bridge

The fabric is local rubble with the single ring of flat face voussoirs of very rough construction.

There is a large triangular cutwater on the upstream side only, and it rises to the top of the low kerbs that enclose a track, 1.6 metres wide, so providing a small refuge. However, 20th-century wooden rails have been affixed to the faces of the bridge and cut the refuge off from access.

A build date as early as the 12th century has been suggested for this bridge, presumably on the grounds of style and fabric, but the suggestion is not backed by any tangible documentary evidence, and perhaps the 14th century would be a more realistic estimate. Some restoration has taken place over its long life.

At the Bridge: The view and access from upstream is very good, but the downstream face is inaccessible. There is no formal parking but a field access road to the northeast end may provide a temporary pull over. There are no amenities or facilities.

10 SOUTHEAST DORSET TOUR

Using Poole as a central starting point these bridges include Crawford Bridge, Wool Bridge, Holme Bridge, Wareham North Bridge, and Place Mill Bridge.

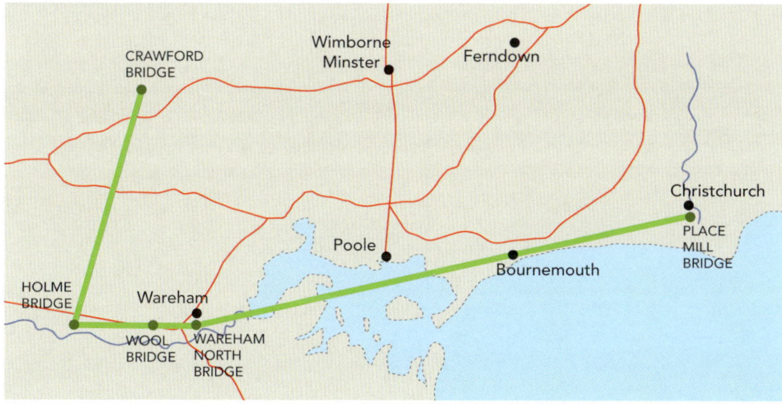

1 Crawford Bridge ★★★

Bridge Name: Crawford Bridge

Location: Crawford Bridge Road across the River Stour, just to the north of Spetisbury. About 9 miles northwest of Poole. Use postcode DT11 9EA for your satnav.

Setting: Village / Countryside

OS Ref: ST 91899 01978

Crosses: River Stour

Orientation: North / South

County: Dorset

Length: 73 metres (including the three northern land arches)

Bridge Type: Multiple Arch

Materials: Stone

Traffic: Road

Build Date: 1400

Authority: Dorset (Unitary Authority)

Designation: Grade I Listed

Directions: From Spetisbury:

- The village of Spetisbury is approached on the A350.
- Just prior to the village of Spetisbury, turn north off the A350 onto Crawford Bridge Road. Follow 100 metres to bridge.

Driving Time: From Poole – 20 minutes.

Crawford Bridge – east face

Crawford Bridge – west face

Pyramid capped western cutwater

Information: The River Stour has several branches as it crosses this low broad plain and Crawford Bridge sits at the junction of two of them. It carries a minor road branching off the A350 across the river from Spetisbury to Tarrant Crawford and is probably the most famous of the many bridges that cross the River Stour.

Although the first documentation of a bridge here dates to 1235, it is thought that the present structure was built around 1400 and extensive work was done in 1506. Thereafter repairs followed at intervals, until in 1819 when major changes were made as the road was widened. The Quarter Sessions orders of 1719 refer to great expenditure on the bridge's maintenance. The bridge was apparently widened on the downstream (east) face to 3.6 metres wide, and the cutwaters on that face were not replaced.

The bridge encompasses nine river arches, ranging in span from 3.6 to 6 metres, giving a length of 66 metres. There are also three similar but smaller flood arches of brick in the northern causeway and at the south end is a short stretch of brickwork with no arch. The fabric is coursed rubble and ashlar. All the arches are approximately semi-circular and heighten slightly toward mid-stream, causing the road deck to rise gently from the abutments to a central point between the fifth and sixth arches from the south. The road kinks slightly to the east between the seventh and eighth arches *(Robertson, 2020)*.

The steeply pitched stone coping

The three flood arches in the northern causeway

On the west side, each pier has a triangular cutwater, and on each alternate pier these projections are either capped or carried up to road level to form four pedestrian refuges. On the eastern (widened) side there are no cutwaters and no refuges. This downstream (east) side is much plainer but is also much more photographed simply because the riverbank is accessible on that side.

The parapet and spandrel walls on the southeastern face are of chequered flint and ashlar, with some patches of rubble. They are noticeably different from those on the northeastern face. Both sides have parapets that are capped by steeply pitched ashlar coping. Near the centre of the east side is a large stone inscribed 1719, presumably reset in its present position when the bridge was widened in 1819.

At the Bridge: There is no formal parking near the bridge but there are pull over places to the north. There are no facilities or amenities at the bridge or in Spetisbury.

2 Wool Bridge ★★★

Bridge Name: Wool Bridge
Location: Just off the A352 outside the village of Wool, and beside Woolbridge House. Use postcode BH20 6HQ for your satnav.
Setting: Countryside / Suburban
OS Ref: SY 84452 87153
Crosses: River Frome
Orientation: North / South
County: Dorset
Length: 75 metres
Bridge Type: Multiple Arch
Materials: Stone
Traffic: Pedestrian
Build Date: Early 15th century
Authority: Dorset (Unitary Authority)
Designation: Grade II* Listed
Directions: Within Wool:

- You will come into Wool from the A352. Follow eastward into town to the big roundabout by the station where the A352 turns northward and west crossing the rail tracks, signposted Wareham.
- Follow 400 metres north to the second road on the left. The bridge is right there.

Driving Time: From Crawford Bridge – 25 minutes.

Information: Documentary research has found that a bridge is recorded to have crossed the River Frome in this location in 1343, although the place name 'Wullebrigg' is first mentioned in 1244 and the bridge may have been constructed by the Cistercian monks of nearby Bindon Abbey sometime after its foundation in 1172.

The structure encompasses five segmental, but close to semi-circular arches, each resting on three unusually wide ribs. The fabric is random rubble with simple single arch rings. It appears to have undergone several phases of development during the 18th, 19th, and 20th centuries, including strengthening and widening, and appears to have been repaired on several occasions. It was lengthened in the later 19th century, with an additional arch added at the southern end.

There is a discernible 'S' shape to the bridge. Each of the four broad piers has large cutwaters upstream, and smaller ones downstream, and all rise to parapet level to form refuges. At the south end, a brick flood arch was added in the 19th century, and rather untidy repairs in brick are found in various places. The largest arch spans 4.5 metres, and the width is 3.3 metres; it has never been widened.

Wool Bridge is situated close to the British Army base of Bovington Camp and witnessed the first tanks in 1916, which had to cross the bridge after their arrival at Wool station some 300 metres to the south. Perhaps unsurprisingly, regular crossing by 25–30 tonne tanks led to damage in 1917 and 1918. A photograph of the time shows that the crew of one Mark V tank named 'Dee' had a lucky escape after crashing through the parapet and ending up on the bank.

A tank fallen off Wool Bridge, 1918 (Image courtesy of Bovington Tank Museum)

In order to prevent a similar scenario during the Second World War, the end arches and the north and south approaches of Wool Bridge were widened, and the parapets removed for the passage of tanks and other large military vehicles for the D-day assault. The parapets were only reconstructed in the early 1960s.

After centuries of scouring by the river the bridge partially collapsed in January 2018 at the southwestern end. A temporary dam was installed, diverting the river water through the undamaged northern three arches of the bridge and the riverbed was pumped dry to allow stabilisation and reconstruction to begin. The original stone was recovered from the riverbed for reuse and was supplemented with stone sourced from the same Purbeck-Portland bed on the Isle of Purbeck that was originally used. Wessex Archaeology took advantage of the opportunity to conduct investigations into the bridge's original construction and these showed that the bridge had been

Wool Bridge – east face and Woolbridge House

The west face showing the newly repaired section

The eastern parapets with smaller refuges

founded on timber foundations for over 500 years. The bridge reopened in November of 2018 and has now been removed from Historic England's Heritage at Risk Register.

The bridge features in Thomas Hardy's novel, *Tess of the D'Urbervilles,* and is linked with the adjacent Woolbridge Manor, the home of the Turberville family where Tess Clare (née Durbeyfield) spent her disastrous wedding night.

At the Bridge: Wool Bridge is now closed to vehicular traffic and access is reasonable all around the bridge. There is a public green space to the southern end that allows access to the west face. There is parking available at both the northern and southern ends.

3 Holme Bridge ★★★

Bridge Name: Holme Bridge

Location: Holme Bridge Road, East Stoke, Purbeck, carried the B3070 across the River Frome to the west of Wareham until it was bypassed relatively recently. Use postcode BH20 6AF for your satnav.

Setting: Rural Countryside

OS Ref: SY 89049 86642

Crosses: River Frome

Orientation: North / South

County: Dorset

Length: 24.5 metres

Bridge Type: Multiple Arch

Materials: Carstone Sandstone

Traffic: Road

Build Date: 15th century

Authority: Dorset (Unitary Authority)

Designation: Grade I Listed

Directions: From Wool Bridge:

- Return to the A352 and head east for 3½ miles to the B3070 Lulworth Road on the right, signposted Lulworth Castle.
- Turn right (south) and follow across the rail tracks 300 metres to the bridge. Lulworth Cove is only 6 miles to the south on this road.

Driving Time: From Wool Bridge – 7 minutes.

Holme Bridge – east face

Information: The old Holme Bridge runs parallel to the new Holme Bridge about 20 metres to the east. It is still possible to drive across this bridge, diverting from the B3070 on the right. Historical evidence shows that there has been a bridge on the site since medieval times and before that a ford.

The oldest part of the structure is the centre, and it consists of three segmental stone arches, spanning 3.6 metres, 4.2 metres, and 3.6 metres, springing from piers with upstream (west) cutwaters that are extended upwards to parapet level to provide four refuges. It seems most likely that this part of the bridge dates, as Jervoise suggests, to the 15th century.

Since then, three more arches have been added; firstly, a fourth segmental arch at the north end, probably in 1674 (and distinguishable from the older arches because each face of the arch has one rather than two arch rings), secondly an 18th-century brick arch at the south end, and finally a 19th-century stone arch with brick spandrels at the north end *(Robertson, 2020)*.

The newer arches also rest on piers with upstream cutwaters, extended upwards to provide refuges, giving six all-told, but there are only two on the downstream (east) face. The width of the carriageway is 3.7 metres and there is no evidence that it has been widened *(Pevsner & Newman, 1972)*.

The military, pictured in 1951, adding a temporary crossing spanning the River Frome after Holme Bridge near East Holme was damaged by military transport in 1945. In 1963, the Bailey Bridge was replaced with the current bridge, superseding the original Holme Bridge (© Bournemouth Daily Echo, *1952, used with permission)*

Holme Bridge – west face

The fabric of the three oldest arches is carstone (a form of sandstone) and limestone coursed rubble, and some effort has been made to preserve a match of colours in the later modifications.

Damage by tanks during the Second World War necessitated replacement of the old parapet with the present brick walls topped with stone copings and splayed on each end. The boat access ramp created during this effort can still be seen on the north end between the bridges. It wasn't until the late 1940s and after a fatal traffic accident that the County Council was persuaded to replace the parapets.

The bridge was the site of a Civil War confrontation in February 1644. The town of Wareham was largely in support of the Royalist cause and on 27 February 1644 a fierce battle took place here. Forty-five Royalist men from Wareham, both on horseback and on foot, fought the Roundheads for five hours, driving off 300 and killing 40 of them. There is an information board about this battle near the bridge.

Local residents recall that during the Second World War there were two German airmen captured while hiding under the bridge. The story seems to be verified by army records that show a Messerschmitt Bf110 was shot down over Purbeck and the crew parachuted into captivity. A local farmer recovered the cockpit canopy and used it as a cloche for his courgettes for many years.

At the Bridge: Access is reasonable around the bridge. There is formal parking at the north end of the bridge. Good views can be obtained from the adjacent new bridge.

Holme Bridge – southernmost arch west face

Holme Bridge – a pedestrian refuge with a seat

4 Wareham North Bridge ★★

Bridge Name:	Wareham North Bridge
Other Names:	Pontun de Pedle
Location:	North Bridge, North Street, in Wareham, across the River Piddle just south of the A351 bypass roundabout. Use postcode BH20 4AH for your satnav. This bridge is only a few miles from Holme Bridge.
Setting:	Town / Suburban
OS Ref:	SY 92140 87814
Crosses:	River Piddle or Trent
Orientation:	North / South
County:	Dorset
Length:	17 metres
Bridge Type:	Multiple Arch
Materials:	Stone
Traffic:	Road
Build Date:	1483
Authority:	Dorset (Unitary Authority)
Designation:	Grade II* Listed
Directions:	In Wareham: • Follow the A351 to the Saxon roundabout just north of Wareham. • Turn right (south) and follow to the bridge.
Driving Time:	From Holme Bridge – 15 minutes.

Information: Wareham North Bridge carries traffic into the north of the walled town of Wareham across the River Piddle and south from the A351 bypass. A bridge here was first mentioned in the 14th century, and Leland described a bridge of six arches in the 16th century *(Leland & John, 1549).*

The bridge today has three arches of different styles and eras, the northern one being pointed and probably of medieval origin but very plain with a width of 3.6 metres. The central and southern arches, which date from c. 1670, are segmental and span 4.5 metres and have double arch rings. There are two deep, upstream cutwaters on the west side with refuges above, and modern parapets matching the original materials and style.

Wareham North Bridge – west face from river level

A decorative string course runs horizontally below parapet level across the west face. The parapets have rounded coping, look relatively modern, and the refuges above the two large triangular cutwaters were probably rebuilt rather than built new. There are generous pedestrian walkways on both sides *(Robertson, 2020)*.

The eastern face looks significantly different, and it seems to be accepted that the bridge was largely rebuilt in 1670, but it is unknown how much of the previous bridge was incorporated. Thereafter it was widened in 1846 to 5.7 metres, almost certainly on the downstream, eastern face, and again a century later, to a recorded 10.8 metres width. There are no refuges on the eastern side of the carriageway.

There are enough medieval features to allow dating for at least some of the bridge earlier than the 15th century.

At the Bridge: The bridge is overgrown and difficult to view. Parking could be problematic and requires a short walk from the village to the south. A water pumping station on the southeast corner may allow some views of the eastern face.

Wareham North Bridge – east face

Wareham North Bridge – pedestrian refuge

Wareham North Bridge – one of the central cutwaters on the west side

5 Place Mill Bridge ★★

Bridge Name:	Place Mill Bridge
Location:	Christchurch, east of Boscombe in the marina area where Quay Road becomes Convent Walk. Take the A3060 southeast. Use postcode BH23 1BY for your satnav.
Setting:	Urban / Town Centre
OS Ref:	SZ 16018 92403
Crosses:	Mill Run, which flows from the Dorset River Avon and becomes a tributary of the River Stour near Christchurch Priory.
Orientation:	North / South
County:	Dorset
Length:	8 metres (including the abutments)
Bridge Type:	Multiple Arch
Materials:	Stone
Traffic:	Road (with width and weight restrictions)
Build Date:	15th century
Authority:	Bournemouth Christchurch and Poole (Unitary Authority)
Designation:	Grade II* Listed
Directions:	From Christchurch: • Follow the B3073 to Christchurch and all the way to the end of the road signposted Christchurch Priory. Use Quay Road not Church Street.
Driving Time:	From Wareham North Bridge – 50 minutes.

Information: A part of the historic Place Mill, the Place Mill Bridge is immediately south of Christchurch Priory and spans a millstream shortly before it runs into the River Stour, which itself then runs into Christchurch Harbour. The restored Anglo-Saxon mill is mentioned in the Domesday book with a value of 30 shillings. The monastic corn mill, later also used for fulling cloth for the wool trade for all those Christchurch mercers, finished its intended working life of fulling cloth and corn grinding in 1908.

The small bridge is built of non-coursed rubble and it encompasses two rounded segmental arches, with single flush arch rings with a grotesque corbel head in the central pier on both faces.

The roadway is cobbled and 2.6 metres wide. Recent inspection of the

Place Mill Bridge – wing wall

Place Mill Bridge – east face

vaulting suggests that it has never been widened. There are no cutwaters.

The parapets are of the same material without coping and overhang the lower substructure by about 3 centimetres. They are thought to be a relatively recent addition.

The bridge is confidently described as medieval by both Jervoise and Historic England, presumably 15th century or earlier, largely it seems, because the adjacent monastic mill is recorded then *(Jervoise, 1930).*

At the Bridge: This bridge is in the heart of a recreation area. There is ample paid parking and facilities and refreshment abound. Access to the bridge is easy, and the surroundings are very pleasant.

The interesting and bypassed old Iford Bridge (not to be confused with the medieval Iford Bridge in Somerset) is 4 miles upriver from here but it is 17th–18th century and not medieval.

Place Mill Bridge – west face

Place Mill Bridge – the roadway

GLOUCESTERSHIRE

Because of its location in Tewkesbury, quite near middle England and not close to any bridges in southern England, this bridge is not included in one of the tours but is treated separately.

King John's Bridge ★★★★

Bridge Name:	King John's Bridge
Other Names:	The Long Bridge (historical name)
Location:	In Tewkesbury on Mythe Road (A38). Use postcode GL20 5BS for your satnav.
Setting:	Town / Urban
OS Ref:	SO 89371 33231
Crosses:	River Warwickshire Avon
Orientation:	Northwest / Southeast
County:	Gloucestershire
Length:	42 metres (not including Beaufort Bridge or the Western Causeway)
Bridge Type:	Multiple Arch
Materials:	Stone
Traffic:	Road
Build Date:	1190
Authority:	Tewkesbury (District Authority)
Designation:	Grade II* Listed
Directions:	To King John's Bridge: • Follow the M5 north to J9, Tewkesbury. • At the big roundabout, follow the A438 1½ mile west into Tewkesbury. • In the centre of town, at the tall stone cross, turn right (north) onto the High Street (A38). Follow north. • At the first mini- roundabout, at Ye Olde Black Bear, Mythe Road turns west off the High Street. • Turn left (west) onto the bridge.

King John's Bridge – western face

Postcard from 1904 – the south side of King John's Bridge

Information: There are two arms of the River Avon here; the Mill Avon to the east, and the Old Avon to the west, once crossed by a single long bridge, thus the historical name 'Long Bridge'. Today there are two bridges connected by a causeway across a central island. Frequently repaired and rebuilt, major works in 1639 appear to have been substantial, and included filling in the arches which sat on the island between the two arms of the Avon. By 1675 documents refer to two distinct stone bridges, King John's Bridge over the Mill Avon, and Beaufort Bridge over the Old Avon *(British History Online, 1968)*. Beaufort Bridge over the Old Avon has been replaced and is today a modern metal structure, and this record is concerned with the more southerly King John's Bridge *(Jervoise, 1930)*.

Tradition relates that this bridge across the Avon Mill was built by King John, and certainly in 1205 the Bailiff of Tewkesbury was assigned two oaks for making a bridge. The first records of this stone bridge suggest that John built the bridge before his accession to the throne. The name King John's Bridge did not become current until the 19th century; earlier it was called the Long Bridge or, in the Middle Ages, the bridge towards Mythe *(Elrington, 2018)*.

King John's Bridge that we see today is built of coursed ashlar sandstone. There are five low segmental arches and the first, second, and third arches from the northwest are lower, with heavy chamfered ribbed vaults. The northernmost arch is usually dry except in times of flood. The fourth arch from the northwest is an exception and it was probably entirely rebuilt as a navigation arch of greater height, most likely during a major restructuring in 1824 when the entire roadway level was raised *(Robertson, 2020)*.

King John's Bridge – eastern face looking north

King John's Bridge c. 1910 – eastern face showing the Olde Black Bear pub

The northernmost arch – east face

There are triangular cutwaters rising to form pedestrian refuges in the parapets on both sides, but these are occupied today by flower tubs. There are generous pedestrian walkways on both sides. The coping is modern.

By the early 20th century, the bridge was a patchwork of stone piers, brick parapets, and an early iron walkway, as seen in the old postcard from 1904. A major reconstruction in 1962 rebuilt and widened the bridge by at least a third to its present 8 metres. Some of the masonry on the eastern side appears to have survived the 1962 rebuild and this side is visually older that the western face.

To the northwest the abutments become a causeway and continue to the west for an additional 27 metres, crossing a low floodplain. On the north side is a plaque giving historical information.

On the downstream side, to the west, a set of 14 steps break cleanly through the parapet and lead down to the riverside walk (the Severn Way) on the island. The Mill Avon remains the only navigable arm of the river.

There is also a King John's Bridge in Ireland (not included in this work).

At the Bridge: The Olde Black Bear Inn is on the southwest corner. There is a parking area on the right after the bridge. There is good access to river level upstream and downstream. All facilities and amenities are available in Tewkesbury.

Heavy and modern ribs

King John's Bridge – the eastern cutwaters with a couple of pigeon visitors on the drain

King John's Bridge – the roadway looking north

HAMPSHIRE

There are three medieval bridges in the county of Hampshire: New Alresford Bridge, Fordingbridge Bridge, and Titchfield Bridge. However, these have not been organised into a tour because Titchfield Bridge is closer to West Sussex, Fordingbridge is quite close to South Wiltshire, and New Alresford Bridge is not at all viewable. Nonetheless, I have included information about New Alresford Bridge here because it is one of the oldest bridges in England and is quite historical.

New Alresford Bridge

Bridge Name:	New Alresford Bridge
Other Names:	Soke Bridge
Location:	New Alresford, on the north side of New Alresford, a few miles east of Winchester. Use postcode SO24 9DA for your satnav.
Setting:	Town / Suburban
OS Ref:	SU 58803 32925
Crosses:	River Itchen / Alre
Orientation:	Northeast / Southwest
County:	Hampshire
Length:	A mere 2 metres
Bridge Type:	Multiple Arch
Materials:	Stone and Brick
Traffic:	Road
Build Date:	1190
Authority:	Winchester (District Authority)
Designation:	Grade II* Listed and Scheduled Monument
Directions:	From Winchester: • Follow the M3 to exit 9. • Take the A31 east 6 miles to New Alresford. • At the approach to the town, at the big roundabout, turn left (northeast) onto the B3047, also called Alresford Road and The Avenue and follow around the town to the north side known as Old Alresford. • At a major intersection with the B3046, also Broad Street, turn left (north) and follow ¼ mile to The Old Fire Station. Park on the Broad Street and walk from here. A gravel road runs off to the right (east) and the bridge is on this road.
Driving Time:	From Winchester – 20 minutes.

New Alresford Bridge

Information: New Alresford Bridge is a late 12th-century stone single-arched bridge, spanning the overflow channel from Old Alresford Pond. The bridge and pond were created by Godfrey de Lucy, Bishop of Winchester (1189–1204), as part of a scheme to make the River Itchen navigable from its source at Bramdean to Winchester and Southampton. Alresford Pond, which was created and originally covered 200 acres, acted as a reservoir, in which the water of several local streams was collected to be channelled through the River Alre to the River Itchen.

New Alresford Bridge was constructed around 1190 and comprises a single two-centred Gothic arch of cut stone voussoirs, which remains visible on the downstream (northwest) side. There are three arch rings, with the lower two chamfered and in two orders.

Underneath the arch at water level are rectangular recesses, which may have supported a timber framework during the construction of the bridge.

The arch is flanked by two stepped stone buttresses, of which the easternmost is encased within the wall supporting the neighbouring patio.

The medieval bridge, which measures approximately 3 metres wide and spans slightly more than 2 metres, was modified, and extended in at least two stages. The bridge was widened on the upstream (southeast) side with a 3-metre-wide brick arch at an unknown date before 1870. During the 17th century a brick parapet was added on the downstream side, topped by copings, which are possibly the original reused 12th-century stones. The upstream face of the bridge was modified in 1881, when a red brick arch and parapet were added.

At the Bridge: Unfortunately, this iconic bridge, one of the oldest survivors in England, can be crossed but not viewed, except from private property.

11 KENT TOUR

There are seven bridges in this Kent tour. That seems like a lot, however, six of them are in a cluster located within a few miles of one another. Using Maidstone as a central starting point these bridges are arranged from north to south and include Aylesford Bridge, Teston Bridge, East Farleigh Bridge, Yalding Town Bridge, Twyford Bridge, Laddingford Bridge, and Hertsfield Bridges. All the bridges in Kent lie in the west part of the county.

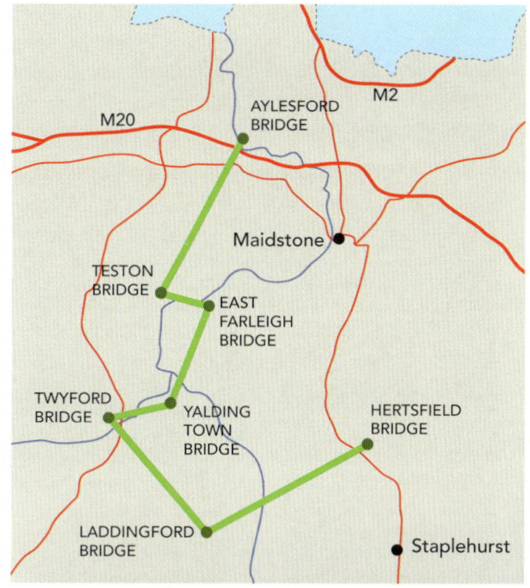

Aylesford Bridge from the bypass

1 Aylesford Bridge ★★★★

Bridge Name:	Aylesford Bridge
Location:	In Aylesford 100 metres south of St Peter's Church, 4 miles northwest of the county town of Maidstone. Use postcode ME20 7BA for your satnav.
Setting:	Town / Urban
OS Ref:	TQ 72942 58930
Crosses:	River Medway
Orientation:	North / South
County:	Kent
Length:	81 metres (including the buried arches)
Bridge Type:	Multiple Arch
Materials:	Stone
Traffic:	Pedestrians and bicycles
Build Date:	1250
Authority:	Tonbridge and Malling (District Authority)
Designation:	Grade I Listed and Scheduled Monument
Directions:	From Maidstone: • Get on the M20 and follow west to Junction 6. • At the big roundabout follow south to the junction with the A20. • At the roundabout turn right (west) and follow for 500 metres to Hall Road. • Turn right (north) and follow under the M20 to the T junction with Station Road. • Turn right (northeast) and follow to the bridge.
Driving Time:	From Maidstone – 20 minutes.

Aylesford Bridge from river level

Information: Aylesford Bridge is one of a group of four fine medieval bridges that cross the River Medway near to Maidstone. The other three are Twyford, East Farleigh, and Teston, and when account is taken also of the nearby bridges at Laddingford and Yalding over Medway tributaries, it is fair to say that such a tight-knit collection is almost unrivalled in the country *(Challis & Savage, 1986)*.

This old single-track bridge crosses the River Medway and originally gave direct access to the old town centre of Aylesford. Jervoise credits this bridge as 'one of the

Gothic (Two-Centred) Arches

One of the defining elements of Gothic architecture was the pointed arch. The two-centred or Gothic arch first came into use in England in the late 12th century and early bridge builders adopted its ability to bear heavy loads. The use of the pointed arch in turn led to the development of the pointed rib vault, both of which are typical characteristics of medieval bridges. The basic Gothic arch is equilateral, in that the width is equal to the height, however, this forms the basis of many variants.

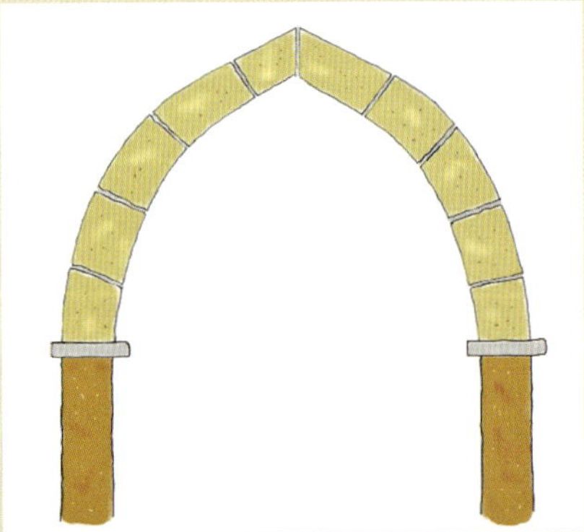

Gothic arches can be narrowed (non-equilateral) arches with a pointed opening. This was considered a more sinuous and elegant successor to the previously dominant Roman arch style. Gothic arches have been used in cathedrals and bridges of the Middle Ages across Europe. Developmentally, the Gothic arch follows the Norman arch in English bridge building.

Aylesford Bridge – north face

most beautiful bridges in Kent' *(Jervoise, 1930)*. Originally built in 1250 of local Kentish ragstone by the local Carmelite Priory nearby, it has seven arches, the largest being the central arch. However, prior to 1824, this large arch was two arches. In that year it was enlarged into one long segmental arch with an 18-meter span, removing the central pier to allow passage for larger river traffic. An incongruent sandstone was used for this newer central arch, but it is not unattractive. The arches at each end are mostly buried by the riverbank, but still visible, leaving only five observable ones. The bridge has angled approaches on both ends and is today no longer used for traffic, as the traffic now uses a new modern bridge just upriver. The bridge, however, is open for pedestrians *(Robertson, 2020)*.

There are three pointed and double-chamfered Gothic style arches to each side of the central segmental rounded arch. The arch vaults are smooth without ribs. The bridge is about 4 metres wide between the centres of the stone-coped parapet. The stone piers have cutwaters on both the upstream and downstream sides on rebuilt concrete foundations revealed only at low tide. On each side are 1-metre-high parapets containing octagonal and triangular angled pedestrian refuges resting on buttresses over the piers. There are two to the south of the central arch and six to the north. Below the bridge are large starlings sitting on a bed of timber.

The name Aylesford derives from 'Ægel's ford' – Ægel being a chieftain who controlled the crossing of the river.

Aylesford Bridge – drawn by William Henry Bartlett, Engraved by B. Winkles, 1810 (Public Domain)

Aylesford Bridge – the refuge 'balconys'

At the Bridge: The bridge no longer carries traffic. There is some limited public parking at the south end of the bridge, otherwise park in the parking area at the north end of the adjacent new bridge and use the footpath through the park. A public footpath runs alongside both sides of the River Medway. Access is good around the bridge. Facilities and amenities are available in the town. The best views are afforded in the morning from the new bypass bridge to the east.

Aylesford Bridge – the buried southern arch

2 Teston Bridge ★★★

Bridge Name:	Teston Bridge
Location:	Off the A26 south of Teston. On the B2163 between Teston and West Farleigh. Use postcode ME18 5BX for your satnav.
Setting:	Rural / Countryside
OS Ref:	TQ 70887 53269
Crosses:	River Medway
Orientation:	Northwest / Southeast
County:	Kent
Length:	54 metres (including the flood and towpath arches)
Bridge Type:	Multiple Arch
Materials:	Ragstone
Traffic:	Road
Build Date:	15th century
Authority:	Maidstone (District Authority)
Designation:	Grade I Listed and Scheduled Monument
Directions:	From Aylesford Bridge: • Reverse directions and return down Hall Road to the A20. • Turn left and follow 200 metres to the first road on the left, the B2246, Hermitage Lane. • Turn right (south) and follow for 2 miles into the village of Barming. • In Barming cross over the first major crossroads (Heath Road) and proceed to the junction with the A26, Tonbridge Road. • Turn right (west) and follow for 2 miles to Teston. • Just before Teston turn left (south) onto the B2163, Teston Lane, and follow 100 metres to the bridge.
Driving Time:	From Aylesford Bridge – 20 minutes.

Information: Teston Bridge is out in the countryside and carries the B2163 over the River Medway. It dates to the late 15th century and is constructed of Kentish ragstone and coursed rubble, tending in places towards semi-dressed ashlar and includes six semi-circular round-headed arches. There are three spanning the river itself and the central arch is taller; two smaller arches to the northwest act as flood arches. The northern river arch was the original towpath arch and now acts as the footpath under the bridge. The central arch has double chamfered arch rings, but the rest are single chamfered arch rings. The vaults are themselves smooth in all cases *(Robertson, 2020)*.

The more decorative central arch was rebuilt in the 1790s with slightly greater height, and a width of 7.2 metres. The flood arches are thought to have been reconfigured in 1830 and have a width of 6.2 metres. The parapets have ashlar coping and have possibly been renewed at a later date. Thomas Spooner's will of 1526 left money for the repair of this bridge *(Jervoise, 1930)*.

There are six pointed cutwaters on the upstream (south) side and four on the downstream (north) side. These rise tapering to the level of the parapet, where they form trapezoidal-shaped pedestrian refuges. The carriageway is 3.3 metres wide without any walkway for pedestrians.

In the 1958 film *Dunkirk*, starring John Mills and Richard Attenborough, Teston Bridge features in scenes early in the film that show the soldiers in Belgium, where a bridge is 'blown up' when the Germans are crossing. Many scenes from the famous film were shot in the area including the farm sequence at a location south of Teston.

The River Medway

Bridges in this Book: Aylesford
East Farleigh
Laddingford (River Teise)
Teston
Twyford
Yalding Town (River Beult)

Main Tributaries: River Beult
River Eden
River Bourne
River Tiese

The River Medway near Whatman Park (© Chris Whippet and licensed for reuse under Creative Commons License 2.0)

Also known as Medwege, the River Medway was given the name Vaga by the ancient Britons. Later, the Saxons added the syllable mad, meaning 'middle', as the river ran through the middle of the kingdom of Kent.

The River Medway is 70 miles long and flows almost entirely within Kent. It rises in Ashdown Forest and joins the Thames near Chatham. Apart from the Thames, it has the largest catchment area in southern England. The river is navigable as far as Tonbridge by large craft and as far as Penshurst by small craft. There are 11 locks on the river, between Allington and Tonbridge. The river is tidal to Allington Lock.

The river divides Kent in two, those born west of the river are known as Kentish Men, while those born east of the river are Men of Kent. The river was used as a line of defence against possible invasion during the Second World War. By far its largest tributary is the River Beult. The drowned lower portion 12 miles below Rochester forms a tidal estuary navigable by shallow seagoing vessels.

Throughout history it has been a major trading route for Maidstone and until the introduction of the bridges and locks, the horseway was also one of the few crossing points. This can still be found between the College of Priests and All Saints Church.

The River Medway is more recreational now rather than a trading route, but nevertheless an interesting place to explore the Kent countryside. The River itself runs between East Grinstead and Forest Row in East Sussex, through the High Weald, around the Hartfield and Groombridge areas, on to Penshurst and Tonbridge, then to Yalding and Maidstone, and finally joining the Thames Estuary between Sheerness and the Isle of Grain.

Just under 350 years ago, a successful Dutch attack on the largest English naval ships, laid up in the dockyards of Chatham, took place in June 1667 during the Second Anglo-Dutch War. The 'Raid on the Medway' saw the Dutch navy bombard and then capture Sheerness, sail up the River Thames to Gravesend, then up the River Medway to Chatham, where they burned three capital ships and 10 lesser naval vessels and towed away the Unity and the *Royal Charles*, flagship of the English fleet.

In a cultural sense, the river has been a source of inspiration and success. Perhaps the most famous tribute was in Edmund Spenser's 1596 epic poem *The Faerie Queene*, where he described the Medway's 'marriage' to the Thames in extensive detail. Local man George Gilbert wrote a song called *Medway Flows Softly*, the 1999 film *The Mummy* used the site for filming, and the river hosts the annual Maidstone River Festival every year.

Teston Bridge – west face

At the Bridge: Teston Bridge Country Park is to the northwest of the bridge and there is paid parking, although the park is very popular. Access is good through the park on both the upstream and downstream sides. There are amenities and facilities at the bridge and sometimes on summer weekends there is an ice cream van.

The northern approach

Teston Bridge – central pier

The towpath arch on the north bank

The sandstone voussoirs

The southern arch western face

❸ East Farleigh Bridge ★★★

Bridge Name:	East Farleigh Bridge
Location:	Station Road in East Farleigh to the southwest of Maidstone. Use postcode ME15 0JG for your satnav.
Setting:	Village / Suburban
OS Ref:	TQ 73480 53518
Crosses:	River Medway
Orientation:	Northwest / Southeast
County:	Kent
Length:	26 metres (not including the approaches)
Bridge Type:	Multiple Arch
Materials:	Ragstone
Traffic:	Road
Build Date:	14th century
Authority:	Maidstone (District Authority)
Designation:	Grade I Listed and Scheduled Monument
Directions:	From Teston Bridge: • Continue on this road, the B2163, southeast for 600 metres to the first road on the left, the B2010, • Turn sharp left (east) and follow the B2010, Lower Road, for 1½ miles to East Farleigh. • Turn left (north) at The Bull Inn onto Station Hill Road and follow for 200 metres to the bridge.
Driving Time:	From Teston Bridge – 10 minutes.

Information: East Farleigh Bridge crosses the River Medway just above East Farleigh lock. It dates to about the 14th century and underwent repair in 1843. The first documentation of the bridge dates from 1324 and it has been described by Jervoise as 'probably the finest medieval bridge in the south of England' *(Jervoise, 1930)*.

East Farleigh Bridge – south face

The central river arch

Arch ribs and ragstone fabric

East Farleigh Bridge – western face

The north face

The roadway

The 'squinch' from across the river

It is built of coursed Kentish ragstone with ashlar coping stones on the 1-metre-high parapets. The bridge is narrow, only wide enough to permit traffic to pass in one direction at a time. The southern approach to the bridge, on Station Road, is angled and the bridge is slightly cambered. There is a substantial 43 metre retaining wall on the south end rising steeply to meet the level of the bridge deck. The bridge features sizeable, pointed cutwaters on each side that act as buttresses rising to the level of the stone parapet. These are protected by modern timber piles. The bridge is only 3.3 metres wide and there are no refuges in the road deck and only very narrow pedestrian walkways.

The bridge has five pointed arches including four main arches spanning the river. The two central arches have chamfered ribs and are slightly higher. On the north bank is a smaller arch with stone voussoirs – a later addition that spans the tow path, now a riverside footpath. There is also a very unusual blind arch (known as a squinch) spanning the angle between the bridge and retaining wall on the south approach and acting as a buttress supporting the bridge at this end. Between the arches are pointed cutwaters rising to the level of the stone parapet.

During the Civil War, General Fairfax crossed East Farleigh Bridge on 1 June 1648 to outflank the Earl of Norwich whose Royalist troops were camped on Penenden Heath. Significant numbers of cannon balls have been recovered from the area surrounding the bridge together with a handgun (now lost). Trenches dug on the Barming side of the bridge produced many bones of men and horses as well as a cannon, which was kept outside the Victory Pub for many years. It is clear that there was Royalist opposition at the bridge, but Fairfax reported the crossing was relatively easy. The subsequent Battle of Maidstone was one of the fiercest fought of the Civil War, ending with the Royalist surrender.

At the Bridge: Parking at the bridge is difficult at either end. There is some parking as you approach the bridge from the south on the right. Alternatively, the East Farleigh rail station at the north end of the bridge has a paid car park. A footpath runs along the north bank of the river. The Victory Pub sits opposite the railway station. There is access to good views of the bridge all around.

4 Yalding Town Bridge ★★

Bridge Name: Yalding Town Bridge

Location: Yalding, B2010 in the centre of the village. Use postcode ME18 6EL for your satnav.

Setting: Town / Urban

OS Ref: TQ 69734 49974

Crosses: River Beult

Orientation: Northeast / Southwest

County: Kent

Length: 170 metres (including the causeway)

Bridge Type: Multiple Arch

Materials: Ragstone

Traffic: Road

Opened: 15th century

Authority: Maidstone (District Authority)

Designation: Grade I Listed and Scheduled Monument

Directions: From East Farleigh Bridge:

- Reverse directions and get back to the B2010, Lower Road.
- Turn left (west) and follow for 5 miles to the village of Yalding.
- The bridge is in the centre of Yalding on this road.

Driving Time: From East Farleigh Bridge – 15 minutes.

Information: Yalding Town Bridge carries the High Street (B2010) across two branches of the River Beult, the main tributary of the River Medway at Yalding. Two bridges cross the main streams and a second arm of the Beult, now disconnected and isolated. A causeway connecting them crosses a central island. Lees Road makes a sharp turn to the north to lead into the village at the point where the B2010 and the B2162 split.

This bridge dates to at least the 15th century and was probably built on the site of an earlier wooden bridge. In

Yalding Town Bridge – north face of the south bridge

Smooth vault ceiling on the southernmost river arch, north face

The refuge in the southwest parapet

The northern bridge from across 'the island'

1474 and 1475 money was left in two wills for the upkeep of the bridge. It is also referred to in the mid-16th century by John Leland, the Royal Antiquary of King Henry VIII *(Leland & John, 1549).*

The main bridge itself is small compared to the great causeway to the north of nearly 135 metres in length to cross a broad flood plain. There is a cobblestone pedestrian walkway on the upstream (east) side that contains a refuge, of sort, used primarily by passing cars. The remains of an ancient lamp hanger can be found on the corner post of this refuge.

The bridge was originally 3 metres wide but was widened in 1848 to 4.2 metres by building a parallel structure alongside it. A comparison of the northern pointed arches to the southern semi-circular arches shows a clear transition in the arch styles. An examination of the vaults confirms that two bridges sit alongside one another with a common roadway surface *(Parsons, 1973).*

The two bridges have seven arches, three of which at the north bridge are pointed, with three at the south bridge, of which two are pointed, leaving a single semi-circular arch in the centre of the causeway. The latter is of more recent construction and is dry unless the river is in spate. Jervoise reported in 1930 that the southernmost arch nearest the town 'has been closed up and now forms a cellar for the Swan Hotel' *(Jervoise, 1930).*

The fabric is mainly ragstone rubble throughout, but rougher on the original downstream face. The single flush arch rings are especially rough below the decorative string courses. There are cutwaters between the arches at both faces and the three of them rise to form refuges on the downstream (west) side *(Penn, 1974; Robertson, 2020).*

An archaeological excavation and survey carried out in 1969 found that the stone foundations rest on a layer of brushwood. Other finds included medieval pottery, roof tiles, oyster shells, butchered animal bones, a silver penny of Edward 1 (AD 1272–1307), part of a cresset-lamp, as well as post-medieval pottery and glass bottles. A cess pit was also uncovered.

At the Bridge: Obtaining a face on or side view of either face of this bridge is difficult since all the land surrounding the bridge is privately held. Some view is offered from the garden of The George Pub in the summer. It is unfortunate that such a notable and interesting bridge cannot really be appreciated, for lack of suitable viewpoints, except on the river. Parking is also unavailable except in the village with a walk to and across the bridge.

5 Twyford Bridge ★★

Bridge Name:	Twyford Bridge
Location:	B2162 in Yalding near the Anchor Inn and very near Laddingford Bridge to the south. Use postcode ME18 6HG or your satnav.
Setting:	Rural / Countryside
OS Ref:	TQ 69067 49778
Crosses:	River Medway
Orientation:	Northwest / Southeast
County:	Kent
Length:	55 metres (including the approaches)
Bridge Type:	Multiple Arch
Materials:	Stone and Brick
Traffic:	Road
Build Date:	1475
Authority:	Maidstone (District Authority)
Designation:	Grade I Listed and Scheduled Monument
Directions:	From Yalding Town Bridge: • Continue across the bridge to the T junction with the B2162, Lees Road. • Turn right (west) and follow for 600 metres around the curve to the right, Hampstead Lane, still the B2162. • Follow to the bridge.
Driving Time:	From Yalding Town Bridge – 5 minutes.

Information: Twyford Bridge carries the B2162 across the River Medway, immediately downstream of the inflow of the River Teise, hence the name is a corruption of 'twin ford'. A bridge is recorded at Twyford in 1325 and in wills of 1475 and 1488. There is documentation to show that there has been a bridge on the site since the early 14th century, but it seems generally accepted that the bridge we see today was built in the second half of the 15th century *(Jervoise, 1930).*

Twyford Bridge from the riverbank

The northern Tudor style arch

Horseshoe (Keyhole/Moorish) Arch

Horseshoe arches are some of the oldest known arches and are also called the Moorish arch and keyhole arch. They are the emblematic arch of Islamic architecture. Like its name suggests, this arch is in the shape of a horseshoe that is more curved than semi-circle. The curved arch line extends beyond the semi-circular line of the arch. Horseshoe arches can take rounded, pointed, or lobed form.

When the springing point is very narrow in a horseshoe arch, it is called a keyhole arch.

It is a very early form of arch and historians speculate that the Romans learned the use of arches from the Middle East and developed their semi-circular arch from this form.

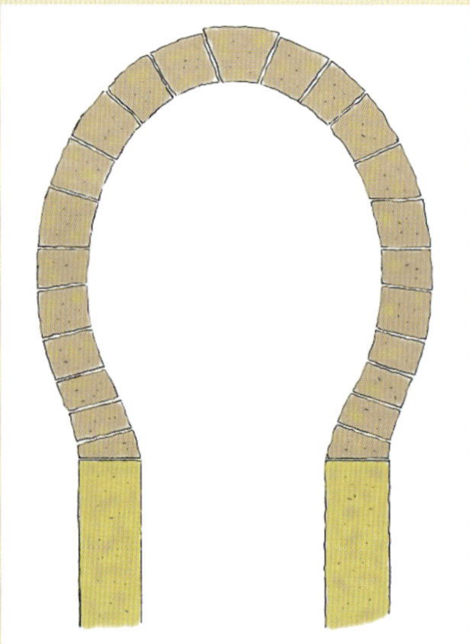

The bridge has three slightly pointed Tudor style arches which are irregular in shape, the northernmost bordering on horseshoe form. The southernmost arch is more rounded and semi-circular. There are two arch rings of flush voussoirs above each archway, and the vaulting of all the arches is smooth. The fabric is quite small-grade, slightly coursed rubble. The red brick parapets, a relatively modern addition, detract from the overall attractiveness of the bridge. There are cutwaters on the broad piers both upstream and downstream and they rise to form six broad triangular refuges, three on each side. There are no pedestrian walkways *(Robertson, 2020)*.

In the southern causeway there is a flood arch that is today used as a pedestrian underpass. The total length of the bridge is 36 metres, with the largest arch spanning 5.1 metres and the piers are around 6 metres wide. The width of the carriageway, which has never been increased, is 3.6 metres and traffic is signal controlled in both directions.

The central cutwater on the east face

The chamfered coping

Twyford Bridge – east face

The pedestrianised flood arch

At the Bridge: Hampstead Weir and footbridge are 100 metres to the west. The Boathouse restaurant is at the north end of the bridge. There is a picnic area and park to the south end of the bridge with ample but paid parking. The bridge can be viewed easily from most angles. There is a footbridge across the adjacent lock that provides the best overall view.

5 Laddingford Bridge ★

Bridge Name:	Laddingford Bridge
Other Names:	Gravelly Ways Bridge
Location:	Just north of Laddingford, on a minor road called Gravelly Ways Lane. Use postcode ME18 6BY for your satnav.
Setting:	Rural / Countryside
OS Ref:	TQ 69074 48841
Crosses:	River Teise
Orientation:	Northeast / Southwest
County:	Kent
Length:	10 metres
Bridge Type:	Multiple Arch
Materials:	Stone
Traffic:	Road
Opened:	14th century
Authority:	Maidstone (District Authority)
Designation:	Grade I Listed and Scheduled Monument
Directions:	From Twyford Bridge: • Reverse direction back down the B2162 for 200 metres and turn right (south) at the first road to the left called Lees Road. • Follow for 900 metres to the first road on the right, Gravelly Ways. • The bridge is right there.
Driving Time:	From Twyford Bridge – 5 minutes.

Information: Laddingford is a small bridge that goes unnoticed by hundreds of car passengers each day. The bridge is constructed of coursed and roughly dressed masonry with two pointed Tudor style arches and has been much repaired. The single arch rings are chamfered, and the lower part of the bridge fabric is rubble, made of quite large, roughly squared, stone blocks.

The bridge is just over 4 metres wide and nearly 9 metres long without any accommodation for pedestrians. The

Laddingford Bridge – the two medieval arches

The western face and the utility pipes

parapets show multiple instances of repairs in modern brick. The view of the western face is ruined by a set of modern utility pipes stretching across the river directly in front of the medieval structure.

The bridge is likely to date to the 14th century, although the later red brick parapets were rebuilt at a later date and are adorned with rounded stone coping.

The single pier with its pointed cutwaters on both sides is narrow for a bridge of this configuration, in this region, and rests on a later concrete starling.

The western parapet

Laddingford Bridge – east face (© David Anstiss, and licensed for reuse under Creative Commons License 2.0)

At the Bridge: Access to the bridge at riverbank level is difficult and involves climbing, although there are green pasture fields all around. There is no parking or place to stop near the bridge but perhaps in front of a line of houses to the east. There is a garden centre 100 metres beyond the southwest end of the bridge.

The roadway

6 Hertsfield Bridges ★

Bridge Name:	Hertsfield Bridges
Location:	Cross-at-Hand, off the A229, not far from Aylesford Bridge and East Farleigh Bridge. Use postcode TN12 0RL for your satnav.
Setting:	Rural / Countryside
OS Ref:	TQ 78250 46762
Crosses:	River Beult
Orientation:	North / South (both)
County:	Kent
Length:	90 metres
Bridge Type:	Multiple Arch
Materials:	Kentish Ragstone and Brick
Traffic:	Road
Opened:	Early 15th century
Authority:	Maidstone (District Authority)
Designation:	Grade II* Listed

Directions: From Laddingford Bridge:

- Return to the centre of Yalding on the B2162 and follow southwards for 3 miles to a little hamlet called Collier Street.
- Turn left onto Green Lane, signposted Marden. Follow for 3 miles to the junction with Hunton Road.
- Turn right (southeast) and follow for 4¼ miles. Do not turn into Marden. Follow to the T junction with the B2079.
- Turn left (north) and follow ¾ mile to the junction with the A229.
- Turn right (south) and follow 1¾ miles to the village of Cross-at-Hand.
- Turn left onto Chart Hill Road, signposted Chart Sutton, in a hamlet called Cross at Hand, follow north 1½ miles to the bridge.

Driving Time: From Laddingford Bridge – 35 minutes.

Southern Bridge – east face

Information: The River Beult splits just west of this point and two bridges, and a long causeway cross the two arms of the river and a large low flood plain. The southern bridge of two slightly pointed Tudor style arches, crosses the main river flow. The lower of the double, flush, arch rings are chamfered on both faces. A smaller single-arch bridge 30 metres to the north crosses another lesser branch of the Beult. The causeway connecting them encompasses five small, pointed flood arches.

It is thought that the structures date to the 14th century, though there has been much repair work and the out-of-character parapets have been rebuilt in buff-coloured

Northern Bridge – east face

brick with black engineering brick coping and unsightly pipe guard railings.

The main part of the fabric is Kentish ragstone rubble. The width of the roadway is slightly more than 3 metres along most of the 90-metre length of the causeway and bridges. The riverbanks are inaccessible near the bridge, and little can be seen from the road. There is an untidy interaction between the arch rings and the corbelling below the parapets.

There is a small weir immediately adjacent to the southern bridge. The approaches are narrow on both ends and the bridge is single file traffic only.

Hertsfield Bridges – roadway

At the Bridge: There are no parking or stopping places nearby and visiting this bridge will require some walking. There are no facilities or amenities at the bridge.

12 LONDON TOUR

There are only three bridges in London that have portions dating to the medieval period. They are arranged from west to east, but unlike the other bridge tours, directions to these are given from the M25. Attempting to drive through central London is insanity, so the suggestion is that each visit is approached from the M25 and then returned to the M25. The bridges included are Hanwell Bridge, Clattern Bridge, and Eltham Palace Bridge.

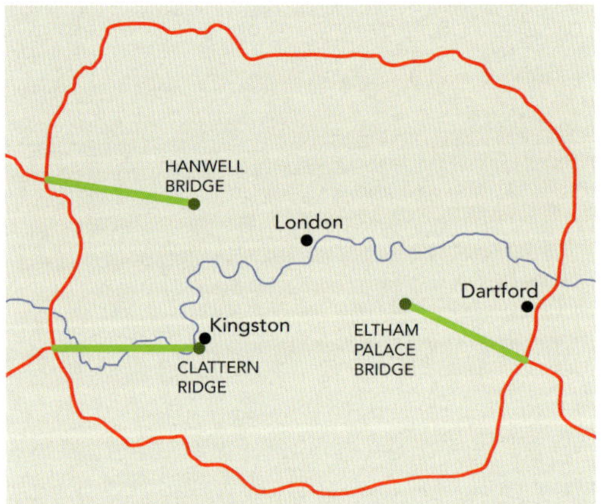

1 Hanwell Bridge ★

Bridge Name:	Hanwell Bridge
Other Names:	Brent Bridge
Location:	In Hanwell on Uxbridge Road in west London, just east of Southall. It is north of the River Thames and carries the Uxbridge Road (A4020) over the River Brent. North of the M4 and south of the A40. Use postcode W7 2NJ for your satnav.
Setting:	City / Urban
OS Ref:	TQ 15096 80120
Crosses:	River Brent
Orientation:	East / West
County:	Greater London Authority
Length:	18 metres
Bridge Type:	Multiple Arch
Materials:	Stone and Brick
Traffic:	Road
Opened:	Before 1396
Authority:	Ealing (London Borough)
Designation:	Grade II Listed
Directions:	From Exit 16 on the M25: • Follow the M40 eastward towards London. This becomes the A40, Western Avenue, after 2 miles. Follow eastwards an additional 7 miles into London. • When you pass under a pedestrian footbridge, get in the left lane. At the Greenford flyover, exit left at the Greenford Road exit ramp, signposted Greenford A4127. • At the big roundabout take the third road (south) onto Greenford Road, signposted A4127 Southall, Greenford. • Follow south for almost 2 miles. Stay on this road, do not turn off. Eventually you will come to the intersection of the A4020. There is a railway overpass bridge on the left. • Turn left (east) and follow for 1¼ miles. As you pass Ealing Hospital on the left, the bridge is ahead 100 metres on this road. If you pass The Viaduct Pub on the right, you've gone too far.
Driving Time:	From exit 16 on the M25 – 40 minutes.

Hanwell Bridge – south face

Concrete balusters

Information: Hanwell Bridge is in west London, north of the River Thames and it carries the Uxbridge Road (A4020) over the River Brent. The road may have originated as a trade route in the early Middle Ages, and though the date at which the river was first bridged here is unknown, references to 'Brent Bridge' and its need of repair have been found as early as 1396. The name Hanwell is in all probability derived from a spring that rises close to the local church.

As was normal in the region then, the original bridge would have been wooden, but in 1500 it was rebuilt in stone, and it had again been largely rebuilt in brick by 1675.

The bridge incorporates four arches, two large central arches of a 5-metre span, which handle the river flow, and two small arches on either end that are of 2 metre spans. The oldest and only medieval arch on the east end is mostly overgrown and buried by the bank. However, its medieval characteristics can be seen in the south face.

In 1762, the turnpike trustees rebuilt and widened the bridge to the north (upstream). From 1815 the county took responsibility for its upkeep, and the bridge was widened again

Hanwell Bridge – north face

to the north and largely faced with stone in 1906 *(Addison,1980)*. These widenings can be clearly seen in the vaults of the pedestrian arch to the west end.

On the north face there are three stone piers with rounded cutwaters which rise to form pilasters supporting the parapets above that are concrete balusters with 'pagoda' shaped coping stone. The fabric of the north side of the bridge is rusticated stone with dressed fine ashlar voussoirs, perhaps a result of the 1906 rebuild. The vaults have a brick lining.

The southern face is made of brick with double brick arch rings that are flush with the face. The piers have rusticated stone pilasters rising to parapet level. There are no cutwaters on the south side.

The Grand Union Canal (formerly the Grand Junction Canal by William Jessop) opened in 1798 and joins the river a little below the bridge. Around the same time the River Brent was straightened to form part of the Grand Junction Canal, and it may be that its course shifted to pass under the eastern arches of Hanwell Bridge.

The Wharncliffe Railway Viaduct overlooks the bridge in the park to the north and was built by the renowned engineer Isambard Kingdom Brunel in 1836 to carry the new Great Western Railway from Paddington. It is said that Queen Victoria would ask to have her steam train stopped on the top of the viaduct so she could admire the view on either side.

At the Bridge: There is a public footpath to the west end of the bridge with steps leading down to river level. The nearest rail station is Hanwell. The Viaduct Pub may provide some temporary parking.

Wharncliffe Railway Viaduct

2 Clattern Bridge ★★

Bridge Name:	Clattern Bridge
Location:	In central Kingston-upon-Thames, in southwest London. It carries the High Street over the Hogsmill River directly in front of the Kingston Council Offices. Use postcode KT1 1HD for your satnav.
Setting:	City / Urban
OS Ref:	TQ 17859 69092
Crosses:	Hogsmill River, a small right bank tributary of the River Thames.
Orientation:	Northeast / Southwest
County:	Greater London Authority
Length:	13.5 metres
Bridge Type:	Multiple Arch
Materials:	Stone and Brick
Traffic:	Road
Opened:	12th century
Authority:	Kingston upon Thames (London Borough)
Designation:	Grade I Listed and Scheduled Monument
Directions:	From Junction 12 on the M25: • Exit eastwards on the M3 into London and follow for 5½ miles to the next exit, number 1, Sunbury-on-Thames. • At the roundabout follow the A308, Staines Road, eastwards, signposted Kingston. Follow for 4 miles past Hampton Court Palace. • At the first roundabout turn left (northeast) following the A308 into Kingston. • At the second roundabout turn right across Kingston Bridge and the River Thames. • Unfortunately, once you are across the bridge, Kingston has a terrible one-way system and pedestrianised streets that makes it nearly impossible to drive to the bridge. However, walking is easy, and Kingston is nice, so find a place to park (I used the John Lewis Car park) and walk southwards to the old High Street. The bridge is directly opposite the Kingston Council Offices and just south of the town centre market.
Driving Time:	From exit 12 on the M25 – 40 minutes.

Clattern Bridge – northwest face

Information: Clattern Bridge is in Kingston-upon-Thames, in southwest London, and carries Kingston High Street over the Hogsmill River, a small east bank tributary of the River Thames. Originally, there was a Saxon bridge on this site, and it is thought that the Normans then built a slightly bigger and more robust bridge around 1175, although the earliest mention of this post-Saxon bridge in a document that can be found today, is that of 1203.

There seems to be a consensus between Jervoise and the Historic England listing that the bridge should be dated to the late 12th century, which makes it one of the oldest in the country, and some of the features of the bridge are consistent with such a build date *(Historic England, 2021)*. Nonetheless, the bridge has been much modified and augmented *(Jervoise, 1930)*.

The more ancient downstream (northwest) face shows that the original bridge was constructed with three slightly stilted semi-circular arches, the two to the northeast spanning 3 metres, the other, now beneath a Tudor building, somewhat smaller. Each arch has two rings of dressed stone voussoirs, with the remainder of the lower part of the bridge's substructure made up of rubble.

The southeast face

The cast iron railings of the southern parapet

The Coronation Stone

Column head at the Coronation Stone

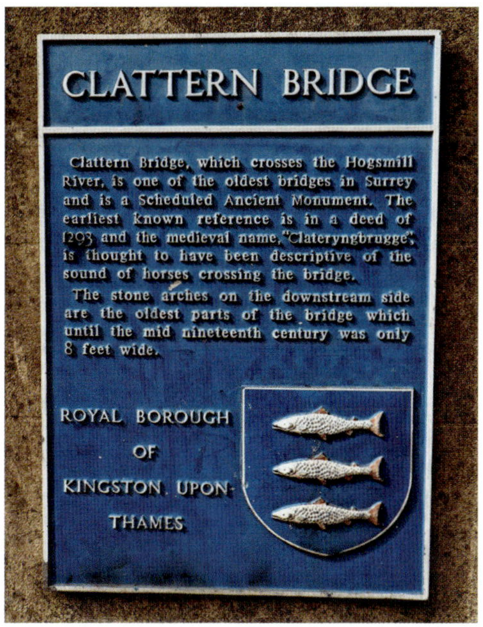

The bridge plaque

The upper red brick parapet with its stone coping, was a 1758 addition to the bridge when the Court of Assembly voted for 'widening and enlarging Clattering Bridge', and, at the same time, the addition of its footpath along the northwest corner of the bridge. The solid parapet on this north side supports a central panel, above which is the base of an octagonal stone shaft.

The south side of the bridge is visibly different and has been twice extended, in 1758 and 1852. This 19th-century, dark red brick south face has three clearly visible half round, one centred (Norman-Romanesque) flush arches in brick with stone dressings. The two cutwaters are decorated by stone half pilasters with cubic capitals, each surmounted by a column with a scallop capital. Between the columns are cast iron railings, which form the parapet, with alternating columnar shafts and two tiers of cusped circles *(Robertson, 2020).*

A plaque on the north parapet suggests that it was originally 2.4 metres wide, and that it acquired its name from the noise of horses crossing it. The three salmon on a blue background is not just a comment on the Kingston residents' love of a fish supper. One of the Domesday Book entries for Kingston mentions three

The Norman (Romanesque) Arch

The Norman arch is an adoption of the semi-circular arch by the post-Conquest Normans in England. Developmentally, it follows the Roman arch and was used in English bridge building until the Gothic style gained popularity in the late 12th century.

It is similar in style and construction to the Roman arch in that they are semi-circular in form, but usually have a series of arch rings in offset depths and are often embellished with masonry decoration. The Norman arch is a defining feature of Norman architecture.

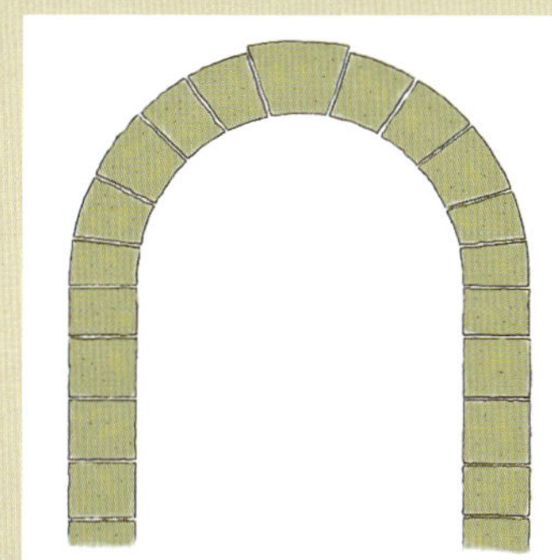

Clattern Bridge – the north side pedestrian walkway

The Tudor building extending over the third arch

Rubble voussoirs forming two arch rings

salmon fisheries in the Thames there, hence the inclusion of them on the county's badge.

In 2012, special tiles were affixed to smooth the underside of the bridge (on the riverbed) so that the local eel population could migrate up the Hogsmill River with greater ease. As late as 1775, women were ducked into the water for any number of supposed crimes. Commendably, there has been no effort to create a pastiche of the ancient bridge still easily viewed downstream from the passageway.

To the east of the bridge is the Coronation Stone of Kingston on which the West Saxon Kings are traditionally said to have been crowned during the 10th century. It was placed in its present position in front of the Kingston Council offices in 1850 on a plinth that has the names of the seven kings believed to have been crowned on it inscribed around the side.

At the Bridge: Bridge views are available from the High Street. Local parking is available at the Rose Car Park. The nearest rail station is Hampton Wick.

The downstream passageway

The stone half column pilaster

3 Eltham Palace North Bridge ★★

Bridge Name:	Eltham Palace North Bridge
Location:	In Eltham within the grounds of Eltham Palace, southeast of Greenwich off the A205 equidistant between the A20 and the A2. The car park and entrance are off the A208, Court Road. Use postcode SE9 5QE for your satnav.
Setting:	City / Urban
OS Ref:	TQ 42461 74050
Crosses:	Eltham Palace moat
Orientation:	Northeast / Southwest
County:	Kent (London)
Length:	28 metres
Bridge Type:	Multiple Arch
Materials:	Stone with brick parapets
Traffic:	Pedestrian
Build Date:	1392
Authority:	English Heritage
Designation:	Grade I Listed
Directions:	From Exit 3 on the M25 (make certain that it's the A20-London Exit-3 and not the M20-Maidstone Exit 3): • Turn northward on the A20 into London and follow for 7 miles to the intersection with Court Road, the A208. This becomes Sidcup Road. • Turn right (north) and follow 600 metres to the Eltham Palace car park entrance. Do not get this mixed up with the earlier Green Lane exit – it is the next right-hand turn.
Driving Time:	From exit 3 on the M25 – 15 minutes.

Eltham Palace North Bridge – southeast face

Eltham Palace North Bridge – northwest face

Information: Eltham Palace North Bridge is in southeast London, between Woolwich and Chislehurst, giving access to the Eltham Palace complex.

The history of the bridge begins with Anthony Bek, Bishop of Durham, who acquired the site in 1295 and rebuilt the manor house. During this effort he also constructed a defensive perimeter wall of stone and brick inside the newly dug moat. Ten years later, Bek presented the manor to the future Edward II in 1305, though he lived there until his death in 1311. Both Edward and his father had frequently stayed at Eltham. By the early 14th century, Eltham had become one of the largest and most frequented royal residences in the country. Edward III (r. 1327–77) spent much of his youth there and frequently visited it as King.

Henry VIII (r. 1509–47) spent much of his boyhood at Eltham and was the last monarch to spend any substantial amount of money or time there. By the 1530s, he rarely came to Eltham at all, preferring Greenwich or Hampton Court. Elizabeth I (r. 1558–1603) only visited Eltham occasionally and over the next two centuries Eltham Palace was used as a farm and the buildings were tenanted.

In 1933, the American millionaires Stephen and Virginia Courtauld, were looking for a semi-rural property within easy reach of central London, and they took a 99-year lease of Eltham Palace from the Crown. They built a modern home on the site of the 19th-century buildings, while retaining as much as possible of the historic palace, and it is their Art Deco interiors within their home that Eltham is known for today.

A portrait of Geoffrey Chaucer from the Welsh Portrait Collection at the National Library of Wales (Public Domain)

Although there is no documentary evidence, it is assumed that the bridge, originally built of wood, was constructed at the same time as the moat sometime after 1296 because by 1390 a new bridge was required. This was built of stone in 1392 and is the bridge we see today. Geoffrey Chaucer was then Clerk of the Works to Eltham Palace, and he supervised the construction of the bridge. Chaucer wrote the *The Canterbury Tales* in about 1386. Today the moat has been mostly filled in and the bridge spans the only remaining water-filled section.

Eltham Palace North Bridge – northwest face

Eltham Palace North Bridge – ribs and vaulting of the northern arch

Eltham Palace North Bridge – the gatehouse window which was used to see who was crossing the bridge

Tudor (Four-Centred) Arch

The four-centred arch, also known as a depressed arch or Tudor arch, is a low, wide type of arch with a slightly pointed apex. It is much wider than its height and gives the visual effect of having been flattened under pressure. It is a low, wide type of arch with a slightly pointed apex.

Its structure is achieved by drafting two arcs that rise steeply from each springing point on a small radius, and then turning into two arches with a wide radius and much lower springing point.

This type of arch, when employed in bridge design, lends itself to very wide spans.

It is known as a Tudor arch as it was a common architectural element during the reign of the Tudor dynasty (1485–1603) and can be seen in many medieval bridges across England. It is sometimes also referred to as a 'flattened Gothic arch'. It appears in Late Gothic architecture of the 15th and 16th centuries.

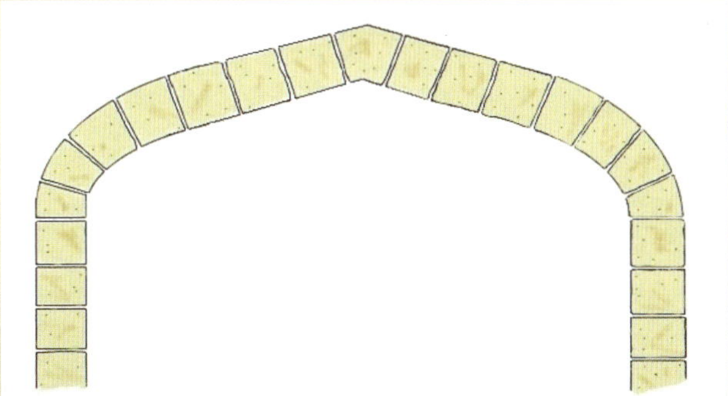

The roadway into the Palace

The remains of the gatehouse

A Bridge at Eltham Palace *by Henry Adlard (1799–1893), engraving (Public Domain)*

Detail of the Courtauld house exterior

The bridge itself encompasses four, four-centred Tudor arches of different widths that are sharply pointed, bordering on Gothic. The largest having a nearly 7.2-metre span. Only the two central arches actually cross the moat with the two outer ones spanning grassy verges, the northern one a public footpath. This footpath provides an excellent (and dry) opportunity to study the medieval vaults and ribs of a classic bridge of the era. The bridge is built of coursed dressed stone blocks of different sizes. The arches are classic examples of four-centred Tudor arches because they are pointed, a strong clue to the build date, with a single flush but highly chamfered arch ring and each has four dressed, equally highly chamfered arch ribs, the outside ones acting as adornment for the rings.

A protruding string course sits just above the point of each arch, which are separated by low cutwaters that rise as columns to be capped just below the later red brick parapets. They enclose a cobbled driveway 3 metres wide. The partial remains of the original gatehouse still stand at the southern end.

At the Bridge: Eltham Palace is now owned and operated by English Heritage. The bridge is only accessible when the Palace is open (there is an admission charge; **https://www.english-heritage.org.uk/visit/places/eltham-palace-and-gardens/**). The nearest rail station is Mottingham.

13 EAST OXFORDSHIRE TOUR

Using Wallingford as the starting point these bridges are arranged from south to north and include Wallingford Bridge, Culham Bridge, Abingdon Bridge, Ock Bridge, and Little Godstow Bridge.

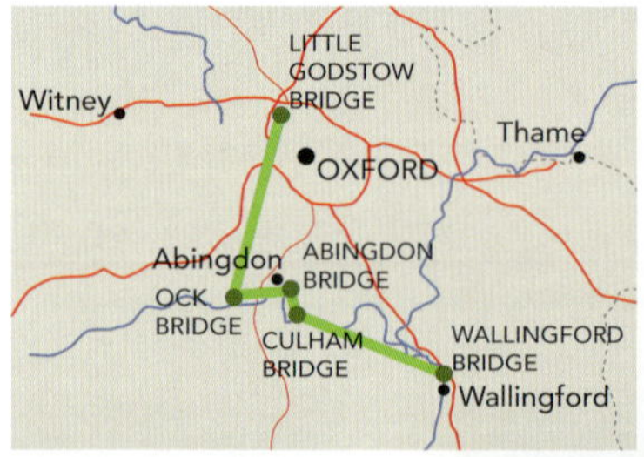

1 Wallingford Bridge ★★★

Bridge Name: Wallingford Bridge
Location: The bridge crosses the River Thames on the A4130 at Wallingford's east side. Use postcode OX10 0BL for your satnav.
Setting: Town / Suburban
OS Ref: SU 61003 89468
Crosses: River Thames
Orientation: East to West
County: Oxfordshire
Overall Length: 300 metres
Bridge Type: Multiple Arch
Materials: Mixed Stone and Brick
Traffic: Road
Build Date: 12th century
Authority: South Oxfordshire (District Authority)
Designation: Grade I Listed
Directions: To Wallingford Bridge:

- The A4139 is the main route through Wallingford and changes names several times in the process.
- The bridge is a main feature of the town and is easy to find on the A4139 on the east side of the town centre area on High Street.

Information: Wallingford Bridge is a medieval road bridge over the River Thames, which connects the towns of Wallingford and Crowmarsh Gifford in Oxfordshire. It crosses the Thames on the reach between Cleeve Lock and Benson Lock. The bridge and causeway together are over 300 metres long and contain 19 arches, five of which cross the main river course and the rest cross a broad flood plain to the east. Several of these arches have chamfered support ribs in their vaults. It has balustraded parapets along its entire length.

Reclaimed stone from the Holy Trinity Priory

Wallingford Bridge – the north face of the river arches looking east

Chamfered arch rib

The ballusters on the steps

Wallingford Bridge and the eastern causeway – south face

The short cutwater on the southern face

Early graffiti under one of the arches

Tradition assigns the date of AD 600 to the building of the first bridge at Wallingford. In 1066 William the Conqueror is reputed to have crossed the River Thames at Wallingford on his way to be crowned at London. The first documentary reference to a bridge across the Thames between Wallingford and Crowmarsh Gifford is from 1142, when King Stephen besieged Wallingford Castle nearby. The first stone bridge is credited to Richard, first Earl of Cornwall, and the four remaining arches of that first bridge are believed to contain 13th-century elements *(Lyte, 1980)*.

Wallingford Bridge is a bit of a patchwork quilt. Major repairs used stone from the dissolved Holy Trinity Priory in 1530 and some of this carved and sculpted stone diaper work can still be seen in the arch vaulting. In 1646 four arches of the bridge were removed by Colonel Blagge during the siege of Wallingford and wooden drawbridges substituted; but in 1751 these four arches were rebuilt of brick with stone facings. In 1809 five river arches, which had been damaged by floods, were taken down and three wider arches erected in their place. At this same time the whole bridge was widened by 2.1 metres on the north side to produce a roadway of about 7 metres in width, and a tollhouse was erected midway across the bridge and the toll keeper is reputed to have lived under the toll house. Because of the widening, the arches on the upstream side are rounded, while those on the downstream side are pointed *(Salzman, 1972)*.

Even casual observation of the arches (many of which you can walk under) reveals that the lower arches of the ancient medieval bridge are encased

Wallingford Bridge – smooth ashlar of the rebuilt central causeway

The north face of the river arches

The widening on the north face can clearly be seen

The seating area in the northern parapet once held the toll house

within the structure of the newer widened bridge. They can be clearly seen along with the iron reinforcements that the builders of 1809 simply laid masonry over. You can just imagine the construction company foreman saying, 'Just cover it with a bit of cement and we can all get down the pub for a swift half. No-one will ever notice'. The rest of the bridge is made of flintstone, local stone, rubble, extensive brickwork, and dressed ashlar stone *(Robertson, 2020)*.

In 1881 the tollgate and house were removed and in 1912 the south wall was buttressed between arches numbers five and eight, and a flight of steps leading to the meadow on the north side was built. The bridge and spire of Wallingford Church are often pictured together.

Dame Agatha Christie lived in Wallingford, and her fertile imagination gave fruit to the mystery stories beloved by so many. The queen of the 'whodunnit' is still one of the UK's best-selling authors and must have crossed this bridge many times.

At the Bridge: Traffic is one way and controlled by a stoplight. There is a public park and parking on the northeast side. The bridge and causeway are easily accessible. Facilities are available in the car park and amenities are easy to find in the town.

Wallingford Bridge – the steps leading up to the bridge roadway

Wallingford Bridge – iron reinforcements buried under the widened face

2 Culham Bridge ★★★

Bridge Name: Culham Bridge

Location: Culham off the A415 south of Abingdon. Use postcode OX14 4LX for your satnav.

Setting: Rural / Suburban

OS Ref: SU 50094 95758

Crosses: River Thames

Orientation North / South

County: Oxfordshire

Length: 42 metres

Bridge Type: Multiple Arch

Materials: Oolitic Limestone

Traffic: Disused, Footpath

Build Date: 1422

Authority: South Oxfordshire (District Authority)

Designation: Grade II* Listed and Scheduled Monument

Directions: From Wallingford Bridge:

- Head east ¼ mile on the A4130 out of Wallingford to the intersection with the A4074.
- At the roundabout turn left (north) signposted Oxford & Watlington and follow for 5½ miles to just outside Berinsfield and the junction with the Abingdon Road, A415.
- Turn left (west) onto the A415 signposted Abingdon and follow 4¼ miles to The Burycroft Road (minor road) on the left. Turn left into The Burycroft Road and immediately find parking. The bridge is shrouded in foliage on the north side of the road.
- *Note: If you suddenly find yourself arriving at Abingdon, don't panic. Just visit Abingdon Bridge first and then turn back to visit Culham Bridge. It is only a short distance, under a mile, south of Abingdon Bridge off the A415.*

Driving Time: From Wallingford Bridge – 25 minutes.

Culham Bridge – west face

Information: Culham Bridge is a medieval bridge crossing what is today a backwater of the River Thames at Culham in Oxfordshire, near the town of Abingdon. The bridge crosses Swift Ditch, which was at one time the main navigation channel of the River Thames until Abingdon Lock was built in 1790. It is felt by many that this channel was cut in about 1052 by the Benedictine monks of Abingdon Abbey under the direction of Abbot Ordric. A large area of land thus became *Andersey Island*, bounded by the main river and this new cut. The bridge was started in 1416 and opened in 1422 and formerly carried the A415 road from Abingdon to Dorchester, Oxfordshire, but was superseded in 1928 by a modern road bridge less than 20 metres to the east.

Culham Bridge was built by Geofrey Barbour who also built Burford Bridge in Abingdon. It is built of coarse local limestone with rubble fill and has five slightly pointed segmented arches of varying widths and heights. One arch has reinforcing ribs in the vaults. There are cutwaters of the same stone on the west side but none on the east side. The deck is today about 6 metres in width, but it was widened and rebuilt at the east face in the 18th century.

During the English Civil War, the bridge was of great strategic importance. After the Royalists left Abingdon in May 1644, Parliamentarian forces seized the bridge and attacked convoys making their way to Oxford. Royalists attempted to recapture the bridge and demolish it in 1645. This resulted in a skirmish on 11 January known as the battle of Culham Bridge, which they lost. The commander of the Royalist forces, Sir Henry Gage, while boldly leading his men in a third assault on the enemy was hit by a bullet and killed. The battle is commemorated by a metal plaque attached to the bridge parapet. The roadway (now a footpath) is overgrown.

During the Second World War, two concrete pill boxes were built on the bridge, each housing anti-tank guns, and part of the parapet was removed to make way for them. The bridge was subsequently restored, at which time, presumably, the rectangular refuge corbelled out above one of the piers was added. The bridge was classified as an ancient monument, also being awarded Grade II* status in July 1963 *(Pevsner, 1974)*.

At the Bridge: There is a public footpath across the bridge and down to the river. There is no formal parking at the bridge but a wide verge at the entrance to a public footpath may provide a temporary pullover. There are no facilities or amenities at the bridge.

The bridge plaque

Spandrel walls

The four-centred Tudor southern arch

The roadway – now a public footpath

3 Abingdon Bridge ★★

Bridge Name: Abingdon Bridge

Other Names: Maud Hales Bridge to the south, Hart Bridge to the north (see below). *(The southern part is technically called Burford Bridge but is not the same as another Burford Bridge in the town of Burford in Oxfordshire.)*

Location: On the A415 just south of the main town. This bridge is just north of Culham Bridge across Andersey Island. Use postcode OX14 3HX for your satnav.

Setting: Town / Urban

OS Ref: SU 49952 96870

Crosses: River Thames

Orientation: North / South

County: Oxfordshire

Length: 300 metres (including both bridges and the causeway)

Bridge Type: Arch

Materials: Stone and Brick

Traffic: Road

Build Date: 1416

Authority: Vale of White Horse (District Authority)

Designation: Grade I Listed

Directions: From Culham Bridge:

- Head north on the A415 towards Abingdon. The bridge is only a short distance north of Culham Bridge off the A415.

Driving Time: From Culham Bridge – 5 minutes.

Information: Abingdon Bridge consists of two portions, separated by a small Island known as Nag's Head Island (because of the pub located there). The southern section is known today as Burford Bridge and the northern portion as Abingdon Bridge. To complicate matters further, the section south of Nag's Head Island was previously known as Maud Hales Bridge

View of Abingdon Bridge from the public park on the south bank

The west face showing the Nag's Head

The small pedestrian tunnel through one of the arches

Steps to the roadway on the south side

The Maud Hales flood arches to the south

Capped parapets and pedestrian refuges

commemorating the benefactress who provided three extra flood arches there. The northern section of the bridge from Nag's Head Island to the town was known as Hart Bridge, after the White Hart Inn that stood for centuries at its northern end, at the site of the later Old Gaol *(Leeming & Salter, 1946).*

The whole structure was originally built of stone in 1416 (to replace an older one of timber) by a body known later as 'The Brotherhood of Christ' (now Christ's Hospital), assisted by the wool and cloth merchants of the town. The structures replaced an unreliable trip by ferry across the river and brought the through traffic from London to the west into the town of Abingdon *(Robertson, 2020).*

Much of the original structure remains, although the northern portion, consisting of seven small Gothic arches, has been altered and widened over the years, particularly in 1790. The arches have sharp cutwaters on the western face.

The bridge cannot be seen in the glance of an eye. It is very long, and rests partly on an island. Standing on this island, the Nag's Head Inn projects from the east side of the bridge *(Ditchfield, 1910).*

The southern portion (Oxfordshire side) normally called Burford Bridge (from Borough Ford) once consisted of five small Gothic arches and one slightly larger elliptical one for navigation. However, the bridge needed serious repair and this part, including the towpath arch, was demolished, and reconstructed in 1927–28, with a new higher arch extended greatly to span 18 metres, so replacing three of the four original arches. Along with the approach causeway from the southeast the bridge was widened and strengthened at the same time. The new arches were rebuilt to a Gothic pattern, with some soffit ribbing, and all were faced with the original stone that had been saved (Leeming & Salter, 1946). The causeway across the southern flood plain has three small flood arches and extends the overall length of the bridge to several hundred metres.

The bridges were of strategic importance in the Civil War, and a drawbridge was inserted into the Abingdon Bridge. In January 1645, simultaneous Royalist attacks across Culham Bridge and Ock Bridge to the west of Abingdon, were beaten off by the Parliamentarian garrison of Abingdon (*Brod* et al., *2010*).

Today there is heavy use of the structure by modern 21st-century traffic but there are wide pedestrian walkways. The parapets are solid and contain triangular pedestrian refuges on both sides. There is a pedestrian tunnel through the old towpath arch on the south bank of the river that allows easy access to both sides of the structure and provides excellent close-up views of the ribbed vault. The spire of St Helen's Church forms a well-known backdrop for photographs of the bridge. Adjacent to the east side of the tunnel there are stone steps leading back up to the roadway.

At the Bridge: Access is good with a community park on the south side of the river and some limited parking. Utilise the pay & display parking and green park space area on the left just prior to crossing the bridge.

Abingdon Bridge roadway looking north into the town

4 Ock Bridge ★★

Bridge Name: Ock Bridge

Location: In the town of Abingdon off Ock Street on the B4017, otherwise Drayton Road. Just south of the A415 at the big roundabout. Use postcode OX14 1AA for your satnav.

Setting: Town / Urban

OS Ref: SU 48842 96917

Crosses: River Ock

Orientation: Northeast / Southwest

County: Oxfordshire

Length: 54 metres

Bridge Type: Multiple Arch

Materials: Stone and Brick

Traffic: Road

Build Date: 15th century

Authority: Vale of White Horse (District Authority)

Designation: Grade II Listed

Directions: From Abingdon Bridge:

- Get back on the A415, at this point called Bridge Street heading left (north).
- Cross the bridge into the town and follow for ¼ mile to the intersection with the High Street, second street on the left, opposite the church, signposted Witney.
- Turn left (west) and follow for 1¼ miles, now Ock Street, to the junction with the B4017, signposted Drayton.
- At the mini-roundabout turn left (south) onto the bridge immediately in front of you.

Driving Time: From Abingdon Bridge – 10 minutes.

Information: Ock Bridge in Abingdon carries the B4017, otherwise known as Drayton Road, across the River Ock, a tributary of the River Thames. The Ock Valley has been a feature of this landscape for centuries and a modern public green space, the Ock Valley Walk, runs past the southern end of the bridge.

There was a bridge here before 1101, when the new Abbot Faritius from Malmesbury entered the town at this point and unshod himself to walk

The main stream running through the sixth arch of Ock Bridge

barefoot to his abbey. A chapel 'on the south end of Oke Bridge in Abingdon town' is mentioned in 1547. In the 14th century there was a hospital on the Ock Bridge dedicated to St Mary Magdalene *(British History Online – The Borough of Abingdon, 2004).*

The bridge was rebuilt in the 15th century, widened in the 18th century, and then widened again in 1979 to 1980, all to the west face. Most of the medieval structure of that side has been entombed inside this modern facade. The colour of the stone used in that reconstruction is not in keeping with the original and the parapet is modern. However, there are glimpses of medieval to be found on the eastern side.

The River Ock splits into two branches just west of the bridge and flows through the first and sixth arches, counting from the south end. The surviving eastern medieval parts of the bridge probably date mainly to the 15th century. The east face is of rubble and consists of seven irregularly spaced arches, two of which are semi-circular, and the rest pointed; the fourth arch retains dressed chamfered ribs. Inspection of the eastern face confirms the rubble build with pointed arches and dressed arch rings below the fourth arch and medieval parapet. The concrete starlings of the arch are modern, and the condition so good as to suggest major refurbishment if not rebuilding of parts of that arch.

At the Bridge: This bridge is not far from Abingdon Bridge. There are public green spaces (Ock Valley Walk) at the south end of the bridge on both sides, allowing access to the riverbank through a wilderness of water, nettles, and bushes. Parking near the bridge isn't available so if you see a spot on Ock Street, take it and walk. There is some limited public parking in the residential area behind the flats just before the bridge on the south side of Ock Street.

The modern eastern face (© P. L. Chadwick and licensed for reuse under the Creative Commons License 2.0)

The worn eastern parapet

The sixth arch squinch

5 Little Godstow Bridge

Bridge Name: Little Godstow Bridge

Other Names: Godstow Bridge (but this is actually the adjacent modern bridge built in 1780. Little Godstow Bridge is the more ancient)

Location: Godstow on the west side of Oxford within sight of the A34 bypass. Use postcode OX2 8PN for your satnav.

Setting: Suburban / Rural

OS Ref: SP 48402 09215

Crosses: River Thames

Orientation: North / South

County: Oxfordshire

Length: 12.5 metres

Bridge Type: Arch

Materials: Calp Stone

Traffic: Road

Build Date: 1485

Authority: Oxford (District Authority)

Designation: Grade II Listed

Directions: From Ock Bridge:

- Get back on Ock Street heading west for 1 mile to the intersection with the A34.
- At the big roundabout head right (north) on the A34 for 7¾ miles following the A34 around the west side of Oxford to a little road off the A34 on the left signposted to Godstow & Wytham. *Note: It is important not to miss this exit.*
- Turn left onto this unnamed road signposted Godstow & Wolvercote and follow north into Wytham. Turn right at the first road in Wytham, Godstow Road, and follow under the A34 to the bridge in Godstow. *Note: Wytham has its own interesting bridge, but it is not medieval.*
- The easiest way back to a main route is to stay on this road and continue for 2 miles through Godstow and Wolvercote to the junction with the A40.

Driving Time: From Ock Bridge – 30 minutes.

An obscured shot of the only remaining medieval arch on Little Godstow Bridge

Single way traffic only across this roadway

The navigable channel to the west. This is not medieval

The date stone in the parapet of the old bridge commemorating its rebuilding in 1892

Information: The River Thames splits just northwest of this bridge and the river's two arms form a good sized island above Godstow Lock. Thus, there are two bridges at this point and the northern one is the more ancient. These Godstow Bridges carry local traffic between Wytham and Wolvercote.

The river under the smaller northern bridge becomes a weir stream adjacent to the well-known Trout Inn (of *Inspector Morse* fame). This bridge has three arches and only the northernmost one is medieval. This arch is limestone rubble spanning 3.6 metres and has a single flush arch ring. It has several medieval characteristics and, based on its appearance, it may well date from around 1500. The two other arches are rounded segmental having been rebuilt in 1892. The roadway on this bridge has a slight hump and a width a little greater than 3 metres. In the east parapet there is a date stone of 1892 commemorating the rebuilding of the bridge.

The southern and larger bridge (Godstow Bridge) crosses the navigable Thames with two wide span elliptical arches. A handsome bridge, but not medieval. Connecting the two bridges is a short causeway built on the island.

At the Bridge: The Thames River walk hugs the south bank of the river and passes in front of the ruins of Godstow Abbey, near the Trout Inn. The easiest parking is at the Trout Inn, but it is often quite busy. The entire structure is overgrown and well obscured by vegetation.

An old lithograph showing Little Godstow Bridge and the Trout Inn before the navigable Thames to the right was widened (used with permission from 'Where Thames Smooth Waters Glide' website at www.thames.me.uk)

14 WEST OXFORDSHIRE & KEBLE'S BRIDGE TOUR

Using Oxford as the starting point these bridges are arranged from east to west and include New Bridge, Radcot Bridge, Keble's Bridge, and Burford Bridge. Keble's Bridge is officially in Gloucestershire.

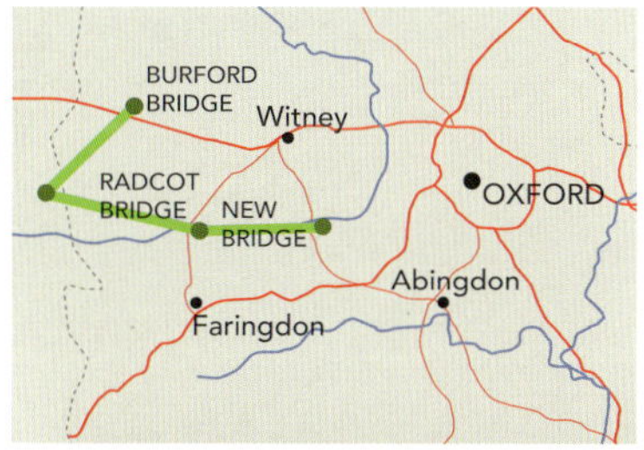

1 New Bridge ★★★

Bridge Name: New Bridge

Location: New Bridge carries the Abingdon–Witney Road (A415) across the Thames. From Kingston Bagpuize, turn north onto the A415 and drive a mile or so to the bridge. Use postcode OX29 7QD for your satnav.

Setting: Countryside / Rural

OS Ref: SP 40365 01404

Crosses: River Thames and River Windrush

Orientation: North / South

County: Oxfordshire

Length: 43.2 metres (including both the north and south sections)

Bridge Type: Multiple Arch

Materials: Taynton Sandstone

Traffic: Limited road

Build Date: 14th century

Authority: West Oxfordshire (District Authority)

Designation: Grade II Listed

Directions: From Oxford:

- Join the A420 at the A34 heading west and follow for 6¼ miles to the junction with the A415 outside Kingston Bagpuize.
- Turn right (north) and follow for 2½ miles to the bridge.

Driving Time: From the A34 – 20 minutes

New Bridge – east face with Maybush Pub in the background

New Bridge – west face showing the cutwaters

Information: New Bridge crosses the Thames at its confluence with the River Windrush. It dates from the 13th century and is built of yellow Taynton stone in the same way as Radcot Bridge, which is slightly older. Both bridges were built by monks in order to improve communications between the wool towns in the south of England and the Cotswold farms. This bridge was named 'New Bridge' as it was the youngest out of the two that were built at around the same time. It was originally much longer than it is now, with 51 arches and being 664 metres long, compared with the current 13 arches: six across the river course and seven across the shallow flood plain near the Maybush Pub. There were once extensive causeways on both the north and south ends but these were demolished and removed *(Carmichael, 1991)*.

It might be considered that there are actually two bridges at this crossing point. Even though they are connected, the two are of distinctly different architectural styles. The northernmost bridge crosses the river itself and its fabric is coursed, dressed limestone rubble. This bridge has a steep humpback and 'still has the six great arches of stone' mentioned by Leland *(Jervoise, 1930)*. All the arches are pointed with widths ranging from 3.6 metres to 5.7 metres. The arches have single flush arch rings and there are four supporting ribs in the soffits of two of the arches, and the outer ones are chamfered. The most northern arch crosses the River Windrush. There are cutwaters on the upstream (west) face rising to refuges and more modern timber cutwaters now protect the old stone ones. The downstream face is flat, without cutwaters. The width between the parapets is 4.5 metres. Obviously there have been repairs over the centuries, some quite extensive, but the bridge's general form is almost certainly unchanged *(Robertson, 2020)*.

The most southerly section of the structure is a causeway that crosses a shallow but wide flood plain containing the Maybush Pub. It is of similar material but different engineering style. Its seven arches are rounded singular segmental style without cutwaters. Above the string course the parapets are of roughly dressed rubble with stone capping but without refuges.

In 1644, in the Civil War, the Battle of Newbridge was fought on the banks of the river. Parliamentarian William Waller attempted to cross the bridge in order to surround Oxford and capture King Charles but was defeated and retreated to Abingdon, where it is alleged, he revenged his loss by destroying the beautiful market cross there.

At the Bridge: The bridge is in a tranquil rural setting, with a public house at either end: the Maybush Pub on the south bank and the Rose Revived on the other. There is parking in the Maybush Pub car park and there is good access to both faces of the bridge. The bridge is controlled by traffic lights, having not been designed to carry modern traffic, and there is an 18-tonne weight limit imposed to protect its ageing structure.

The east face with timber cutwaters

The southern portion across the flood plain

A closeup of the support ribs in the vaulting

2 Radcot Bridge ★★

Bridge Name: Radcot Bridge

Location: South of Radcot and north of Faringdon on the A4095. It carries the road across the river on the reach above Radcot Lock. Use postcode OX18 2SX for your satnav.

Setting: Rural / Countryside

OS Ref: SU 28530 99494

Crosses: River Thames

Orientation: North to South

County: Oxfordshire

Length: 14 metres (Radcot Bridge only)

Bridge Type: Multiple Arch

Materials: Taynton Sandstone

Traffic: Road

Build Date: c. 1200

Authority: West Oxfordshire (District Authority)

Designation: Grade I Listed

Directions: From New Bridge:

- Reverse direction south down the A415 and re-join the A420 heading west.
- Follow for 6½ miles towards Faringdon to the junction with London Road on the right, before Faringdon.
- Turn right (northwest) and follow into the centre of Faringdon.
- At the old market hall, opposite the Bell Hotel, turn right onto the A4095.
- Proceed northward past The Old Crown Coaching Inn. At the cemetery, the road curves right. Follow it for 200 metres where it suddenly makes a sharp left, becoming Radcot Road, signposted Witney A4095, Radcot.
- Follow for 2½ miles to the bridge.

Driving Time: From New Bridge – 30 minutes.

The east face of Radcot Bridge, showing the statue projection in the centre arch

The canal arch – east side

1885 Radcot Old Bridge – The River Thames (used with permission from 'Where Thames Smooth Waters Glide' website at www.thames.me.uk)

Information: The word Radcot means 'cottage by the road' and is mentioned in the Domesday Book as a two-family hamlet near the river with 24 acres of farmland.

There are in fact two stone bridges and a long causeway at this point on the Thames. There is a bridge over the canal bypass to the north, and Radcot Bridge to the south. Radcot Bridge itself is now on a backwater since the construction, in 1787, of that 'new cut' for the Thames and Severn Canal. From Radcot Bridge the road runs northwards and traverses a narrow island to the second channel of the Thames. This 'new cut' serves as the current barge and canal route. Known as Radcot New Bridge, or locally as Radcot Canal Bridge, it was built in 1787 and repaired in 1848.

There has been a bridge of some sorts at the Radcot Thames crossing since the 10th century, but the first stone bridge was completed in 1225 and parts of this still stand to make this the oldest 'proper'

Sheep washing at Radcot Bridge in 1885. The projection on the bridge's east side may have formerly supported a statue of the Virgin (© British History Online with permission)

The pointed northern arch and yellow spandrels

bridge across the Thames. Jervoise calls Radcot Bridge 'one of the best examples of a medieval bridge over the Thames' *(Jervoise, 1930)*. The only craftsmen in those days who had the necessary skills to perform the task were attached to the religious houses, so the builders were probably the Cistercian monks from nearby Faringdon.

Radcot Bridge is built entirely of yellow limestone from Taynton in Oxfordshire and bears the unmistakeable marks of early medieval construction. The arches are ribbed internally, and the ascent is very steep. The bridge as it now exists has two sharply pointed outer arches flanking a slightly rounder rebuilt central arch, all of limestone ashlar. The coped parapet has a triangular projection over the central arch on the eastern side, which may formerly have contained a statue of the Virgin Mary. According to tradition the statue was destroyed during the Civil War. The western side has a plinth on which a cross may once have stood.

The Battle of Radcot Bridge was fought near the bridge in December of 1387 during the troubled reign of Richard II, between King Richard's troops, led by Robert de Vere, and an army captained by Henry Bolingbroke, Earl of Derby. After a fierce fight, De Vere was defeated and fled to France. Much of the bridge was destroyed during the battle but was reconstructed in 1393. Apparently, a monument, now lost, was put on the repaired bridge in 1393 *(British History Online – Langford Parish: Radcot, 2000)*.

The west face showing a slightly flatter central arch

At the Bridge:

Adjoining the bridge is the Swan Inn. Access is reasonably good to view the eastern face, with parking possible in the pub car park; the western face, which seems very similar, can only be viewed in entirety from the river or private land.

The roadway across both bridges (© David Luther Thomas and licensed for reuse under this Creative Commons License 2.0)

3 Keble's Bridge ★★

Bridge Name: Keble's Bridge

Other Names: Kebles Clapper Bridge

Location: The village of Eastleach about 3½ miles north of Lechlade-on-Thames and south of Burford. The bridge is just southeast of the road that connects the two parts of the village of Eastleach, which are divided by the River Leach, a tributary of the River Thames. Use postcode GL7 3NQ for your satnav.

Setting: Village / Rural

OS Ref: SP 20111 05214

Crosses: River Leach

Orientation: Northwest / Southeast

County: Gloucestershire

Length: 9.5 metres (including the abutment projections)

Bridge Type: Clapper

Materials: Granite Stone

Traffic: Pedestrians and ducks

Build Date: 15th century

Authority: Cotswold (District Authority)

Designation: Grade II Listed

Directions: From Radcot Bridge:

- Continue north on the A4095 to Clanfield. In Clanfield the road turns into the B4020. Do not follow the A4095 east but instead stay on this road, now the B4020.
- Follow north through Black Bourton and Alvescot.
- Turn left just west of Alvescot (poorly signposted) and follow the B4477 for 2¼ miles into Broughton Poggs.
- At the intersection in Broughton Poggs turn left (south – still the B4477) and follow 400 metres to the intersection with the A361.
- Turn left (south) and follow 300 metres to the next intersection signposted Southrop, Fyfield.
- Turn right (west) and follow 2½ miles to a triangular intersection signposted Fyfield & Eastleach.
- Turn right (north) and follow ½ mile to the next triangular intersection signposted Eastleach.
- Turn left west and follow to Eastleach. At the triangular intersection turn left (west) and follow 150 metres into this picturesque village. The footbridge is not on the road but on a little footpath to the left.

Driving Time: From Radcot Bridge – 45 minutes.

Keble's Bridge – downstream south face

The plinths

The steps to Keble's Bridge

The upstream north face

The bridge clappers

Information: The pretty Cotswold villages of Eastleach Martin and Eastleach Turville are situated on opposite banks of the River Leach but connected by an old stone 'clapper' footbridge known as Keble's Bridge. Named after the early 19th-century churchman, John Keble, who was a curate at the church. However, the Keble family was a well-known local household so the bridge may not be named after him personally. There are two parish churches looking at each other across the clear waters of the little river.

The clapper bridge has a series of four low limestone rubble piers and projecting earthen abutments that support a row of wide bridging flagstones. Some of the slabs are irregular in shape. The width of the pathway is about 1.2 metres and sits about 1 metre above the water. The four piers produce five stream channels, and one pier has a set of concrete-topped steps affixed to its downstream face leading into water.

At the Bridge: The twin villages Eastleach Martin and Eastleach Turville are among the most picturesque locations in the Cotswolds with their two adjacent parish churches facing each other across the river Leach. Access is very good. A public footpath runs alongside the river, and the river is a popular wading spot in the summer months.

4 Burford Bridge ★★

Bridge Name: Burford Bridge

Location: The village centre of Burford northwest of Oxford on the A361 (not to be confused with Burford Bridge at Abingdon). Use postcode OX18 4BD for your satnav.

Setting: Village Centre

OS Ref: SP 25179 12504

Crosses: River Windrush

Orientation: North / South

County: Oxfordshire

Length: 22.5 metres

Bridge Type: Multiple Arch

Materials: Stone

Traffic: Road

Build Date: 15th century

Authority: West Oxfordshire (District Authority)

Designation: Grade II* Listed

Directions: From Keble's Bridge:

- Reverse directions and proceed back to the A361 at Broughton Poggs.
- Turn left (north) and follow 6 miles straight across the big A40 roundabout, down the street named The Hill into the village centre, to the bridge on the north side of town.

Driving Time: From Keble's Bridge – 35 minutes.

Information: Documentary sources agree that Burford Bridge was built in the 15th century, although there was a bridge in some form on the site at least a century earlier. Historic England states that it was heavily remodelled in 1791 and restored at some point in the 20th century, with rebuilding of the southern arch possibly a part of that exercise.

The fabric is coursed squared yellow Cotswold ashlar. There are four segmental arches, spanning about 4 metres each, with

Burford Bridge – west face

The east parapet walls with pedestrian niches

Triangular coping on the parapets with niche refuges rising from the cutwaters

double arch rings in two orders, of which those on three, are chamfered. Even at normal water level there is little clearance above the water, and this makes observation difficult. There are cutwaters both upstream and downstream that rise to form refuges and prominent string courses on both faces *(Robertson, 2020)*. There are short sections of causeway both north and south made from undressed rubble with chamfered coping. The total length of the bridge is 22.5 metres and the width between the parapets is 4.5 metres. The parapets are quite high at over a metre and the string course protrudes noticeably.

At the Bridge: Access to river level is difficult and involves climbing fences. Access is fair downstream, though the low arches limit what can be seen from the riverbank. The east face is surrounded by private gardens and is inaccessible. Burford is an active Cotswolds tourist village so parking can be a problem, especially in the summer. If you can find a spot on the High Street in town, take it and walk. There is no parking at all on the north side of the bridge. There is a free public car park with limited spaces on Church Lane. There are plenty of facilities and amenities in the village High Street.

Burford Bridge – west face

15 EAST SOMERSET TOUR

Using Bristol as the starting point these bridges are arranged from north to south and include Tun Bridge, Stanton Drew Bridge, Bow Bridge, Wyke Champflower Bridge, and Buckland Dinham Packhorse Bridge.

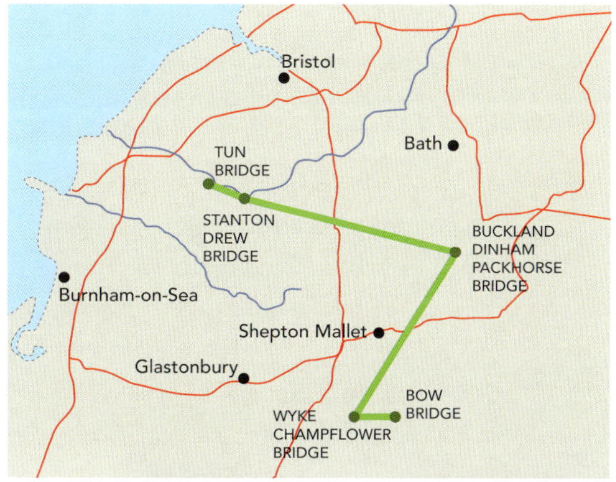

1 Tun Bridge ★★

Bridge Name:	Tun Bridge
Location:	In Chew Magna on Tunbridge Road at the south side of the village of Chew Magna, which is a few miles south of Bristol. Use postcode BS40 8SP for your satnav. This bridge is only 3 miles west of Stanton Drew bridge.
Setting:	Village / Suburban
OS Ref:	ST 57696 62916
Crosses:	River Chew
Orientation:	North / South
County:	Somerset
Length:	22 metres (actual span)
Bridge Type:	Multiple Arch
Materials:	Sandstone and Limestone
Traffic:	Road
Build Date:	Late 15th century
Authority:	Bath and Northeast Somerset (Unitary Authority)
Designation:	Grade II* Listed
Directions:	From Bristol: • Take the A37 southwards for 3 miles from the Bristol Airport Road bypass to the B3130. • At the B3130 turn right (west) and follow for another 2½ miles to the centre of Chew Magna. At the roundabout turn sharply left onto Tunbridge Road, signposted Bishop Sutton, and follow 80 metres to the bridge.
Driving Time:	From Bristol – 20 minutes.

The central cutwater – western side

Tun Bridge – western face

The main river arches – eastern face

The vinegar plague bowl in the eastern cutwater at parapet level

Vinegar Stones

Vinegar stones (or plague stones) are found all across England in villages that existed during the plague eras of 1348 through 1393 and then again, in the 15th century. These stones, with hollowed out depressions, were positioned at strategic locations around communities, such as at bridges, stone fences, footpaths, and the base of stone crosses. A number of plague stones are known to be reused bases from historic crosses.

Vinegar was placed in the depression to disinfect coins during the plague years. Vinegar was used as a disinfectant in the belief that it prevented the plague from spreading. Centuries before our modern understanding of disease control and transmission, people commonly believed the plague was passed through bad smells and dousing the coins in strong-smelling vinegar would remove the odour and prevent passing the infection.

Residents placed the coins in the vinegar and outsiders would place food or goods next to the stone. This practice allowed communities to continue essential trading and buy food from outsiders while minimising the fear of contagion.

There are two plague stones associated with bridges in this book: one at Tun Bridge in Chew Magna and another at Coombe Bisset in Wiltshire.

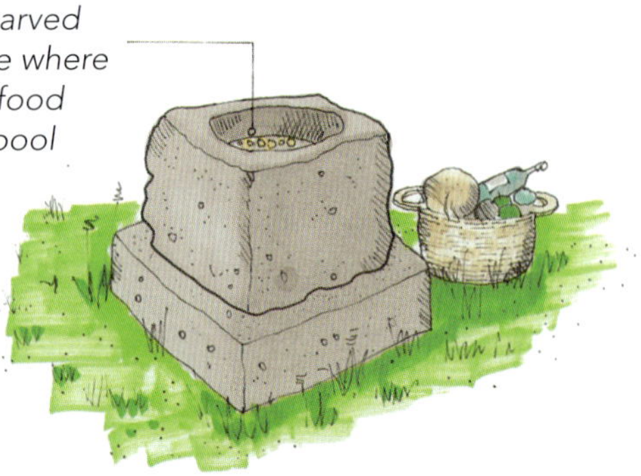

Information: Tun Bridge carries a minor road over the River Chew, a tributary of the Bristol River Avon, at the south side of the village of Chew Magna, which is a few miles south of Bristol. Jervoise calls this 'an exceptionally fine medieval bridge' *(Jervoise, 1930)*.

There are three Gothic pointed arches, the two larger with offset double arch rings, a small one with a single arch ring, which suggests it might be of later construction. The fabric is largely sandstone and limestone rubble, though the dressed voussoirs are of freestone.

There is limestone coping to the parapets, which are about 1 metre high. The parapets and the string courses, together with at least one of the small cutwaters, are more recent modifications.

The two faces of the bridge seem to differ only in the tops of these cutwaters. One is carried to parapet level and neatly capped and topped with a vinegar basin on the east face. It may have been used in the past for food but today is a rainwater collector. There are two cutwaters with offsets to the west side *(Robertson, 2020)*.

The total length is 22 metres, while the width between the parapets is 4.8 metres, which given its build date is wide.

At the Bridge: Access is good upstream and adequate downstream to identify features of interest.

Tun Bridge – unusual funnel shape to the northern arch showing widening and a small arch underneath

2 Stanton Drew Bridge ★★

Bridge Name:	Stanton Drew Bridge
Location:	In the village of Stanton Drew a few miles east of Chew Magna. Use postcode BS39 4ER for your satnav.
Setting:	Countryside / Rural
OS Ref:	ST 59678 63446
Crosses:	River Chew
Orientation:	North / South
County:	Somerset
Length:	12 metres (actual span), 24 metres with the causeway approaches
Bridge Type:	Multiple Arch
Materials:	Limestone
Traffic:	Road
Build Date:	13th century
Authority:	Bath and Northeast Somerset (Unitary Authority)
Designation:	Grade II* Listed and Scheduled Monument
Directions:	From Tun Bridge: • Reverse directions and go back east on the B3130 out of Chew Magna for 1¼ miles to the intersecting road to Stanton Drew. *Note: There is a unique little house sitting in the centre of a triangular intersection.* • At the intersection, turn right (south) and follow 250 metres to the bridge.
Driving Time:	From Chew Magna – 7 minutes.

Information: Surrounded by countryside, the fabric of this bridge is a mixture of local limestone rubble and dressed limestone used in the arch rings and ribs. There are two, pointed Gothic river arches, each with chamfered arch rings surmounted by a second ring of voussoirs, on each face.

Stanton Drew Bridge – eastern face

Arch ribs supporting the southern arch

The smaller cutwater – western face

There are four ribs beneath each arch, with the outer faces of the outer ribs chamfered. To the south is a segmental arch with double flush arch rings, crossing a path, but no doubt also serving as a flood arch.

There are 1-metre-high parapets to each side with rubble coping. There are no pedestrian walkways but on the east side the parapet has a strange junction to the southern approach creating a large, refuge-like, 45-degree angle in the wall. A long causeway leads southward into Stanton Drew village.

Upstream there are two large cutwaters with pyramidal stone tops, but downstream there is a single rather smaller cutwater of similar design. On the east side there is an oval plaque with an illegible inscription.

The bridge may well date to the 14th century, though unsurprisingly it has been repaired since then. There is an inscription on the outside of the downstream parapet marking a repair of 1809. The bridge was damaged and repaired in a great flood in 1968 *(Robertson, 2020)*.

The road deck has a width of 3.9 metres. There is an exposed 20th-century steel girder that supports an outward extension of the bridge into a bend in the road on the north side. It sits above older corbelling forming a squinch, all of which was no doubt incorporated to ease access at some great cost to the appearance *(Pevsner, 1958)*.

At the Bridge: Access is reasonable, but views of the bridge are obstructed by shrubs and trees. There is no formal parking but a field entrance on the north side may provide a temporary pullover.

Stanton Drew Bridge – northern arch – east face

The coping stones

The unusual angle in the eastern parapet

③ Bow Bridge ★★

Bridge Name: Bow Bridge

Other Names: Bruton Packhorse Bridge

Location: In Bruton, a village 7¾ miles southeast of Shepton Mallet. Bruton is not far from Wyke Champflower. Use postcode BA10 0ED for your satnav.

Setting: Village / Suburban

OS Ref: ST 68357 34821

Crosses: River Brue

Orientation: North / South

County: Somerset

Length: 9 metres

Bridge Type: Single Arch, Packhorse

Materials: Stone

Traffic: Pedestrian

Build Date: 15th century

Authority: South Somerset (District Authority)

Designation: Grade I Listed and Scheduled Monument

Directions: From Stanton Drew Bridge:

- Make your way back to the A37.
- Turn right (south) and follow the A37 for 12 miles to just south of Shepton Mallet.
- Just south of Shepton Mallet at a roundabout the road splits. Take the A371 southeast towards Castle Cary. Follow for 1 mile.
- At the B3081 bear left (southeast again) signposted Evercreech and follow for 3½ miles through Evercreech and Milton Clevedon.
- Just outside Bruton the road becomes Coombe Street. Follow the road as it curves down into the village centre. At the large triangular intersection in front of the church bear right onto Silver Street.
- The bridge is just off Silver Street, the A359. It is a one-way system, directly across the street from St Mary's Church. This bridge is a footbridge and not on a road.

Driving Time: From Stanton Drew Bridge – 35 minutes.

Bow Bridge – western face

The single graceful arch built on one rib

Information: Bow Bridge was built using locally quarried ashlar stone and has an impressive single 9-metre-span arch with slightly pointed chamfered and recessed double arch rings of large blocks. The narrow vault is smooth without ribs. There are angled parapets and copings forming a slight point in the centre, with walls along the footpath. On the northwest corner are the remains of a plinthed pier. The walkway is less than 1 metre wide, with Keinton flagstones to the south side and stone setts to north.

This bridge has been damaged several times by flooding of the River Brue, the latest during the winter of 1983, with subsequent repair.

On the parapet on the western side of the bridge the remains of a carved shield can still be seen. The shield is thought to bear the dolphin of the Fitzpanes family, who lived at Redlynch in the 15th and 16th centuries, and founded Kings School, suggesting that they may have rebuilt this link between the former Abbey, being opposite the supposed gatehouse of Bruton Abbey, and its Court House in the High Street *(Robertson, 2020)*. It had acquired the name Bow Bridge by 1707. *Note: The Church Bridge is just a few metres downstream and the two are sometimes confused.*

At the Bridge: There is a ford and steppingstones immediately downstream (southwest) that provide a good view of the bridge. Wear your wellies. Access is good at the northwest side of the bridge. There is temporary parking on the street or in the community hall.

Bow Bridge – the footpath looking south

The parapets

The steps leading down to the stepping stones ford

The eastern face

4 Wyke Champflower Bridge ★

Bridge Name:	Wyke Champflower Bridge
Location:	To the south of the village of Wyke Champflower and some two miles west of Bruton. Use postcode BA10 0PW for your satnav.
Setting:	Countryside / Rural
OS Ref:	ST 65706 34046
Crosses:	River Brue
Orientation:	East / West
County:	Somerset
Length:	8.5 metres
Bridge Type:	Multiple Arch
Materials:	Stone
Traffic:	Road
Build Date:	14th century
Authority:	South Somerset (District Authority)
Designation:	Grade II* Listed and Scheduled Monument
Directions:	From Bow Bridge (footbridge): • Follow Silver Street to its T junction. Get in the right lane marked 'Frome'. • Turn right (north) and follow ¼ mile to the second road on the left marked 'Wyke Champflower'. • Turn left (west) and follow for 2 miles through Wyke Champflower (do not turn off). The road becomes a country lane as you head south on Wyke Road. The bridge, noticed by its wooden handrails, is to the south of the village of Wyke Champflower.
Driving Time:	From Bow Bridge – 20 minutes.

Wyke Champflower Bridge – south face

The substantial cutwater on the north side

The roadway

Wyke Champflower Bridge – north face

Information: Wyke Champflower Bridge is out in the countryside and would go unnoticed if you were not looking for it. Records for this bridge begin in 1677 when it was declared a county bridge. It was deemed dangerous in an 1854 inspection report. It has two pointed arches and a central cutwater on both faces.

Today this bridge carries a single-track minor road over the River Brue, some two miles west of Bruton. This quiet road was once part of the ancient Bristol to Weymouth route. The Historic England listing dates the bridge as 15th century or earlier, and states that the fabric is locally quarried stone 'cut and squared' *(Robertson, 2020).*

There are flush double arch rings to two pointed arches without arch ribs, with a span of 3.2 metres each, giving the bridge a length of about 8 metres overall.

The width of the roadway is 3.6 metres, and it is enclosed by a wooden post and rails fence for its entire length rather than parapets.

The large cutwaters on both sides are constructed from the same local rough stone, and form angled buttresses placed centrally between the arches. They extend for up to 1.5 metres out from the pier structure.

Retaining walls on the east side of the bridge appear to be built from the same stone as the arches and the cutwater piers, which suggests a single phase of construction for the whole bridge. There are no revetments on the west side.

The precise date for the construction of the bridge is unknown although it displays features typical of the 14th century and before, particularly its style of arch, which is uncommon after 1500. It is probably the same bridge referred to in a document dating from 1677 as 'the ancient common bridge at Wake Champflower', which records it as being in great decay *(Jervoise, 1930).* This suggests that the bridge has been restored at least once to its original form.

At the Bridge: The bridge is overgrown and access to river level is very difficult. There is no formal parking available, but a small farm access road may afford a temporary pullover.

Wyke Champflower Bridge – central cutwater – south face

The double arch rings

The adjoining stream at the southwest corner

5 Buckland Dinham Packhorse Bridge ★

Bridge Name:	Buckland Dinham Packhorse Bridge
Location:	Just south of the village of Buckland Dinham and just north of a newer replacement that carries the A362 over the Buckland Brook. It is to the northwest of the town of Frome. Use postcode BA11 2QL for your satnav.
Setting:	Rural / Countryside
OS Ref:	ST 75594 50883
Crosses:	Buckland Brook
Orientation:	North / South
County:	Somerset
Length:	11 metres
Bridge Type:	Three Arch
Materials:	Stone
Traffic:	Local foot traffic
Build Date:	15th century
Authority:	Mendip (District Authority)
Designation:	Grade II* Listed and Scheduled Monument
Directions:	From Wyke Champflower Bridge:

- Reverse directions and make your way back to Bruton.
- Take the A359 through Bruton heading northeast towards Frome for 8½ miles.
- At a roundabout outside the village of Nunney Catch take the A361 east, signposted Frome Trowbridge.
- Outside Frome, at the first roundabout, go straight across onto the B3090 Marston Road and head into the centre of Frome.
- At the centre bear left as the road curves, signposted Buckland Dinham A362.
- At the roundabout bear left again and follow the A362 northwest through Frome.
- The bridge is just south of Buckland Dinham on the A362 as it passes over the Buckland Brook. Just shy of Lower Street.

Driving Time: From Wyke Champflower Bridge – 30 minutes.

Buckland Dinham Packhorse Bridge – north face

Information: The Historic England listing describes this ruin as a footbridge adjacent to the ruin of a 'wool drying tower', and indeed both are in a ruinous state. Both are well camouflaged behind overgrowth and private parking spaces next to the A362, ¼ mile south of Buckland Dinham. A new bridge 20 metres south now carries the A362 and this old bridge has been abandoned and forgotten.

Although not officially listed as a packhorse bridge, it displays all the classic characteristics of one. The footway is less than 2 metres wide; it lacks parapets

The central cutwater – north face

The rubble built arch vaults

The western arch – north face

The wool drying tower sluice in a niche

(although modern wooden handrails are present), and it has a humpback shape with ramped up approaches on both ends. It also sits on the route of an ancient trade road. This observation is supported by the presence of the wool drying tower and the fact that wool was a primary economic activity of the area.

The tower is two storeys in height without a roof and badly decayed. There is a small segmental arch at the base of the tower in a niche that once formed a sluice to the river *(Hudson, 1967)*.

There are three segmental arches of local rubble, each of about 2 metres in width, the easternmost one slightly smaller. On the upstream (north) side the two piers have low cutwaters that do not rise above impost level. This structure really is in a perilous state and it is clear that without attention it will not be with us for much longer.

At the Bridge: The brook is shallow and unless in flood, a pair of wellies will allow wading. Access is good but overgrown. There is no parking nearby and a visit will require walking.

16 CENTRAL SOMERSET TOUR

Using Taunton in central Somerset as a starting point, these bridges are arranged west to east and include Hele Bridge, Bradford-on-Tone Bridge, and Haselbury Old Bridge.

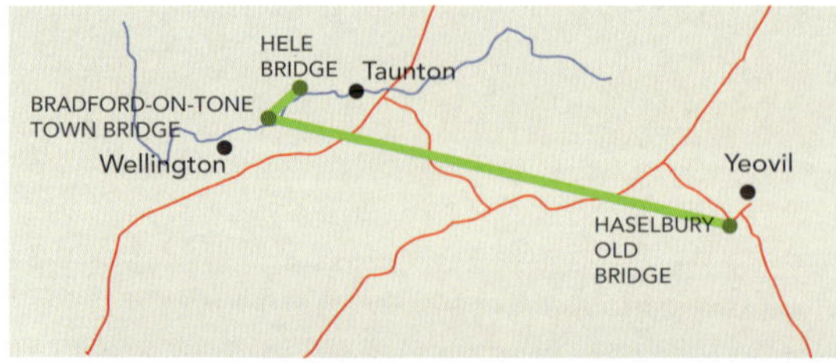

1 Hele Bridge ★★

Bridge Name:	Hele Bridge
Other Names:	Bradford Hele Bridge
Location:	Outside Bradford-on-Tone, a mile and a half to the southwest of Taunton. Use postcode TA4 1AH for your satnav.
Setting:	Rural / Countryside
OS Ref:	ST 18691 24765
Crosses:	River Tone
Orientation:	North / South
County:	Somerset
Length:	22 metres
Bridge Type:	Multiple Arch
Materials:	Stone and Concrete
Traffic:	Road
Build Date:	15th century
Authority:	Somerset West and Taunton (District Authority)
Designation:	Grade II Listed
Directions:	To Hele Bridge: • From Taunton take the B3227 west out of Taunton for 2 miles. • Turn south (left) onto Allerford Road, signposted Allerford and follow for 1 mile. • At the T junction tun left and follow ½ mile to the bridge.
Driving Time:	From Taunton – 15 minutes.

Hele Bridge – west face

Hele Bridge from downstream

This OS cut mark can be found on the south parapet of Hele Bridge (© Adrian Dust, and licensed for reuse under Creative Commons License 2.0)

Information: Hele Bridge carries a minor road over the River Tone. The bridge consists of three pointed arches of approximately 4 metre spans that have double arch rings.

The bridge has been brutally widened, at both faces by removing the upper part of the structure, and affixing rolled steel joists (RSJs), on which brick parapets sit, thus overhanging the cutwaters, and protruding beyond the substructure of the bridge. This modification, which increased the width of the roadway by 0.7 metres to 4.2 metres, was carried out early in the 20th century and was harshly criticised by local inhabitants and is similarly dealt with in the Historic England listing. In truth, far worse has been done to widen old bridges, and this procedure had the merit of at least leaving the substructure of the medieval bridge untouched, and visible. Nonetheless, the bridge was restored in 2002 by replacing the steel beams with reinforced concrete and the brick parapets with the more appropriate masonry visible now. Today's parapets are of roughly coursed stone with splayed end walls and stone coping *(Robertson, 2020)*.

The surviving lower part of the bridge, which has been dated to the 15th century, is fabricated from local

Hele Bridge in the 1920s (from the website Bude and Beyond, R. Wilcox, 2014)

Hele Bridge – east face (© Derek Harper, and licensed for reuse under Creative Commons License 2.0)

random rubble with ashlar dressed soffits. There are double, chamfered arch rings in two orders, and cutwaters cut off at the level of the top of the arches, though they may have risen higher before the widening operation described above *(Pevsner, 1958).*

In 1617 the Bradford parishioners pleaded at the Quarter Sessions that they should be freed from paying the enormous costs of repairing Hele Bridge on the grounds that it lay 'in the uttermost boundes of our parishe and none of us have occasion to travell to the markett that way'. The Justices of the Peace for Somerset subsequently enrolled it as a County Bridge.

It was badly damaged when Taunton was besieged in 1645 during the Civil War. Several years later the Justices were still trying to raise funds to repair that damage along with many other war-damaged bridges *(Page, 1978).*

There is another Hele Bridge in Dulverton that dates to the late 16th century and thus is not included in this book.

Hele Bridge – west face (© Roger A. Smith, and licensed for reuse under Creative Commons License 2.0)

At the Bridge: Access is fair downstream though foliage obstructs the view. There is no formal parking, but a field access and footpath may provide a temporary pullover. The Allerford Inn is less than a mile to the west.

2 Bradford-on-Tone Town Bridge ★★

Bridge Name Bradford-on-Tone Town Bridge
Other Names: Bradford Bridge
Location: In Bradford-on-Tone 3 miles southwest of Taunton, off the A38 and only 2 miles southwest of Hele Bridge. Use postcode TA4 1HF for your satnav.
Setting: Rural / Countryside
Orientation: Northwest / Southeast
OS Ref: ST 17192 22998
Crosses: River Tone
County: Somerset
Length: 8 metres
Bridge Type: Two Arch
Materials: Stone
Traffic: Road
Build Date: 13th to 15th centuries
Authority: Somerset West and Taunton (District Authority)
Designation: Grade II* Listed and Scheduled Monument
Directions: From Hele Bridge:

- Continue across Hele Bridge and turn right (south) and follow for just under a mile to the T junction.
- Turn right (west) on Bradford Bridge Road and follow to the bridge.
- 150 metres northwest of the White Horse Inn.

Driving Time: From Hele Bridge – 20 minutes.

Bradford-on-Tone Town Bridge – east face

Information: This bridge is a stone-built structure with two four-centred pointed arches with double arch rings chamfered in two orders, surmounted by a third flush arch ring. The smooth soffits without ribs have been partly renewed in brick.

There is a central pier with cutwaters to both sides, which are capped at the level of the parapets. There are splayed abutments on the west end of the bridge, which has restored parapets and a 3-metre-wide carriageway.

The bridge was built at some point between the 13th and 15th centuries. By 1667 it had been adopted as a 'County Bridge'. A marker stone was installed to show the area on either side of the bridge that was the responsibility of the local

Bradford-on-Tone Town Bridge – central cutwater

Justices of the Peace. It can still be seen near the White Horse Inn.

The bridge was restored in 1698 (it bears a date stone on the southern parapet recording this fact) and again in the late 19th century. Major repairs have been made several times since then.

The fabric is random rubble of local stone, and it still carries vehicular traffic today. The bridge is Grade II* listed *(Robertson, 2020).*

In 2000, a lorry went through the parapet of the bridge, but the damage, although still visible, has since been repaired.

At the Bridge: There is a small parking area on the west end of the bridge and access is good.

The northern aproach

The northern arch soffit

3 Haselbury Old Bridge ★★

Bridge Name: Haselbury Old Bridge

Location: Southwest of Yeovil off the A30 west of Haselbury Plucknett. Use postcode TA18 7NR for your satnav.

Setting: Countryside / Rural

OS Ref: ST 45847 10969

Crosses: River Parrett

Orientation: East / West

County: Somerset

Length: 7.2 metres

Bridge Type: Arch

Materials: Ham Stone

Traffic: Road

Build Date: 14th century

Authority: South Somerset (District Authority)

Designation: Grade II* Listed and Scheduled Monument

Directions: From Taunton:

- Take the A303 southeast for 15 miles to the Crewkerne A356 junction.
- Exit and turn right (south) and follow 5 miles into Crewkerne.
- In the village centre turn left (north) on East Street, the A30, and follow for ¾ mile to a major turning on the left signposted Merriott.
- Turn left and follow for 150 metres to the first turning on the right signposted Haselbury Mill.
- Turn right and the bridge is just there.

Driving Time: From Taunton – 40 minutes.

Haselbury Old Bridge – north face

Information: Haselbury Bridge now carries a minor road over the River Parrett, having been bypassed by the A30, a few miles northeast of Crewkerne. The fabric is generally of coursed rubble of Hamstone, but the arch rings and ribs are dressed ashlar. There are two slightly pointed, segmental arches, spanning just over 3 metres each, and they both have two chamfered arch rings in two uneven orders, and, unusually for the area, the soffits are supported by four chamfered ribs *(Robertson, 2020)*.

There are cutwaters upstream and downstream on the central pier, which are roughly capped below the parapets. The parapets are of large, coursed stone with plain coping and iron cramping links. The southwest corner is splayed to accommodate the road junction.

Masons' Marks

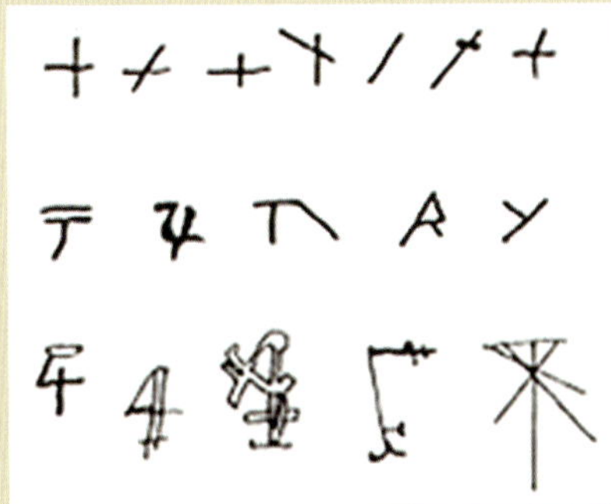

A few examples of masons' marks

If you closely examine an old village church and carefully look at the stonework of the walls, piers, and arches, it is almost certain that, before long, you will find some stones bearing curious marks. These marks are masons' marks, a series of sophisticated symbols that, for the past 4,000 years, have been inscribed on stones and used by designers and builders to enable instructions to be transferred with ease. These were also an integral part of medieval bridgebuilding. The mark may be a simple X, it may be a sort of W, or it may take one of many forms, but it will almost certainly be some straightforward geometric combination of straight lines. Curves and circles were used only occasionally.

Most modem scholars are now agreed that there are three categories of masons' marks:

1. The first is the quarry mark, which is used to show where stone came from and where it was to be shipped. This was usually carved on the roughly cut stone block and was part of the quarry-master's tally system. Quarry marks were unlikely to survive the process of cutting up the stone and dressing it for use in the bridge, and to be sure their purpose was served once the block had been delivered to site.
2. Assembly marks are the second category, and these are the marks that can often still be seen on the faces of the stone, since they were part of the process of construction. This enabled complex sections of things like arch ribs, or voussoirs to be built up in the correct order. The marks form a progression of assembly in many cases, and they are often still visible in the finished bridge. Sometimes the sequence was based on a version of Roman numerals, at other times a domino system was used in which the end of one block had the same symbol as the end of the next block, which in turn had a different symbol on its other end to relate to the next one.
3. And finally, contemporary documents describe the different ways that masons were paid, with piecework frequently the norm, and it is this that accounts for the use of the third category, 'banker'-masons' marks. Masons marked their stone to let the paymaster know how much work they had done. Used as a sign of ownership, or responsibility for work completed, the mason who put his mark on a stone admitted or claimed that he had worked the stone.

In many grand houses and churches of the era these marks were carefully removed to provide a clean 'dressed' surface *(Alexander, 2008)*.

Detail of the four chamfered arch ribs

Haselbury Bridge – masons' marks

Haselbury Bridge – masons' marks

Haselbury Old Bridge – south face

The coping stones and cramps on the north parapet

Detail of the central cutwater north face

The riverbed has been paved below the arches, presumably to prevent scouring, and smooth the water flow. The bridge has a length of 7.2 metres, and the width of the roadway is 3.6 metres, accommodating only single file traffic.

The bridge was repaired in 1844 at a cost of 40 pounds, soon after it had been bypassed by the main Crewkerne to Yeovil road some 150 metres to the south.

During recent repairs to the stonework, an opportunity was taken to examine the substructure of the bridge in some detail. During that examination, a number of masons' marks were recorded. These were marks of individual ownership of responsibility for work done or possibly assembly marks that were used to ensure the correct installation of important pieces of stonework *(Alexander, 2008)*.

This bridge is dated to the 14th or 15th century on the grounds of style, there being no documentation referring to its original construction. Jervoise described it as one of the most interesting bridges in Somerset (Jervoise, 1930).

At the Bridge: There is no formal parking. The Haselbury Mill Hotel is just down the street.

The unusual iron reinforcing cramp in the first rib of the eastern arch south face

17 WEST SOMERSET TOUR

Using Minehead as a starting point, these bridges are arranged west to east and include Horner Packhorse Bridge, West Luccombe Packhorse Bridge, Gallox Bridge, Landacre Bridge, Tarr Steps Bridge, Barle Bridge, and Bury Bridge.

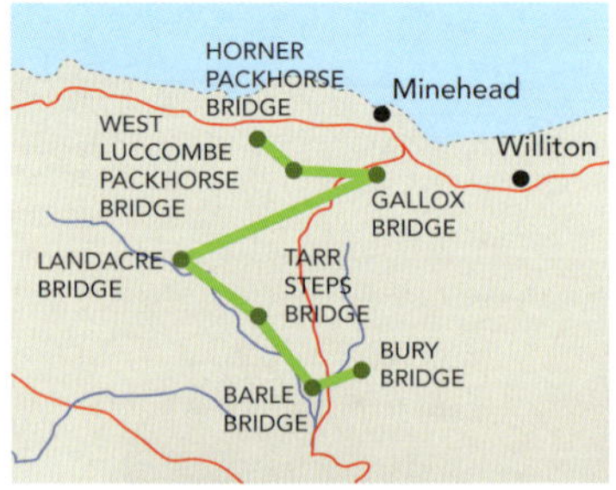

1 Horner Packhorse Bridge ★★

Bridge Name: Horner Packhorse Bridge
Other Names: Hacketty Way Bridge
Location: In the hamlet of Horner, south of Porlock heading towards Luccombe within Exmoor National Park. Use postcode TA24 8 for your satnav.
Setting: Rural / Woodland
OS Ref: SS 89722 455491
Crosses: Horner Water
Orientation: Northwest / Southeast
County: Somerset
Length: 5 metres
Bridge Type: Multiple Arch
Materials: Red Sandstone
Traffic: Road
Build Date: c. 1500
Authority: Somerset West and Taunton (District Authority)
Designation: Grade II* Listed and Scheduled Monument
Directions: To Horner Packhorse Bridge:

- From Minehead take the A39 west towards Porlock for 5½ miles.
- Before you get to Porlock turn left (south) onto a road signposted West Luccombe, Horner.
- Follow south on this road ¾ mile through the hamlet of West Luccombe on to the hamlet of Horner. Do not turn off. You will pass over an interesting little bridge; this is not it. Travel a little further south.
- The bridge is not on the road but is accessible via a footpath called Hacketty Way just south of the lane that leads to the parking area.

(Note: Google Maps has mislabelled this bridge and guides you to West Luccombe Packhorse Bridge, which is only ½ mile north of this bridge.)

Driving Time: From Minehead – 20 minutes.

Horner Packhorse Bridge – north face

Information: This beautiful example of a packhorse bridge carries the Hacketty Way footpath across the Horner Water (stream) just west of the hamlet of Horner. It has only one high segmental arch spanning 5.4 metres and a roadway width of 1.2 metres carrying a narrow-cobbled pathway.

It is built of coursed red sandstone rubble and the parapets are swept back at approaches. The arch is either very irregular in shape or represents an effort

Under the arch west abutment

Horner Packhorse Bridge – south face

The footpath

The east abutment and wing wall

to produce a four-centred arch, which would imply a construction date of around 1500 *(Robertson, 2020)*.

There are single, flush, dressed arch rings at each face. The most noticeable feature, given the other dimensions, is the height of the arch above the small river. The pathway is cobbled, but there is no ford beside it, and it does not lead anywhere in particular.

This bridge is very well preserved. On the west side there are apparent pony trekking routes through the woodland.

At the Bridge: There is good all-round access and there is a parking area with facilities to the east down a small lane.

Exmoor National Park

Ancient Exmoor is one of the most remote places in England. Lying mainly within the boundaries of West Somerset and north Devon, Exmoor National Park is the smallest of our national parks, encompassing only 170,000 acres. It embraces a unique landscape of moorland, woodland, valleys, and farmland that nature and humans have crafted over thousands of years. Exmoor was designated a National Park in 1954.

Despite its situation in the west country and proximity to many of England's most popular tourist destinations, it has retained a timeless and unexploited charm. Its medieval villages embrace their local produce, while burial mounds, standing stones and Roman forts provide compelling scenery for visitors to enjoy with their friends and family.

Exmoor derives its name from the River Exe, which has as its main tributaries the Barle and the Haddeo. There are many smaller rivers in the north portion of Exmoor known as the 'waters', Weir Water, Horner Water, and Badgworthy Water are but a few. There are about 483 km of named rivers on Exmoor.

One of Exmoor's many Tors

The East Lyn River, Exmoor National Park

Exmoor is an excellent place to explore the outdoors through walking, cycling, and horse riding. Footpaths and bridleways weave through the park's ancient oak woodlands and go alongside its rivers and open heather-covered moorland.

Exmoor's northern coast

Surprisingly, there are 37 miles of coastline in Exmoor, as well as the highest sea cliffs in England. The landscape also features rare coastal woods, which are of scientific interest. The exposure to the Bristol Channel makes it a diverse area where vast exploration leads to new discoveries like its wild red deer and Exmoor ponies. Its dark nighttime skies further grant visitors the opportunity to stargaze, while its seas and inland waters offer tourists of all abilities the chance to canoe, kayak, and fish. For visitors that choose to remain on land, Exmoor is the perfect place to rock climb, mountain bike, and trail run.

Exmoor has been the setting for several novels including the 19th-century *Lorna Doone: A Romance of Exmoor,* by R. D. Blackmore, and Margaret Drabble's 1998 novel *The Witch of Exmoor.* The park was featured on the television programme Seven Natural Wonders twice, as one of the wonders of the West Country.

2 West Luccombe Packhorse Bridge ★★

Bridge Name: West Luccombe Packhorse Bridge

Location: In the hamlet of West Luccombe south of Porlock heading towards Horner within Exmoor National Park, less than half a mile upstream from Horner Packhorse Bridge. Use postcode TA24 8HT for your satnav. *(Note: Google Maps has mislabelled this bridge calling it Horner Packhorse Bridge which is only ½ mile south of this bridge.)*

Setting: Rural / Woodland

OS Ref: SS 89877 46107

Crosses: Horner Water

Orientation: Northwest / Southeast

County: Somerset

Length: 7 metres

Bridge Type: Single Arch

Materials: Red Sandstone

Traffic: Pedestrian

Build Date: Late 15th century

Authority: Somerset West and Taunton (District Authority)

Designation: Grade II* Listed and Scheduled Monument

Directions: From Horner Packhorse Bridge:

- This bridge is only ½ mile from Horner Packhorse Bridge.
- Turn back north on this same road. Just before the little stone bridge you passed over earlier, the bridge is on the left (west).

Driving Time: From Horner Packhorse Bridge – 3 minutes.

Information: There are two ancient packhorse bridges within a mile of one another; West Luccombe and Horner. West Luccombe Packhorse Bridge crosses the Horner Water, less than half a mile downstream from Horner Packhorse Bridge and is also thought to be late medieval dating from the 15th century.

West Luccombe Packhorse Bridge – south face

The footpath

West Luccombe Packhorse Bridge – north face

Although it has been restored over the years it retains most of its original form and features. This is a well-preserved packhorse bridge. It is built of red sandstone rubble and has a cobbled carriageway, which measures up to 1 metre wide and 7 metres long.

The single, pointed segmental arch spans 4.5 metres, and there is a single flush arch ring made of shaped voussoirs *(Robertson, 2020)*.

The north end of the span is supported on a rock face, the south end on a robust masonry abutment.

The parapets have saddleback coping and are less than 1 metre high. They are swept back at the approaches. In fact, the previously mentioned rock face has been rendered partly artificial by the masonry extension of the bridge abutment on the downstream side. The bridge now provides farm access, but its longer-term history is unknown. It is easily viewed from all sides *(Hinchcliffe, 1994)*.

At the Bridge: There is good all-round access and there is a parking area with facilities to the east down a small lane.

The east abutment and impost

3 Gallox Bridge ★★★

Bridge Name:	Gallox Bridge
Other Names:	Dunster Packhorse Bridge, Gallows Bridge, Gallocksbrigge Bridge, or Gallocks Bridge
Location:	In the village of Dunster, 1½ miles southeast of Minehead. Use postcode TA24 6SR for your satnav.
Setting:	Town / Suburban
OS Ref:	SS 98952 43204
Crosses:	River Avill
Orientation:	North / South
County:	Somerset
Length:	5.5 metres (not including the causeway)
Bridge Type:	Two Arch
Materials:	Stone
Traffic:	Pedestrian (Road traffic uses the adjacent ford)
Build Date:	15th century
Authority:	English Heritage and Somerset West and Taunton (District Authority)
Designation:	Grade I Listed and Scheduled Monument
Directions:	From West Luccombe Bridge: • Return to the A39 and turn right (east) and make your way 7 miles back through Minehead to Dunster on the A39. • At the Dunster stoplights turn right (south) onto the A396 signposted Dunster Medieval Village. • Follow the A396 through Dunster, past the medieval wool market all the way through town. Turn left (south) onto Park Street at the Foresters Arms Inn and follow a short distance to the bridge at the bottom of Park Street. *(Note: Do not try to drive right up to the bridge as there are no turning spaces. Use the car park.)*
Driving Time:	From West Luccombe Bridge – 35 minutes.

Gallox Bridge and causeway

The east face

Gallox Bridge – west face

The central cutwater west face

Gallox Bridge

Information: Gallox Bridge once carried packhorses bringing wool from Exmoor villages to the Somerset market town of Dunster and was once part of the main route into Dunster from the south. The bridge crosses the River Avill at the southern end of the village, at the base of the hill on which Dunster Castle sits, at a point that may have been the limit of tidal flow during the medieval period. Local belief is that ships could once navigate up the Avill as far as this bridge. The approach from the village is via a raised causeway. The name Gallox is believed to be derived from gallows as the village gallows were nearby. The bridge is first mentioned in a document of 1475 but is almost certainly older than this.

The bridge is semi-circular in shape and has two pointed arches and a roadway width of 1.2 metres and is 10.5 metres long. The arches are built with double arch rings comprised of two rows of upright voussoirs arranged around the curve of the arch. On the upstream (west) face of the bridge, a stone cutwater guides the river current through the two arches. The bridge has low parapets and, on the town (north) side, the parapet is continued along the footpath for some way beside the river, in order to prevent flooding.

Alongside the bridge is an ancient ford – undoubtably older than the bridge.

At the Bridge: Parking is in the small parking lot between Park Street and Mill Lane, or in the main Dunster parking area off the A396. The bridge is an open site and is accessible at any time.

4 Landacre Bridge ★★★

Bridge Name:	Landacre Bridge
Other Names:	Known locally as Lannacre Bridge
Location:	On Landacre Lane between Withypool and Hawkridge. A minor road a few miles west of Withypool. Use postcode TA24 7SD for your satnav.
Setting:	Countryside / Rural / National Park
OS Ref:	SS 81645 36128
Crosses:	River Barle
Orientation:	Northeast / Southwest
County:	Somerset
Length:	20 metres
Bridge Type:	Multiple Arch
Materials:	Stone
Traffic:	Road
Build Date:	15th century
Authority:	Somerset West and Taunton (District Authority)
Designation:	Grade II* Listed and Scheduled Monument
Directions:	From Gallox Bridge: • Return to the A396 and take it southwards for 8½ miles through Wheddon Cross to Edbrooke Road on the right. • Turn right (west) at the triangular intersection signposted Withypool and follow for 5 miles towards Withypool. • Before Withypool you will come across the junction with the B3223 signposted Simonsbath. • Turn right (northwest) and follow 1¼ miles to a large triangular intersection. • Turn left (west) onto Chibbet Hill Road (eventually becoming Landacre Lane) and follow for 2 miles to the bridge.
Driving Time:	From Gallox Bridge – 40 minutes.

Landacre Bridge – east face

Landacre Bridge – east face

Landacre Bridge northern arches on the east face

Information: Landacre Bridge spans the River Barle, a tributary of the River Exe, upstream from Withypool. It encompasses five stilted, pointed arches, each spanning 2.7 metres, giving the bridge a total length of nearly 20 metres, when the four robust piers are considered. Each of the piers supports triangular cutwaters capped off at parapet level with hipped tops, both upstream and downstream.

The fabric is rubble, coursed in the cutwaters, and the double flush arch rings are made up of roughly dressed voussoirs. The parapet walls are 0.6 metres high with saddleback coping of up-ended slate and they extend for 22.7 metres on either side of the single carriageway. The ends of the parapet walls are set with large single blocks and are splayed outwards, extending beyond the span of the bridge for 4.9 metres on the northwest side and for 1.5 metres on the southeast side. An Ordnance Survey benchmark on a stone slab is embedded in the inner face of the north parapet wall *(Robertson, 2020)*.

The width of the roadway is just less than 3 metres, the bridge has not been widened, and perhaps the only surprise is the fact that it is so exactly horizontal with not a semblance of a hump.

Its form and fabric are compatible with a 15th-century build date, though the first

Ordnance Survey Benchmarks

Before the days of GPS and satellite-based geographic information system (GIS) earth measuring technologies, Ordnance Survey mapmakers and architects measured altitudes above sea level from triangular marks with a single horizontal line – known as benchmarks. The first systematic network of levelling lines and associated benchmarks was initiated in 1840. In the Victorian era over 35,000 benchmarks were carved throughout the UK and their locations are recorded in the OS database. Thousands more have been added since. These obscure marks are like secret symbols carved on buildings and bridges all around mainland Great Britain. Hidden in plain sight, we walk past them every day without realising what they are and their purpose. The UK's network of 500,000 benchmarks all stem from a single 'mother benchmark' at the tidal measuring station in Newlyn in Cornwall.

Benchmarks were always carved into static vertical structures like bridges, buildings, and monuments, never carved into kerbstones, which could be moved at any time after flooding or road changes. There are many included in this book.

There is a benchmark database (separate from the OS database) of surviving benchmarks and an unusual hobby has sprung up called 'Benchmark Bagging'.

The network has had little maintenance since the early 1980s when satellite technology took over. Many benchmarks are now 'lost' due to building work, demolition, and the widening of bridges and roads. Although the main network is no longer being updated, the full record is still in existence and the markers will remain until they are eventually destroyed by redevelopment or erosion.

Landacre Bridge – the southernmost pointed segmental arch

Landacre Bridge – the cutwaters on the west face

documentation was in the early 17th century, and it has obviously been well maintained and not much altered since.

At the Bridge: In a beautiful setting on Exmoor National Park, Landacre Bridge is by some margin the most photogenic arched bridge on Exmoor. Access is good around the bridge and there is parking at the west end of the bridge but no facilities. It is a popular spot for seeing Exmoor ponies and wild swimming.

5 Tarr Steps Bridge ★★★

Bridge Name:	Tarr Steps Bridge
Location:	This bridge is remote, between Hawkridge to the south and Liscombe to the north. Use postcode TA229QA for your satnav directions.
Setting:	Rural / Isolated / National Park
OS Ref:	SS 86776 32116
Crosses:	River Barle
Orientation:	Southwest / Northeast
County:	Somerset
Length:	55 metres
Bridge Type:	Clapper
Materials:	Granite and Slatestone
Traffic:	Pedestrian
Build Date:	Early medieval
Authority:	Somerset West and Taunton (District Authority)
Designation:	Grade I Listed and a Scheduled Ancient Monument
Directions:	From Landacre Bridge: • Turn around and make your way back to the B3223. • Turn right (south) and follow for 4 miles to the third major intersection signposted Liscombe, Tarr Steps. • Turn right (west) and follow 1¼ miles towards Liscombe to a triangular intersection. • Turn left (south) and follow ½ mile to the steps.
Driving Time:	From Landacre Bridge – 25 minutes.

Information: Tarr Steps Bridge is a beautiful and photogenic example of a clapper bridge crossing the River Barle, a tributary of the River Exe in the heart of Exmoor, 2¾ miles southwest of Winsford. The slabs are of a local grit sandstone weighing between 1 and 2 tonnes apiece. Even at this weight the slabs are frequently washed off their piers during floods and have on occasions been washed up to 46 metres downstream, requiring re-setting as recently as 2016. They have now all been numbered to facilitate replacement.

There are 17 spans, of which 12 are single slabs, four are paired and one is of three stones' width. The slabs sit on stone piers about 1 metre above the river. Smaller flat slabs have been placed on both sides of the piers acting as cutwaters protecting the piers against scouring. Much damage to the bridge has been due to debris such as branches floating down with floodwaters and battering the bridge. Debris used to be removed once a year by farmers from the Hawkridge sides of the river but since the flood of 1952 it has been trapped by cables strung across the river upstream of the bridge *(Pevsner, 1958)*.

The bridge was badly damaged by floodwater on 22 December 2012 when the steel wires upstream designed to protect the bridge from damaging debris, were broken by falling trees washed down the river. Floodwaters carried away part of the bridge again on 21 November 2016, and it has since been rebuilt.

Unsurprisingly, given its impressive scale, there have been many theories about the origins of the bridge, with some taking it back to prehistoric times. One rationale for the suggestion of a prehistoric date includes evidence that several prehistoric tracks converge here, although the presence of a bridge as a result of this remains unproven. Secondly, dating it by the place-name association of 'Tarr'. The Celtic 'Tochar' or 'Toher' means 'causeway' (across water) *(Robertson, 2020)*.

More realistically it has been suggested that it was built in the 15th or 16th century to give access to a corn mill. Of course, that is not to say that all or even most of the masonry visible now has been there for up to 600 years, because in recent times, parts have required rebuilding on several occasions.

Local legend has it that the 'steps' were first laid in place by the devil. Obviously, the locals of the time were none too happy to have the devil in their midst, particularly as he would not allow anyone to cross here. Witnesses observed a black cat attempt the crossing, only to disappear in a puff of smoke midway. The vicar somewhat bravely decided to try his luck. Following a mid-bridge confrontation, with much gesticulating and intimidation, the devil backed down. It was

Tarr Steps Bridge, showing 14 of the 17 spans

One method of transport across the ford

The deck slabs

subsequently agreed that anyone could cross unharmed. The devil did, however, request the right to sunbathe on the stones should he fancy it.

At the Bridge: As isolated as it is, the bridge sits next to the Tarr Farm Inn, a five-star hotel on the north bank and there is parking available. (*Note: there is a deep ford to the north side of the bridge, but it is only advisable to cross the River Barle at this point with a four-wheel drive or SUV.*)

Tarr Steps Bridge – stone slabs protecting the piers

6 Barle Bridge ★★★

Bridge Name:	Barle Bridge
Other Names:	Dulverton Bridge
Location:	Carries the B3222 across the River Barle into Dulverton. Use postcode TA22 for your satnav.
Setting:	Town / Suburban
OS Ref:	SS 91207 27823
Crosses:	River Barle
Orientation:	East / West
County:	West Somerset
Length:	25.5 metres
Bridge Type:	Multiple Arch
Materials:	Stone
Traffic:	Road
Build Date:	Medieval
Authority:	Somerset West and Taunton (District Authority)
Designation:	Grade I Listed and Scheduled Monument
Directions:	From Tarr Steps Bridge: • Reverse directions and make your way back to the B3223. • Turn right (south) and follow 3½ miles, all the way into the centre of Dulverton. The road becomes Lady Street. • At the town centre (The Lion Hotel) turn right (southwest) and follow through town to the bridge. The road becomes the B3222.
Driving Time:	From Tarr Steps Bridge – 35 minutes.

Information: Barle Bridge carries the B3222 over the River Barle, a tributary of the River Exe, in the centre of the village of Dulverton. It is a stone bridge of medieval origin that has five segmental pointed arches, with double arch rings. The old causeway and ford once used to cross the river sat next to the bridge before it was widened in the early 1800s *(Page, 1978)*.

Barle Bridge – south face

The bridge is constructed with local stone, random cut rubble, with rubble voussoirs and a protruding ashlar string course. The bridge has stone parapets with flat copings without pedestrian refuges or designated walkways. It was repaired in 1866 and again in 1952–3 after flood damage.

There are four cutwater buttresses with three-tier stepped coping between the four arches on both sides. Some of the weather capping has been restored. The pointing on the town end is somewhat old but the stone coping is comparatively new. The cutwaters on the north side have been repaired recently *(Robertson, 2020).*

The will of John Sydenham 1558 of Combe Dulverton was said to give six shillings and eight pence to the maintenance of the bridge at Dulverton.

Carved stones on the outside of the north parapet record that the bridge was repaired in 1624 and subsequently widened by about 1½ metres on the upstream side in 1819 by John Stone. Access from scaffolding during repairs to the bridge in July 2013 enabled photographs of the two date stones to be taken. One reads:

> *'Dulverton Bridge (was re?) paired un ye yeAre oF ovr (Lo?)rd GOD 1684'*

The remaining section of inscription could not be deciphered although a number of individual letters are visible. It may mention a donor as 'OF SOM' can be made out. The other inscription reads:

> *'Bge Widned 1819 by John Stone' (bridge widened 1819)*

At the Bridge: A small public park on the east end of the bridge allows easy access and a good viewpoint. There is ample parking on the east end of the bridge and the Bridge Inn pub is adjacent to the car park. All facilities and amenities are available in Dulverton.

Barle Bridge – north face

The squinch in the southwest corner

The parapet and string course

7 Bury Bridge ★★★

Bridge Name: Bury Bridge

Location: The hamlet of Bury a few miles east of Dulverton off the A396 within Exmoor National Park. Use postcode TA22 9ND for your satnav.

Setting: Hamlet / Rural

OS Ref: SS 94467 27456

Crosses: River Haddeo

Orientation: North / South

County: Somerset

Length: 20 metres

Bridge Type: Multiple Arch, Packhorse

Materials: Slatestone

Traffic: Pedestrian and limited small vehicular traffic (bicycles etc.)

Build Date: Medieval

Authority: Somerset West and Taunton (District Authority)

Designation: Grade II* Listed and Scheduled Monument

Directions: From Barle Bridge:

- Turn around and make your way back into Dulverton following the High Street (B3222) east past the Rock House Inn, out of town. The road becomes Jury Hill Road.
- Follow for 1½ miles until it intersects with the A396.
- Turn right (south) and follow for only ¼ mile to the first road to the left signposted Brompton Regis.
- Bear left, but then the road immediately splits again.
- Bear right onto that minor road and follow 1 mile into the hamlet of Bury and the bridge.

Driving Time: From Barle Bridge – 25 minutes.

Bury Bridge – west face

Bury Bridge – east face

Bury Bridge – the southernmost arch

The ford, looking south

Information: Bury Bridge is a narrow medieval stone bridge that crosses the River Haddeo, a tributary of the River Exe, alongside a paved ford, which allows a minor road to pass through the village of Bury, at the southeast of Exmoor. The bridge lies on the line of an ancient road called 'Fort Lane'. The bridge is described in the Historic England listing as a packhorse bridge, but it does not display the standard features of a packhorse bridge, specifically no, or very low, parapets, although the ones we see today may have been added later *(Robertson, 2020)*.

The rubble-built bridge is of local flat slatestone masonry and has four arches – the two to the south are pointed, the other northern ones are rounded segmental, implying perhaps a later rebuild. There are single flush arch rings. Two of the arches span 2.1 metres, a third 2.4 metres, and the largest 3 metres. The width between quite high parapets of the same stone is 2 metres. The coping is upturned slate. The roadway is cobbled with a few areas of recent repair.

Each pier has a triangular cutwater buttress upstream, but on the downstream side there are three large if truncated cutwaters associated with the segmental arches, while there seems to be none between the pointed arches.

It has been suggested that the bridge might date to the 14th century, or at least that the pointed arches do. If so, it has been remarkably well maintained.

At the Bridge: Apart from the danger of getting wet feet, or a marooned car, access is good. Parking in Bury is limited and there are no public amenities.

The footway

18 SURREY TOUR

All of the medieval bridges in Surrey are in the west part of the county within a few miles of one another and lie between Farnham and Guildford. Using Farnham as a starting point, these bridges are arranged from west to east and include Tilford West Bridge, Tilford East Bridge, Elstead Bridge, Somerset Bridge, Eashing Bridges (Upper & Lower), and Unstead Bridge.

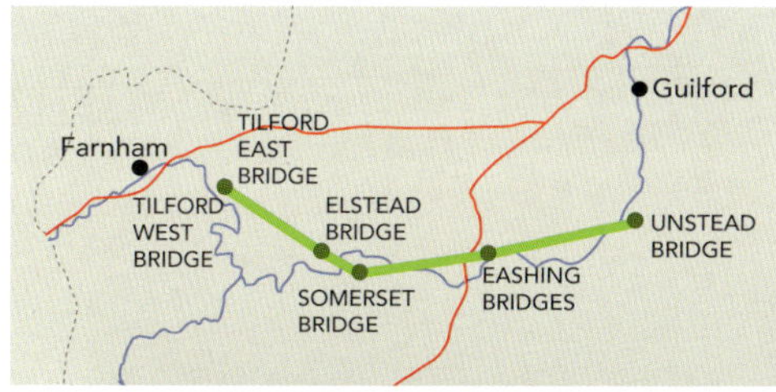

1 Tilford West Bridge ★★

Bridge Name: Tilford West Bridge
Other Names: Tilford Northwest Bridge
Location: Village of Tilford, on the Green over one branch of the River Wey. Use post code GU10 2BU for your satnav.
Setting: Village / Rural
OS Ref: SU 87174 43524
Crosses: River Wey
Orientation: North / South
County: Surrey
Length: 19 metres (including the buried arch)
Bridge Type: Multiple Arch
Materials: Ironstone
Traffic: Pedestrians and bicycles
Build Date: 13th century
Authority: Waverley (District Authority)
Designation: Grade I Listed and Scheduled Monument
Directions: From Farnham:

- From the A31 in Farnham, exit left (southeast) at Farnham Station Road and the B3001 and turn left (southeast).
- Follow for only 200 metres and bear right (south) onto Tilford Road, signposted Tilford, just past Farnham Station.
- Follow for 3½ miles to Tilford Commons. You will actually cross over the River Wey beside Tilford West Bridge.
- Find a place to park on the Green and walk to both bridges. Tilford West Bridge is located at the northwest corner of the commons and Tilford East Bridge is located to the northeast corner of the commons.

Driving Time: From Farnham – 25 minutes.

Tilford West Bridge – east face

Information: There are two medieval bridges in Tilford, within ¼ mile of one another. Like Tilford East Bridge, this bridge carries Tilford Street across the River Wey, but unlike Tilford East Bridge, this one does not carry traffic. Tilford New Bridge was constructed alongside to replace a semi-permanent crossing built by the army in 1941. Tilford East and West Bridges were obviously built as two separate structures and so are treated separately here.

This bridge is one of a series of bridges built over the Wey by the monks and lay brothers of Waverley Abbey, nearby, in the first half of the 13th century. Waverley Abbey was the first Cistercian Abbey in England, but it was dissolved in 1536 during the dissolution. Six of these bridges remain and all are included in this work. They are Eashing, Unstead, Somerset, Elstead, and the two at Tilford. Similarities in construction suggest that they were built around

Tilford West Bridge – east face

The rounded cutwater

Tilford West Bridge – west face

the same time, possibly after the floods of 1233, when many of the earlier bridges were destroyed *(Malden, 1911)*.

The fabric of the bridge is local iron-stone rubble with thin slabs in two concentric rows forming the voussoirs of the arches. There are no parapets, but 20th-century wooden posts and rails have been added. Four arches remain visible, a fifth arch is buried in the south bank and now marked only by a cutwater and buttress. The arches increase in height and width to the centre where the largest spans 3.9 metres. The arches vary in shape with four being slightly pointed segmental and two elliptical segmental. The vault soffits are smooth without ribs. There are small ridged or diamond-shaped cutwaters to the upstream (east) side and rounded cutwaters to the downstream (west) side. As with Tilford East Bridge, there has clearly been considerable refurbishment, unsurprising when it is remembered that it is estimated to be over 700 years old *(Robertson, 2020)*.

At the Bridge: The Barley Mow Pub on the north side of the green lies almost exactly halfway between these two bridges. The bridge is an important feature of the village green. There is parking nearby on the village green from where you can walk to the bridge. The bridge is easily viewed from the bypass downstream but there is no access upstream. Waverley Abbey is only a few miles west of this bridge (**https://www.english-heritage.org.uk/visit/places/waverley-abbey/**).

② Tilford East Bridge ★★

Bridge Name: Tilford East Bridge

Other Names: Tilford Northeast Bridge, Tilford Packhorse Bridge

Location: Village of Tilford, Tilford Street, on the Green. Use postcode GU10 2BU for your satnav.

Setting: Village / Rural

OS Ref: SU 87386 43449

Crosses: River Wey

Orientation: East / West

County: Surrey

Length: 34 metres (including the previously buried arch)

Bridge Type: Multiple Arch

Materials: Ironstone

Traffic: Road

Build Date: 13th century

Authority: Waverley (District Authority)

Designation: Grade I Listed and Scheduled Monument

Directions: From Farnham:

- From the A31 in Farnham, exit at the B3001 and turn left (southeast).
- Follow for only 200 metres and bear right (south) onto Tilford Road, signposted Tilford, just past Farnham Station.
- Follow for 3½ miles to Tilford Commons. You'll actually cross over the River Wey beside Tilford West Bridge.
- Find a place to park and walk to both bridges. Tilford West Bridge is located to the northwest of the commons and Tilford East Bridge is located to the northeast of the commons.

Driving Time: From Farnham – 25 minutes.

Tilford East Bridge – south face

The eastern arches of Tilford East Bridge

The newly uncovered easternmost arch

Tilford East Bridge – north face

Information: The Council has recently refurbished the superstructure of this bridge and most of the wooden railings are new. The fabric is local rubble ironstone with thin slabs forming the voussoirs of arches. There are no parapets, but 20th-century wooden posts and rails have been added. There are now seven visible arches since the Council dug out and cleared the seventh easternmost arch that had been buried in the bank.

The arches increase in height and width to the centre where the largest spans 3.9 metres. The arches vary in shape with four being slightly pointed segmental and two elliptical. On the village side the bridge is brick lined, and must date from a rebuild, perhaps in the 16th century. The original arches have single flush arch rings. The arch to the east side is elliptical and brick edged. There are ridged or diamond shaped cutwaters to the upstream side and rounded cutwaters over keeled starlings to the downstream side *(Pevsner, 1971)*.

A corbelling arrangement on the upstream face has added 0.6 metres to the width but there is still only single file traffic. There is a 1 metre pedestrian walkway on the north side.

At the Bridge: The Barley Mow Pub on the north side of the green lies almost exactly halfway between these two bridges. The bridge is an important feature of the village green. There is parking nearby to the south of the bridge. Waverley Abbey is only a few miles west of this bridge (**https://www.english-heritage.org.uk/visit/places/waverley-abbey/**).

3 Elstead Bridge ★★

Bridge Name: Elstead Bridge

Location: Farnham Road, Elstead on the B3001 over the River Wey, just to the west of the village of Elstead. Use postcode GU8 6DE in your satnav.

Setting: Village / Rural

OS Ref: SU 90539 43805

Crosses: River Wey

Orientation: West / East

County: Surrey

Length: 22.5 metres (not including the buried arches)

Bridge Type: Multiple Arch

Materials: Bargate Stone

Traffic: Road

Build Date: 13th century

Authority: Waverley (District Authority)

Designation: Grade I Listed, and Scheduled Monument

Directions: From the Tilford Bridges:

- Proceed across Tilford East Bridge. This is Tilford Street.
- Follow for 1½ miles to the T junction with the B3001, Waverley Lane.
- Turn right (east) and follow for 2 miles to the bridge just before Elstead.

Driving Time: From Tilford Bridges – 10 minutes.

Information: Elstead Bridge carries the west bound traffic on the B3001 across the River Wey. A new bridge has been built directly adjacent to the old one to carry the eastbound traffic and the bridge is done few favours by the close proximity of this modern relief road. Elstead Bridge is constructed of Bargate ironstone with sandstone rubble and includes seven semi-circular arches. The centre two arches have been rebuilt with large block voussoirs forming double arch rings. The remaining three visible arches have rubble-built arch rings. The two

Elstead Bridge – south face

Cutwaters and buttresses on the south face

Two rebuilt centre arches

easternmost arches are buried in the bank. The arches vary slightly in width up to 3.6 metres. The roadway is 3.8 metres wide with no pedestrian walkway on the medieval bridge side *(Robertson, 2020)*. The medieval bridge has been strengthened with three pairs of Victorian ties.

The cutwaters are pointed on the upstream (south) side and rounded on the downstream (north) side. An incongruous brick parapet was added in 1826 and extends westwards above a Bargate stone wall of unknown date and an arch across a subsidiary stream, which was rebuilt in concrete. Brick buttresses for this new parapet sit atop the rounded cutwaters on the north face.

At the Bridge: The Mill Pub restaurant is to the west end of the bridge on the south side of the road. Locals and visitors alike often use the stretch of river downstream of Elstead Bridge for swimming. The river is accessible from the public footpath joining the Farnham Road at the west end of the bridge nearly opposite the entrance to the Mill. There is a car park at the west end of the bridge in the Riverside Gardens.

Elstead Bridge – north face

4 Somerset Bridge ★★

Bridge Name: Somerset Bridge

Location: Just to the east of Elstead, off the B3001 heading north on Shackleford Road. Use postcode GU8 6FE for your satnav.

Setting: Rural / Countryside

OS Ref: SU 92177 43925

Crosses: River Wey

Orientation: Northeast / Southwest

County: Surrey

Length: 21.5 metres

Bridge Type: Multiple Arch

Materials: Sandstone and Brick

Traffic: Road

Opened: 1233

Authority: Waverley (District Authority)

Designation: Grade II* Listed and Scheduled Monument

Directions: From Elstead Bridge:

- Proceed eastwards into Elstead on the B3001, which becomes Milford Road.
- Follow through the village on this road for 1¼ miles to the large triangular intersection with Shackleford Road.
- Bear left (north) and follow for ¼ mile to the bridge. *(Note: the parapets of this bridge are modern and misleading.)*

Driving Time: From Elstead Bridge – 15 minutes.

Somerset Bridge – south face

Somerset Bridge – south face, looking west

Information: Somerset Bridge's substructure is built of sandstone rubble and has three original semi-circular arches. The central arch has single rubble slab slices forming the voussoirs. It is irregular in form but is best described as slightly pointed and 3.6 metres wide. The outer arches have been rebuilt in larger sandstone ashlar blocks, are a little smaller, and are, again, surrounded by rubble in the spandrels. The two cutwaters on each face have pyramidal tops and the starling under the central arch appears to have been reinforced and raised with concrete at some point in time. The carriageway is a bit more than 4 metres wide *(Pevsner, 1971)*.

This bridge has obviously been through a rebuild, perhaps several. In 1565, 300 years after it first opened, the Bridge Commissioners reported:

> *Somersford (Somerset) Bridge is decayed and downe, and the cawsye thereunto adjoining, which bridge is the Queenes bridge, and by her highnes to be mayneteyned, the stones of which bryda were caryed away by James Bromefelde and by him employed upon his own buyldinges and Peper harowe upon the form of Sir Richard Pexall Knight.*
>
> **(Drew, 2001)**

In 1826, an arch with red brick voussoirs and vault lining was added through the angled abutment on the southeast end, presumably to act as a

The central arch of Somerset Bridge – south face

flood arch of sorts, although today it carries a full stream flow. The parapet consists of a later red brick wall of about 1 metre high, which was possibly also added in 1826. It is incongruous to the look of the bridge and has evidence of being repaired many times. Three pairs of Victorian S-ties strengthen the bridge *(Robertson, 2020).*

The plaque half buried by the parapet

There is a plaque half-buried in the ground beside the modern brick parapet on the southern side of the river and downstream side of the bridge. It is greatly worn and damaged and resultantly difficult to decipher. I think it says:

THE WEST SIDE
AND THE WEIR IN THE RIVER
BUILT IN THE YEAR 1826

The word 'WEIR' and the '8' in the date are indistinct.

At the Bridge: Access is fairly good to riverbank level, but the overgrown state of the vegetation limits the views of the bridge. There is no formal parking at the bridge but wide verge spaces at each end may allow for a temporary pullover. There are no facilities or amenities at the bridge.

Somerset Bridge – central arch north face

Somerset Bridge – the cutwater on the north face

5 Eashing Bridges (Upper & Lower) ★★

Bridge Name: Eashing Bridges (Upper & Lower)

Other Names: Lower Eashing Bridge & Upper Eashing Bridge

Location: In Eashing south of Godalming. Use postcode GU7 2QW for your satnav.

Setting: Village / Rural

OS Ref: SU 94647 43825 and SU 94668 43811

Crosses: River Wey

Orientation: Northwest / Southeast

County: Surrey

Length: 31 metres (including both bridges and the connecting causeway)

Bridge Type: Multiple Arch

Materials: Bargate Sandstone

Traffic: Road

Build Date: 13th century

Authority: Guildford (District Authority)

Designation: Grade I Listed and Scheduled Monument

Directions: From Somerset Bridge:

- Reverse direction and go back to the B3001 Elstead Road.
- Turn left (east) and follow 1¼ miles to the intersection with the A3. Do not get on the A3.
- At the intersection's roundabout follow signs for the A283 over the A3 bridge to the next roundabout. Follow the A283 for only 200 metres to the first road to the left, Eashing Lane.
- Turn left (northeast) and follow ½ mile to the first road on the left, Hollow Lane.
- Turn left (west) and follow through the village to the bridge. Stoplight controlled.

Driving Time: From Somerset Bridge – 15 minutes.

The three arches of the eastern bridge – Lower Eashing Bridge

One of the rounded 'beehive' cutwaters on the northern face showing evidence of under-scouring

The southern face of the western bridge

Information: There are two bridges over the two branches of the River Wey at Eashing, separated by only 150 metres. There is a small eyot (island) in between and a short causeway connects them. They are referred to as 'Upper Eashing' (west) and 'Lower Eashing' (east). Because of their proximity to one another and similarity in construction, they are treated together here. Given the 'in-line' configuration of the two bridges, construction techniques of the central causeway, and the levels and widths of the road surfaces, it is likely that the two bridges were once a single bridge *(Renn, 1974)*.

The bridges are built of Bargate and local sandstone rubble and consist of two spans joined by a causeway. Each span originally consisted of five arches, as the cutwaters buried in the banks suggest, yet at present only three are visible under the eastern bridge, and four under the western one. The remaining arches survive but are buried in the banks. All the arches have thin voussoirs set in mortar, some form flush double arch rings, some single arch rings. The cutwaters are pointed on the upstream side and rounded on the downstream side *(Robertson, 2020)*.

The silted-up westernmost arch of the western bridge north face

Thin stone voussoirs

The bridge was repaired in 1766, when a low brick parapet was added. However, the height of the road surface was also raised at some later date bringing it level with the tops of the bricks. The medieval road is buried underneath the modern road surface. Twentieth-century timber rails have been fixed to the oak bearers running through the bridges and four pairs of Victorian ties strengthen the western arches *(Pevsner, 1971)*.

Easing Congregational Chapel in situ (image courtesy of Rural Life Museum at www.rural-life.org.uk)

In 1857, a group of Eashing residents became alienated from the local Congregational Church, so they built a prefabricated church known as Eashing Chapel on land belonging to the owner of the Eashing paper mill. Services were held in the little church until 1870 when Eashing Chapel became reunited with the Congregational Church. The Chapel was deconsecrated and later relocated to the other side of the river in approximately 1950 by 'rolling it across Eashing Bridge', or so the story goes, where it had a varied history with references being found to it being used as a library, a timber store and even a chicken coop. Today the chapel is on display at the Rural Life Living Museum outside Tilford (https://rural-life.org.uk/) *(Penn, 1974)*.

Local legend has it that the bridge is haunted by the monks who built it. Their ghostly apparitions are reported to have been seen on the bridge at night.

Eashing Chapel (image courtesy of Rural Life Museum at www.rural-life.org.uk)

At the Bridge: The Stag on the River pub is just south on the Lower Eashing Road. There is parking to the west end of the bridges. A footpath runs along the east bank of the river. Nettles abound!

6 Unstead Bridge ★★

Bridge Name:	Unstead Bridge
Location:	Off the A3100 on Tilthams Corners Road. The bridge is immediately at the intersection with Unstead Lane. Use postcode GU5 0BT for your satnav.
Setting:	Rural / Suburban
OS Ref:	SU 99311 45435
Crosses:	River Wey
Orientation:	West / East
County:	Surrey
Length:	26 metres
Bridge Type:	Multiple Arch
Materials:	Bargate Stone
Traffic:	Road
Build Date:	13th century
Authority:	Guildford (District Authority)
Designation:	Grade II* Listed
Directions:	From Eashing Bridge: • Reverse direction and make your way back to Eashing Lane. • Turn left (north) and follow as it curves around eastwards to the T junction with the A3100, Ockford Road. • Turn left (north) and follow 3 miles northward. At the roundabout bear left, northward, and follow this road, the A3100, signposted to Guildford, through Godalming. It is confusing but just stay on the A3100 towards Guildford. • After Godalming the road becomes Medrow Road. Follow for 1½ miles. • Turn right (east) onto Tilthams Corner Road and follow ¼ mile over two modern bridges to the T junction with Unstead Lane. The bridge is right there at the junction.
Driving Time:	From Eashing Bridge – 40 minutes.

Unstead Bridge – north face, looking east

The roadway, looking east

The south face, looking east

Unstead Bridge – south face

The triangular cutwater – south side

Information: This bridge carries a minor road across a cut-off oxbow of the River Wey, just north of Godalming. It has five rounded but tapering arches, with two smaller ones on either side of a higher central arch that has a span of 4.5 metres. The fabric is Bargate stone rubble, save for some brick patching. All the arches have rubble-built soffits without reinforcing ribs. The westernmost arch has been rebuilt with an uncharacteristic red brick arch ring and has mostly silted up in recent years. The bridge has triangular cutwaters tapering off below the road level on the south face, characteristic of the other Waverley bridges. The north face has no cutwaters *(Andrews, 1996)*.

The superstructure has recently been renewed without parapets and the width is 3.6 metres between metal balustrade railings.

At the Bridge: Parking is nearly impossible near the bridge and I resorted to pulling over some way down Unstead Lane and walking back. Now that Surrey Council has cleared the excess undergrowth, access is reasonable around the bridge and views of all aspects are available. There is a public footpath across the farmer's field just to the south. There are no facilities or amenities at the bridge.

19 TITCHFIELD & WEST SUSSEX TOUR

Using the M27 west of Southampton as a starting point, these four bridges are arranged west to east and include Stony Bridge, Trotton Bridge, Woolbeding Bridge, and Stopham Bridge.

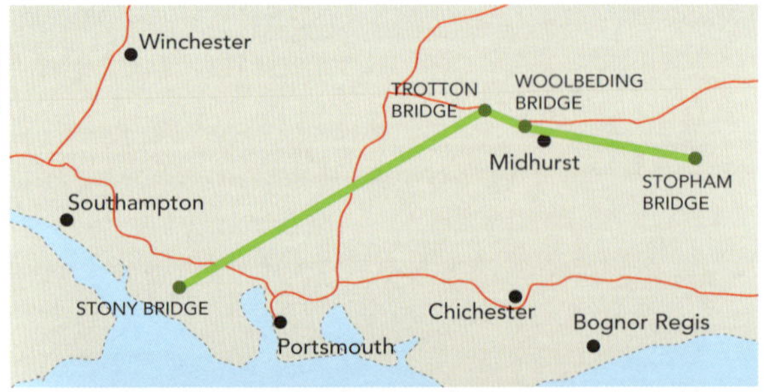

1 Stony Bridge, Titchfield ★

Bridge Name: Stony Bridge, Titchfield
Other Names: Anjou Bridge
Location: Southeast of Southampton in Titchfield just off Mill Lane. Use postcode PO15 5RA for your satnav.
Setting: Rural / Suburban
OS Ref: SU 54364 06605
Crosses: River Meon
Orientation: East / West
County: Hampshire
Length: 9.4 metres
Bridge Type: Multiple Arch
Materials: Stone
Traffic: Road
Build Date: 14th century
Authority: Fareham (District Authority)
Designation: Grade II Listed and Scheduled Monument
Directions: From the M27 junction 11:

- At junction 11 on the M27, at the big exit roundabout for junction 11, head south on the A27, signposted Gosport, Fareham, A27.
- Follow the A27 as it curves west for 4¼ miles to Mill Lane on the right (north) side. Keep following the signs for Titchfield Abbey. Proceed past the Titchfield gyratory. Do not get mixed up with the B3334 intersection there but stay on the A27 heading west. The Titchfield Mill is on the corner of Mill Lane.
- Turn right (north) and follow ¼ mile to the first road on the right, a minor road called Fishers Hill about 100 metres east of the entrance to Titchfield Abbey (worth a visit while you're there).
- Turn right at the Fisherman's Rest pub. The bridge is just there.

Driving Time: From the M27 junction 11 – 15 minutes.

Stony Bridge – south face with the river in spate

The modern brick flood arch in the eastern causeway

Information: This small bridge is also known as the Anjou Bridge, because it is associated in local tradition with the marriage of Henry VI and Margaret of Anjou in 1445 at Titchfield Abbey across the road. This stone structure replaced a bridge built by the monks during the 14th century, which was made of stone piers and a wooden parapet.

Stony Bridge is made of roughly coursed stone rubble and is formed by two slightly pointed arches, each with a width of 2.7 metres and deeply chamfered arch rings. The western arch is segmental in shape, while the eastern is slightly pointed. The arches are very low in relation to the normal river water level and, as a result, if the river is at all swollen the arches become overwhelmed and unviewable.

There is a modern brick flood arch in the eastern causeway with a diversion channel from the river directing overflow through it, probably as a result of the low level of the main river arches.

The parapets are slightly humped and above the cutwater, on the upstream (north) side, is a small refuge for pedestrians. The coping stones have iron cramps to hold them in place. There is no cutwater on the downstream (south) face. The road width between the parapets is about 3.5 metres and at the end of the parapets are stone buttresses.

Stony Bridge was rebuilt in stone during the 17th century under Henry, the 3rd Earl of Southampton, whose grandfather had acquired the Abbey *(Robertson, 2020)*.

At the Bridge: The bridge can be viewed from downstream, but parking nearby is a problem. The bridge is certainly within walking distance of the pub on the corner. There are no facilities or amenities at the bridge. While you're there, Titchfield Abbey is well worth a visit (**https://www.english-heritage.org.uk/visit/places/titchfield-abbey/**).

The northern parapet with refuge

Stony Bridge – the roadway looking west

The upstream diversion chanel

2 Trotton Bridge ★★★

Bridge Name: Trotton Bridge

Location: On the A272 just outside Trotton, to the east towards Petersfield, 120 metres southeast of St George's Church. Use postcode GU31 5EN for your satnav.

Setting: Rural / Countryside

OS Ref: SU 83656 22387

Crosses: River Rother

Orientation: Northwest / Southeast

County: West Sussex

Length: 47 metres

Bridge Type: Multiple Arch

Materials: Stone

Traffic: Road

Build Date: 1400

Authority: Chichester (District Authority)

Designation: Grade I Listed and Scheduled Monument

Directions: From Stony Bridge:

- Reverse directions and return to the A27 heading east. Follow the 4½ miles back to the M27 and join heading east.
- Follow the M27 east for 5½ miles. Do not get on the M275 but instead join the A3(M) heading north. Follow for 11 miles to the third Petersfield exit, the A272.
- From the A3 join the A272 Petersfield Road heading east (no exit number) signposted Petersfield, Midhurst. You will need to follow it east through the village of Sheet where it makes a right (southeast) turn.
- Follow for 4 miles to the bridge.

Driving Time: From Stony Bridge – 25 minutes.

Trotton Bridge from the eastern bank

Five chamfered arch ribs

The south face from the western bank

The western river arch south face

Information: Trotton Bridge carries the busy A272, which connects Midhurst and Petersfield, over the River Rother, about 3 miles to the west of Midhurst. It is the only one of the series of old bridges crossing the river that is still part of a major traffic route, and traffic lights now control one-way passage *(Salzman, 1953)*.

The bridge is built of evenly coursed rubble trending towards ashlar and has five rounded arches, which are close to semi-circular, the central three spanning 5 metres with the two outer arches at each end slightly smaller. The westernmost arch is mostly buried but still visible. Each arch rests on five chamfered ribs, and there are chamfered single arch rings.

The large triangular cutwaters are stepped, and it is suggested by Jervoise that they once extended upwards to form refuges, but that these were removed when the parapets were rebuilt in finer, coursed rubble in the late 20th century. The bridge has not been widened and the carriageway width of 4.5 metres is as built.

The bridge is confidently dated to the very early years of the 15th century, when it was built at the instigation of a Lord Thomas Camois (Camoys) who commanded the rear guard at the Battle of Agincourt in 1415 *(Robertson, 2020)*. A long causeway on the east side forms the abutment.

Trotton Bridge is one of a series of old bridges across the Rother and two are included in this book. Woolbeding Bridge is a few miles to the east.

At the Bridge: Unfortunately, the bridge is very obscured by overgrown foliage and access is poor at riverbank level, but there are a few overgrown pathways. There is no formal parking at the bridge. Just near the bridge, St George's Church grounds may offer some temporary parking. Views at river level are also difficult with overgrown vegetation obstructing any clear view. There are no facilities or amenities at the bridge.

Trotton Bridge – the western buried arch

3 Woolbeding Bridge ★★★

Bridge Name:	Woolbeding Bridge
Location:	Woolbeding Road is just to the northwest of Midhurst off the A272 Petersfield Road, 344 metres northwest of Manor Cottage. Use postcode GU29 9RJ for your satnav. Not far from Trotton Bridge to the west.
Setting:	Rural / Countryside
OS Ref:	SU 87276 22042
Crosses:	River Rother
Orientation:	Northwest to Southeast
County:	West Sussex
Length:	24 metres
Bridge Type:	Multiple Arch
Materials:	Stone
Traffic:	Road
Build Date:	15th century
Authority:	Chichester (District Authority)
Designation:	Grade II* Listed
Directions:	From Trotton Bridge: • Continue eastwards on the A272 towards Midhurst for 2½ miles. • Before reaching Midhurst turn left (north) onto Woolbeding Road. Follow for ¼ mile to the bridge.
Driving Time:	From Trotton Bridge – 10 minutes.

Information: Woolbeding Bridge carries Woolbeding Road over the River Rother, just to the northwest of Midhurst.

The bridge has four semi-circular arches, each segmental and resting on three heavy chamfered ribs. The northernmost arch is mostly buried in sand and allows for a close view of the vault and ribs. The arches have single chamfered arch rings. The masonry is coursed rubble, but the parapets were rebuilt in 1919 using smaller grade, more uniform stone, in places almost ashlar *(Robertson, 2020)*.

There are triangular cutwaters, which are capped at the base of the parapets that act additionally as buttresses between the arches. The bridge is 24 metres long with three quite broad piers and the arches

Woolbeding Bridge – west face

span 4.1 metres. The roadway is 3.2 metres wide between the parapets. The wing walls on the north end are splayed outward. On the south side the abutment turns into a short causeway, which is about 2 metres wider than the bridge.

The bridge was restored in 1919 and the parapets renewed. Further repair work and restoration was carried out in the late 20th century. Despite this repair work and alteration (or perhaps because of it), Woolbeding Bridge survives in a good state of preservation.

The build date of Woolbeding Bridge is normally assigned to the 15th century, along with the others on the river, a date corroborated by the ribs and arch rings. The bridge has distorted a little *(Muckley, 2004)*.

Woolbeding Bridge – west parapet and cutwaters

Three chamfered arch ribs

The east parapet and cutwaters

An old postcard of Woolbeding Bridge

An archaeological excavation and survey were carried out in 1994. This revealed the phased construction of the bridge and the layers of road surfacing across it. The first road surface was of compacted flint, sand, and gravel, which was partly replaced around 1625 by a cobbled surface. The third road surface, dating to about 1828, included wheel ruts indicative of a long, or heavy, period of use. Fragments of medieval pottery and roof tile were also found.

Woolbeding Bridge is one of a series of old bridges across the Rother and two are included in this book. Trotton Bridge is a few miles to the west.

At the Bridge: Access upstream is reasonable with a public footpath running across a sheep grazing field, allowing views of the west face. Another public footpath runs along the south bank of the river to the east. There is no parking or even stopping place nearby. The National Trust's Woolbeding Gardens is 400 metres further along this road (**https://www.nationaltrust.org.uk/ woolbeding-gardens**).

4 Stopham Bridge ★★★★

Bridge Name: Stopham Bridge

Location: Stopham on the A283 two miles west of Pulborough in the South Downs National Park. Use postcode RH20 1DS for your satnav.

Setting: Rural / Countryside

OS Ref: TQ 02983 18379

Crosses: River Arun

Orientation: Southeast / Northwest

County: West Sussex

Length: 75 metres

Bridge Type: Arch

Materials: Ironstone

Traffic: Pedestrian

Build Date: 1422

Authority: West Sussex Council

Designation: Grade I Listed and Scheduled Monument

Directions: From Woolbeding Bridge:

- Return to the A272 Peterfield Road.
- Turn left (east) and follow into Midhurst. In the centre of town, at the roundabout, turn left (north), still the A272, and follow through Eastbourne where the road curves right (east), still the A272. Stay on it.
- Follow for 4¼ miles to Petworth. At the roundabout in the centre of town turn right (south) onto Station Road and follow for ½ mile to the intersection with Haslingbourne Road on the left, signposted Pulborough (A283).
- Turn left (east) onto the A283 and follow for 3¼ miles. The A283 makes a large S curve in the village of Fittleworth but stay on it.
- Follow east across the new bridge over the Arun and then immediately turn right into The White Hart pub, the entrance road to which is on the right. The bridge is accessible from their parking area.

Driving Time: From Woolbeding Bridge – 30 minutes.

Stopham Bridge– north face from the riverbank

The roadway and White Hart Pub

Stopham Bridge – south face

The tall central arch

Information: Stopham Bridge is on the site of an ancient ford across the River Arun, just east of where the River Rother finally joins with the Arun. The bridge once carried the A283 east towards Pulborough until it was bypassed in 1986. The original bridge was constructed of wood in 1309, as a replacement for the Eastover Ferry, which was owned by John Stopham. The earliest stone bridge, possibly with a wooden drawbridge, was constructed in 1422. The bridge has had a chequered history over the centuries, periodically being allowed to fall into ruin and decay followed by repair and reconstruction.

The bridge has 14 arches. The original seven central arches are 3.6 metre spans, with the central arch spanning 4 metres. This central arch was heightened by 1.5 metres in 1822, unbalancing the look of the bridge but allowing for taller river traffic, such as barges headed for the Wey Arun Junction Canal, which had opened in 1816. Six other original arches, three on each end, are semi-circular and make a total of 13 arches. One span was demolished in the Civil War and replaced by a drawbridge, which was subsequently rebuilt as seen in 1822. During a major rebuild in 1865 an eighth flood arch was added to the curved west side making a total of the 14 arches of today's structure.

The bridge is built of local ironstone, though the 1822 modifications to the central arch included brick. There are signs of ashlar courses added above the arches near the centre to give a smooth rise on each side of the new central highpoint of the carriageway. The parapets are of a slightly darker local stone.

Stopham Bridge – south face

South Downs National Park

Beachy Head in the South Downs National Park (© Ian Stannard/WikiCommons)

The South Downs National Park is the newest of the UK's national parks, only being fully covered by the law in 2011. It is the most popular UK National Park, receiving approximately 39 million visitors per year. It spans the countryside between Winchester in the west all the way across the counties of Hampshire, West Sussex, and East Sussex, terminating where it meets the English Channel in the form of the spectacular white cliffs including Beachy Head and the Seven Sisters near Eastbourne. Longitudinally it reaches from Guildford in the north to Chichester in the south and the landscape of all of it is what many would call typically English with gently rolling hills. The name 'Downs' is derived from the Old English word 'dun' meaning 'hill'.

The chalk downlands and woods have inspired artists such as Joseph Mallord William Turner, and the sparkling clean River Itchen was the inspiration for Charles Kingsley's *The Water Babies*. The South Downs have been home to many literary giants including Jane Austen, Mary Shelley, William Penn, John Galsworthy, Hillaire Belloc, Edward Thomas, and Virginia Woolf. Easily accessible from London, the Downs have horse riding and mountain biking, with miles of footpaths and bridleways including the 99 mile South Downs Way.

The South Downs National Park is a haven for any nature-lover with its rolling green and gold hills and busy market towns. It offers a range of views with its white cliffs at Seven Sisters, farmland, and flourishing vineyards. The park's landscapes are home to magnificent wildlife, which offers peacefulness amid its bustling tourist attractions. Guests are led to interact with people and the place, coming together to explore the hidden villages and historic estates within the areas of ancient woodland and lowland heaths. Several traditional country pubs entertain guests who may spend the day walking, cycling and horse riding along the chalk grasslands *(Culture Trip, 2020)*.

Through trails like the South Downs Way, visitors will encounter wildflowers, butterflies, and other intriguing plants and animals. The park is home to a large number of sheep, totalling somewhere between 110,000 and 125,000 at any one time. The South Downs land gives residents and visitors food, wildlife, clean water, and access to the countryside. This landscape, which has been shaped by human use and natural causes, has unmatched biodiversity *(Culture Trip, 2020)*.

Please take a look at **https://visitsouthdowns.com/**.

Stopham Bridge – the south face cutwaters and refuges

There are blunt cutwaters between the arches. Six of these are continued above the water level on the south side as half hexagonal buttresses and form recesses for pedestrian refuges of this shape on the bridge. On the north side the cutwaters are continued the whole height of the bridge and form triangular refuges on the bridge. There are a total of 17 pedestrian refuges, including four in the western approach.

The total length of the bridge is 75 metres including extensions at both ends carried out during the 1865 rebuild. The approaches on both ends are angled and during the 1865 rebuild the western end was re-aligned to give a better approach to Stopham House nearby. The roadway is 3.6 metres in width.

The bridge was badly damaged by army lorries during the Second World War but was repaired in 1991, a fact that is commemorated by a plaque on the river side. In 1986, Stopham Bridge was bypassed and replaced by the new reinforced concrete bridge, located 30 metres north of the old bridge.

At the Bridge: The picturesque White Hart Public House is situated at the southeast end of the old bridge. Access is quite easy, and parking is available in the pub car park. Access to the old bridge and the White Hart is via the old road (now a dead-end side street) on the south side off the busy Stopham Road A283. Broader views are afforded from the bypass bridge.

The roadway, looking west

20 NORTH WILTSHIRE & IFORD TOUR

Using Bradford-on-Avon as a central starting point this tour heads slightly south and then turns north ending up above Swindon. Bridges included are Bradford-on-Avon Town Bridge, Barton Bridge, Iford Bridge in Somerset, Lacock Bridge, and Gumstool Bridge.

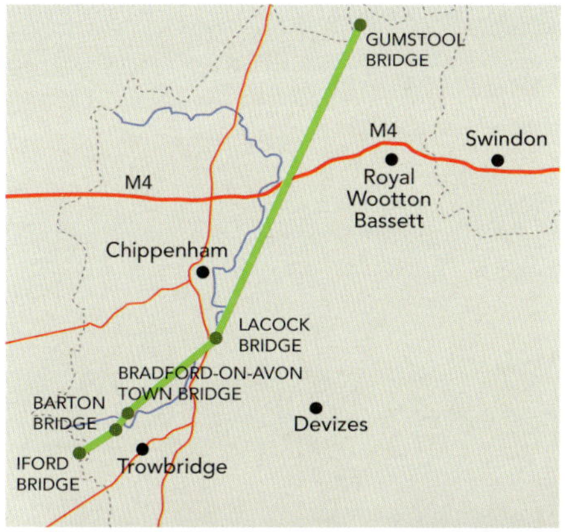

1 Bradford-on-Avon Town Bridge ★★★★★

Bridge Name:	Bradford-on-Avon Town Bridge
Other Names:	Chantry Bridge
Location:	Bradford-on-Avon town centre, Silver Street, on the A363 over the River Avon. Use postcode BA15 1BY for your satnav.
Setting:	Town / Urban
Orientation:	Northeast / Southwest
OS Ref:	ST 82613 60901
Crosses:	River Tone
County:	Wiltshire
Length:	54 metres
Bridge Type:	Multiple Arch
Materials:	Stone
Traffic:	Road
Build Date:	13th to 15th centuries
Authority:	Wiltshire (Unitary Authority)
Designation:	Grade I Listed and Scheduled Monument
Directions:	To Bradford-on-Avon Town Bridge: • This bridge is located directly in the centre of town on the A363.
Driving Time:	Use this bridge as your starting point.

Information: Bradford-on-Avon Town Bridge carries the A363 over the River Avon. It remains busy as it is the town's only road bridge over the Avon, a task it has been performing well for more than 700 years. It is the icon of the town and has been chosen to figure in the logo of many local organisations, including the nearby Bradford-on-Avon Museum.

The first bridge here, to replace the broad ford that gives the town its name ('Broad-Ford'), was made of wood and was mentioned in a deed of 1200. By

The bridge plaque at the south end

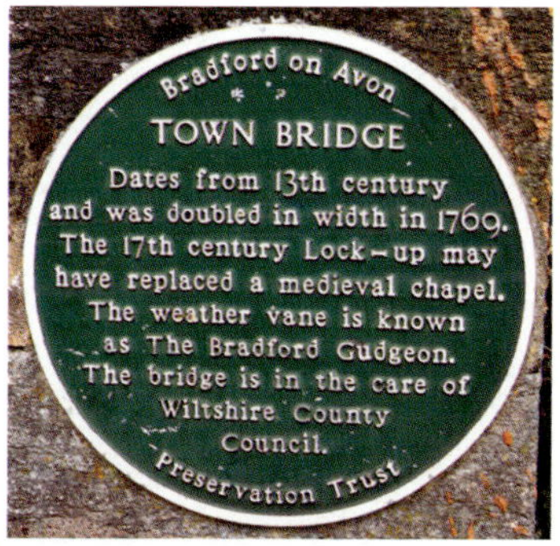

Bradford-on-Avon Town Bridge – east face

The Town Bridge at the begining of the 19th century

The Bradford Gudgeon

Bradford-on-Avon Town Bridge – east face

the time of King Edward II (r. 1307–27), the bridge is recorded as a structure of stone. It suffered serious damage from floods in 1340 and King Edward III decreed in 1350 that the 'bailiffs and good townsmen of Bradeford' could take tolls on goods passing over it for five years to pay for repairs *(Bradford-on-Avon Museum, 1999)*. Fifty years later, in 1400, Pope Boniface IX appealed for funds for further repairs. In 1562 there was complaint that there was no parapet. At that time, the bridge was only 3.3 metres, and it had to wait for more than 200 years, until 1769, to be widened to its present size (with new parapets one assumes); the junction between the old and new can be seen underneath *(Jervoise, 1930)*.

The bridge is largely constructed of stone rubble with dressed voussoirs and cutwaters; the parapets are a relatively late addition. There are nine arches

Bradford-on-Avon Town Bridge – west face from the Bullpit

The chantry chapel (gaol)

ranging in span between 4.2 and 5.4 metres. The small silted up one at the northeast end spans just 2.3 metres, giving a total bridge length of 54 metres. Viewed from the east (upstream), the two southernmost arches are classic medieval Gothic pointed in shape and supported by four narrow vault ribs. These medieval arches are thought to date from around 1300. The remainder are semi-circular with double arch rings in two orders *(Robertson, 2020).*

The downstream (western aspect) is totally different, with all the arches semi-circular with a single flush arch ring surmounted by a prominent keystone; there are no cutwaters on this face. The bridge was widened on the western side in the 17th century (or possibly 1769) to 7.7 metres including footways, and Jervoise suggests that the other arches to be seen from upstream were rebuilt during this 18th century widening. The bridge originally may have been only 4 metres wide *(Jervoise, 1930).*

A watercolour painting by W.H. Allen of a covered wagon crossing the bridge (© Hampshire County Council. Provided by Hampshire Cultural Trust)

The piers have cutwaters on their upstream side only, some stepped and capped at different heights.

The second pier from the southwest end is wider and more substantial than the others and its cutwater is corbelled out to support a small square stone building with a domed roof. This is the original bridge chapel and was almost certainly built together with the 13th-century bridge. The chapel is square in shape with a domed roof topped with a fish-shaped weathervane, which is known as the Bradford Gudgeon, although it does not really resemble a real gudgeon (a small fish). After the dissolution, the building was used as a prison and goods store rather than for worship. An occupant of the cells was said to be 'below the fish and above the water' *(Cook, 1947),* referring to the weathervane. The chapel has four small square window openings with iron bars, two overlooking the river and one on each side.

A narrow arch doorway gives access from the bridge. There is a short chimney stack on the river side of the roof. The timber plank door has iron fittings and bracing around the door. It opens into a lobby with iron drains at both ends. Beyond the lobby are two cells formed by a stone partition wall. The interior has a stone-vaulted roof in line with the dome. There is ironwork bracing to the walls and around the window openings. Further iron fittings

A lock-up bed in the gaol

include a bed, a latrine, and a further door. Another cell bed appears to be of steel. John Wesley, Methodist preacher, apparently spent a night in this lock-up *(Cook, 1947)*.

On 2 July 1643 the town was the site of a skirmish in the English Civil War, when Royalists seized control of the bridge on their way to the Battle of Lansdowne *(Page, 2017)*.

At the Bridge: The Bradford-on-Avon Museum is at the south end of the bridge and there is parking there as well as in several locations to the north of the bridge. It is possible to view most features of the bridge from the War Memorial Park and various paths and alleys in the town.

Bradford-on-Avon Town Bridge postcard (used with permission of Bradford-on-Avon Museum)

2 Barton Bridge ★★★

Bridge Name:	Barton Bridge
Other Names:	Bradford Barton Bridge, Barton Footbridge
Location:	Bradford-on-Avon, within Barton Farm Country Park, south of the town centre. Less than a mile downstream of the famous town bridge. Use postcode BA15 1LF for your satnav.
Setting:	Town / Urban
OS Ref:	ST 82288 60532
Crosses:	River Bristol Avon
Orientation:	Northwest / Southeast
County:	Wiltshire
Length:	20 metres (not including the modern footbridge to the mainland)
Bridge Type:	Multiple Arch
Materials:	Stone
Traffic:	Pedestrian
Build Date:	1340
Authority:	Wiltshire (Unitary Authority)
Designation:	Grade II* Listed
Directions:	From Bradford-on-Avon Town Bridge: • Proceed south on St Margaret's Street to the big roundabout. • Follow the A36, Frome Street, straight across, signposted Frome B3109 and follow south for ¼ mile. • Turn right (west) onto Pound Lane, off the B3109, and follow to the end and the Tithe Barn Workshops. • The bridge crosses the River Avon there.
Driving Time:	From Bradford-on-Avon Town Bridge – 5 minutes.

Information: Barton Bridge is a medieval stone footbridge built around 1340, some 550 metres downstream from Bradford-on-Avon's better-known, and larger, Town Bridge.

Barton Bridge – west face

The more modern footbridge over to the island

Barton Bridge – east face

A by-pass channel around the bridge was created, probably in the early part of the 19th century, to relieve pressure on the main bridge from flood water. This created an island, and the bridge was reached by a ford, with a narrow causeway and modern footbridge at its side.

The bridge now forms part of the Barton Farm Country Park that features historic Tithe Barns. It carries just a footpath from the northwest as it spans the River Avon to the small island, on which there is a Second World War reinforced concrete and brick shell-proof type 24 pillbox. The bridge continues to the southeast end where it traverses the island with 25 metres of stone walling to its upstream side. The attached narrower mid-19th-century footbridge over the side stream is a reinforced clapper bridge formed of two large stone slabs supported on a rectangular stone pier, which has been chamfered on its upstream side.

The fabric of the main bridge is coursed, squared rubble, and the bridge encompasses four pointed arches, uniformly sized with widths of just less than 3 metres, and each with double un-chamfered arch rings in two orders. The vaultings are smooth, without ribs. To either side of the northwest end of the bridge are stone buttresses *(Robertson, 2020).*

Barton Bridge – Tithe Barns

The pillbox on the island

Documentary records suggest that the cutwaters on the upstream side of the bridge are later, yet still medieval, additions that have pyramidal copings. The downstream side is plain without cutwaters. Tall kerb stones (partly buried under a later resurfacing of a formerly cobbled road surface) mark the edge of the roadway. The width is 3.5 metres between the iron railings that have replaced any original stone parapets. The railings were installed during restoration work in 1867–71.

The bridge underwent a scheme of repair in the late 19th century and a significant proportion of the facing stones are from this period, and later. The bridge was restored again in the 1960s and in 2003.

Bradford-on-Avon Rowing Club is located on the northwest end of the bridge. The bridge forms part of a group of remarkable medieval buildings,

Barton Bridge, with the town beyond, in a lithograph by Elizabeth Tackle in the 1850s (used with permission of Bradford-on-Avon Museum)

The west face

including the town's significant 14th-century tithe barn, all contained within Barton Farm Country Park (**https://bradfordonavon.uk.com/barton-farm-country-park/**), which is freely accessible to the public *(McFetrich, 2019)*.

At the Bridge: There is paid parking and a small playground. There are facilities and amenities in the park.

3 Iford Bridge ★★★

Bridge Name:	Iford Bridge
Other Names:	Britannia Bridge
Location:	In the far northeast corner of Somerset between Bath and Trowbridge off the A36. Use postcode BA15 2BA for your satnav.
Setting:	Rural / Countryside
OS Ref:	ST 80021 58898
Crosses:	River Frome
Orientation:	Northeast / Southwest
County:	Somerset
Length:	12 metres
Bridge Type:	Multiple Arch
Materials:	Stone
Traffic:	Road
Build Date:	1245
Authority:	Bath and Northeast Somerset (Unitary Authority)
Designation:	Grade II* Listed and Scheduled Monument
Directions:	From Barton Bridge: • Return to the B3109. • Turn right (south) and follow 1¼ miles to Westwood Road, signposted Iford Manor. • Turn right (west) and follow through Westwood then continue for 1 mile to a small road to the left signposted Iford Manor. • Turn left on this very narrow road, Iford Lane, and follow to the bridge.
Driving Time:	From Barton Bridge – 30 minutes.

Information: Although on a public road, Iford Bridge sits at the entrance to Iford Manor and Gardens. The bridge carries the narrow lane from the A36 across the River Frome, a tributary of the River Avon, and links the villages of Westwood and Hinton Charterhouse.

Iford Bridge and Manor

Iford Bridge – east face

Harold Ainsworth Peto (1854–1933)

Harold Ainsworth Peto was a key link in the history of garden and landscape design, although he is less well known than one of his students, Sir Edwin Lutyens.

In 1854, Harold Ainsworth Peto was born the 5th son of Sir Samuel Morton Peto, a famous Victorian railway engineering contractor, at his home at Somerlayton Hall in Suffolk.

At the age of 17, Peto was apprenticed to the Lucus Brothers builders where he worked in the joinery workshop gaining valuable practical experience. In 1876 at the age of 22 Peto left his apprenticeship and entered a partnership with Ernest George, an established architect and artist. By 1880, the golden age of the Edwardian era was in full flow, and the Peto-George practice grew in popularity amongst the elite and affluent of London. Also, during this time, international interest began in Italian Renaissance Garden layouts and Peto enthusiastically studied the Italianate Garden ideal and developed a fascination for architectural embellishments to garden layout.

In 1886, a young 18-year-old trainee joined the Peto-George partnership named Edwin Lutyens (1869–1944). By this time Peto, age 32, was now an accomplished and knowledgeable architect and became, over the next six years, very influential in the career interests and development of the young Lutyens.

With financial stability, Peto, at age 38, terminated his partnership with Ernest George in 1892 and, due to respiratory illness, left England for a superior climate, establishing a practice in the South of France on the Mediterranean. Simultaneously, a contemporary form of garden design evolved, promoted by Gertrude Jekyll: country house architecture, using local materials, complemented by wildflowers in an Italianate style composition.

Harold Ainsworth Peto (1854–1933) (used with permission, Slocombe, 2019, https://landarchconcepts.wordpress.com/history-of-harold-peto/)

In 1899, Peto purchased Iford Manor in Wiltshire and returned to England and worked continually on the Italianate Garden there until his death.

By the end of the First World War, Peto had influenced both Edwin Lutyens and Gertrude Jekyll, who gratifyingly acknowledged him in her publication *Garden Ornament*.

Harold Ainsworth Peto wrote one book during his life, *The Boke of Iford.*

Peto died, age 79, at Iford Manor in 1933, his distinguished garden design career having spanned 27 years *(Slocombe, 2019).*

Peto's works include:

- Wayford Manor, Somerset
- Easton Lodge for Lady Warwick, Essex
- Hartham Park, Wiltshire
- Villa Maryland, Côte d'Azur, France
- Villa Sylvia, Côte d'Azur, France
- Buscot Park, Oxfordshire
- Heal House, for the Hon. Louis Greville, Wiltshire
- Crichel House, Dorset
- Hinton Admiral, Hampshire
- High Wall, Oxford
- Petwood, Lincolnshire
- Bridge House, Surrey
- Garinish Island, Ireland
- Burton Pynsent, Somerset
- West Dean Gardens, Sussex
- Ilnacullin Island Garden, South of France
- Witanhurst, Highgate in London (was called Parkfield)

Iford is a hamlet that straddles both the River Frome and the Wiltshire/Somerset border. The Manor House is on the Westwood, Wiltshire, side, but the mill is in Hinton Charterhouse, Somerset. The name was first noted in the grant of Westwood in 987 (copied in the 12th century) as *Igford*, meaning a ford with an island.

The Manor House was built in the late 15th or early 16th century, but most of what is visible today is from a rebuilding as an early Georgian house around 1725–30. Inside there is a 16th-century fireplace and 17th-century panelling.

The internationally renowned, Grade I listed, Italianate gardens of Iford Manor were designed by Harold Ainsworth Peto, who made Iford Manor his home from 1899 until his death in 1933. The gardens are characterised by terraces, pools, statuary (even on the bridge), cloisters, and remarkable rural views *(Mawrey, 2018).*

The bridge itself encompasses two deep segmental arches separated by a large central pier that supports triangular cutwaters on both faces. The cutwater on the downstream face is capped below the top of the parapet. The one upstream rises to the roadway and originally formed a pedestrian refuge but now provides a base for a statue of Britannia that was added by Peto in 1910. There are double arch rings of which the lower are slightly recessed. The width of the roadway is slightly less than 4 metres, and it does not appear to have been widened. The north wing walls extend at

Iford Bridge – west face showing the vault soffits

right angles to form revetments to the riverbank and include a small 'squinch' on the northeast corner to support the curve of the roadway.

The fabric is loosely coursed rubble, which varies in regularity. There is some damage to the northern arch on the downstream face. The Historic England listing dates the bridge to around 1400 but describes it as much restored but not enough to detract from its attractiveness.

Iford appears in the antique 'strip maps' of Britannia by John Ogilby, published in 1675. The work has the distinction of being the first ever road atlas of England and Wales. The 100 maps contained within were also the first to work by the principle of one inch to the mile and to use the statute mile of 1,760 yards. Each road map depicts a route in the form of six or seven vertical strips with a compass rose showing orientation; additionally, miles, furlongs, towns, churches, windmills, rivers, hills, and even gallows are depicted. Please see page 87 for more information on John Ogilby.

At the Bridge: Access is good around the bridge, though on a nice day there will probably be many people around. Parking is available in designated areas for the Manor House. More information is available at **https://www.ifordmanor.co.uk/**.

Iford Bridge chamfered parapet coping

Iford Bridge – east face showing the squinch (© David Iliff and licensed for reuse under Creative Commons License)

Statue of Britannia

4 Lacock Bridge ★★

Bridge Name: Lacock Bridge

Other Names: The bridge was formerly known simply as 'Foot Bridge' as it lay near the foot of the hill rising to the west.

Location: In the village of Lacock south of Chippenham, off the A350 on a minor road called The Wharf, connecting the hamlets of Lacock and Bowden across the River Avon within sight of Lacock Abbey. Use postcode SN15 2PQ for your satnav.

Setting: Rural / Countryside

OS Ref: ST 92214 68100 and ST 92325 68089

Crosses: River Bristol Avon

Orientation: East / West

County: Wiltshire

Length: 150 metres (overall including both bridges and all causeways)

Bridge Type: Multiple Arch

Materials: Stone

Traffic: Road

Build Date: 15th century

Authority: Wiltshire (Unitary Authority)

Designation: Grade II* Listed

Directions: From Iford Bridge:

- Reverse directions back through Westwood and return to the B3109.
- Turn left (north) and follow back into Bradford-on-Avon and cross the town bridge. Once across you'll be forced to follow the one-way system to the left, up Market Street. Follow it around through town forming an almost complete circle through town as it curves eastwards. It eventually joins the B3107 at a new roundabout.
- Turn left, signposted Melksham and follow the B3107 for 5¾ miles as it passes through Holt and eventually comes into Melksham.
- At the first roundabout in Melksham bear left (north), signposted Lacock. The road becomes the A350. Follow it towards Lacock.
- Just before Lacock the road splits. Turn right onto Melksham Road, signposted Lacock Village and Abbey.
- Follow for ½ mile to the first roundabout. Bear right onto Hither Way and follow it as it curves to the right and becomes Bowden Hill Road.
- Follow for 500 metres to the bridge.

Driving Time: From Iford Bridge – 35 minutes.

Western Lacock Bridge – north face

Roadway drains in the parapets from the field side

Small 'bumper' kerb stones protecting the leaning causeway parapets

Information: The ancient bridges at Lacock have carried road traffic across the River Avon and its broad water meadows since at least the 14th century. These are two stone bridges, connected by a long causeway. Surviving records of the 17th century indicate that the bridge was too dilapidated to be passable to wheeled traffic, and therefore some percentage of the present fabric is of a later restoration.

The westernmost bridge nearest to Lacock and the Abbey, crosses the river Avon itself and has four pointed segmental arches spanning 4.5 metres each with double arch rings offset from one another, separated by three piers with small cutwaters on the upstream face. The two arches to the west are slightly forward of the left pair. The bridge has stone parapets. To the west end of the structure 19 metres of stone rubble walling form the approaches. To the east end of this bridge 68 metres of similar walling, pierced with square holes for floodwater, form a link across the flood plain to the second bridge over a minor tributary.

The bridge to the east spans a small tributary but in flood season experiences a tremendous amount of high water from the vast flood plain as evidenced by visible water marks in and above the arches. The bridge has five arches built of local stone ashlar. The eastern pair of arches are early 19th century with rounded flush single arch rings and brick lined vaults. This bridge has ashlar parapets with iron cramp linking bands. The parapet carries a date

Eastern Lacock Bridge – south face

Western Lacock Bridge – south face

stone and inscription reading 'G. Banks 1809'. The other three arches are pointed and rebated with upstream (north) cutwaters, and downstream stepped pilasters on the piers and parapets. To the east side of this bridge runs a further 24 metres of rubble stone wall. Both bridges are 4.2 metres wide between the parapets. The roadway has small kerb stone supports for the parapets protecting them, somewhat, from traffic.

In 2003, major repair work on both bridges was carried out with funding from Wiltshire County Council and their condition is now very good, except for the north face of the eastern bridge.

At the Bridge: Access to view the northern faces (upstream) of both bridges is easily gained, but the southern aspect is harder to view, especially of the western bridge. There is no formal parking at the bridge. The nearest pullover place in on the east end of the causeway. Facilities and amenities are available in Lacock. *(Note: While you're there, Lacock Abbey is definitely worth a visit.)* (**https://www.national trust.org.uk/lacock-abbey-fox-talbot-museum-and-village**).

Western Lacock Bridge – the cutwaters – north face

5 Gumstool Bridge ★

Bridge Name:	Gumstool Bridge
Location:	In the village of Ashton Keynes to the northwest of Swindon. Use postcode SN6 6PB for your satnav.
Setting:	Village / Rural
OS Ref:	SU 04507 94206
Crosses:	River Thames
Orientation:	North / South
County:	Wiltshire
Length:	4 metres
Bridge Type:	Multiple Arch
Materials:	Limestone
Traffic:	Road
Build Date:	15th century
Authority:	Wiltshire (Unitary Authority)
Designation:	Grade II Listed

Gumstool Bridge – south side

Directions: From Lacock Bridge:

- Return to Lacock village and get back on the A350 heading north.
- Turn right (north) and follow the A350 for 9½ miles around Chippenham and further north under the M4 motorway. Above the M4 the road becomes the A429, signposted Cirencester. Do not get on the M4.
- Follow the A429 for 3½ miles past Malmesbury to the roundabout north of town. Turn right (east) onto Charlton Road, the B4040, signposted Cricklade, Charlton. Follow for 7¾ miles through Charlton, and Minety to the intersection with the B4696.
- Turn left (north), signposted Ashton Keynes, and follow to the village.
- Turn into the village off the B4696 at Gosditch Street.
- At the junction with the High Road in the village, turn north and follow to Church Walk and the bridge is right there at a small triangular intersection with a cross (missing its top).

Driving Time: From Lacock Bridge – 60 minutes.

Gumstool Bridge – south side

Gumstool Bridge – splayed out parapet walls

Information: Gumstool Bridge crosses the River Thames at a point where it is still a small shallow stream in the village of Ashton Keynes, to the northwest of Swindon. The river runs next to the High Road all the way through the village and every house on the west side can boast that they have a bridge crossing the Thames. The name is purportedly derived from a ducking stool for punishing malefactors, although the shallowness of the river would make it difficult today.

This small and low bridge has two low segmental arches of near-equal size, above which there are parapets only 80 centimetres high. The parapets have steep triangular copings and are splayed outwards at both ends. The fabric is ashlar limestone, which probably accounts for the modern appearance. The voussoirs are very large for the size of the arch. Gumstool Bridge is approximately 5 metres wide, unsurprising given that in 1812 it was taken apart and rebuilt in wider form by inserting extra stonework between the existing faces so as to widen the roadway.

The cross next to the bridge (now missing its cruciform upper part) was taken down and rebuilt a few paces from its original site and sits on a substantial plinth. The cross is thought to date to the 1320s and there is a similar cross in the village centre.

At the Bridge: There are two interesting little bridges, similar in style, which cross the nascent River Thames, just upstream of Gumstool Bridge on the High Road. Access is excellent all around the bridge. The White Hart Inn is at the village centre.

21 SOUTH WILTSHIRE & FORDINGBRIDGE TOUR

These bridges are arranged from north to south and include Salisbury Milford Bridge, Salisbury Crane Bridge, Harnham Bridge, Coombe Bissett Packhorse Bridge, which form a cluster around Salisbury. Fordingbridge is in Hampshire to the south but is included here because of its access from Salisbury.

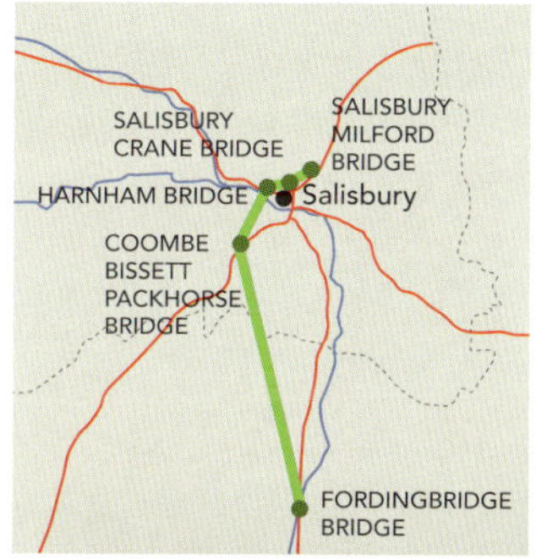

1 Salisbury Milford Bridge ★★

Bridge Name: Salisbury Milford Bridge

Other Names: Milford Mill Bridge

Location: Millford Mill Road near Laverstock, to the east of Salisbury. Use Postcode SP1 1NL for your satnav.

Setting: Rural / Countryside

OS Ref: SU 15760 29764

Crosses: River Bourne

Orientation: Northwest / Southeast

County: Wiltshire

Length: 21 metres (including the connecting causeway)

Bridge Type: Multiple Arch

Materials: Stone

Traffic: Road

Build Date: 15th century

Authority: Wiltshire (Unitary Authority)

Designation: Grade I Listed

Directions: From Salisbury:

- Take the A36 eastwards for ½ mile to the intersection of Petersfinger Road on the left.
- Turn left (north) and follow as it curves sharply left (northwest) and becomes Milford Mill Road.
- Follow for only 100 metres to Queen Manor Road. The bridge is to the left.

Driving Time: From the A36 in Salisbury – 10 minutes.

Salisbury Milford Bridge – southwest corner, looking east

The western pointed arch, south face

Information: Milford Bridge carries Milford Mill Road over the River Bourne, a tributary of the Hampshire Avon, and connects with what is now a suburb of Laverstock. It is one of three medieval stone bridges in Salisbury including the Harnham, and Crane bridges. The bridge and the ford that preceded it are on the 13th-century medieval route from Winchester to the then 'new' city of Salisbury. It is likely too that the Roman road from the small town of

Salisbury Milford Bridge – south face, looking east

Salisbury Milford Bridge – south face, looking west

Sorviodunum (Old Salisbury) to the New Forest also crossed the river at this point.

The bridge has two pairs of archways crossing the river and the former mill stream, linked by a short causeway across a sedimentary island. The westernmost arch is rounded and segmental and is different from the others. All three remaining arches are pointed and all have a width of 2.7 metres each. The two to the west have double arch rings in two orders, but those to the east seem to have single flush arch rings. There are no arch ribs.

The cutwaters that separate the arches are capped immediately below the parapets at each face. The north face has a modern utility conduit across its entire length,

Jervoise refers to the bridge as having been widened to 4.8 metres, but the Historic England listing suggests that it remains as built. There is a prominent string course at road level, and the parapet above has chamfered coping and square piers at either end creating a pleasing look. The fabric is coursed limestone rubble, and the Historic England listing dates the bridge to around 1500, though the Victoria history hints at origins more than a century earlier *(Jervoise, 1930)*.

The well-known artist John Constable (1776–1837) painted many works in the Salisbury area, including a watercolour of this bridge.

The meadow to the south is the location of the deserted medieval village of 'Meleford', as it was called in the Domesday Book of 1086. The men and women who lived their lives in that long gone original village would have probably seen this bridge being built and may have helped with its construction.

At the Bridge: In recent years, the Milford and Area Preservation Group have made great efforts to reduce the overgrown vegetation and introduce legislation that would restrict weight limits and protect the bridge. Access to river level is difficult but some views may be available from the south side. There is no formal parking but there are areas that may allow a temporary pullover.

2 Salisbury Crane Bridge ★★

Bridge Name:	Salisbury Crane Bridge
Location:	Crane Street in Salisbury in the centre of the city. Use postcode SP1 2QB for your satnav.
Setting:	City / Urban
OS Ref:	SU 14148 29835
Crosses:	River Salisbury Avon
Orientation:	Northwest / Southeast
County:	Wiltshire
Length:	14.5 metres
Bridge Type:	Multiple Arch
Materials:	Stone
Traffic:	Road
Build Date:	15th century
Authority:	Wiltshire (Unitary Authority)
Designation:	Grade I Listed
Directions:	From Salisbury Milford Bridge: • Reverse direction and return to the A36. • Turn right (west) and head back towards Salisbury. At the big second roundabout turn left (south) onto Churchill Way South and follow to the next roundabout Exeter Street, signposted Old George Mall. • Follow north (the old cathedral walls should be on your left). At the intersection with New Street the Bell & Crown Pub should be in front of you. • Turn left (west) and follow the road that becomes Crane Street to the bridge.
Driving Time:	From Salisbury Milford Bridge – 25 minutes.

Information: Salisbury Crane Bridge is the surviving part of a medieval bridge of six stone arches, four of which are now visible. It is one of three medieval stone bridges in Salisbury including the Milford Mill and Harnham bridges. It was most likely rebuilt in the 15th century with four segmental arches,

Salisbury Crane Bridge – north face

The cutwaters on the northern face

though there may be traces of another smaller and lower archway buried at its eastern end. The arch at the eastern end is wider and higher than the others.

The south face of the bridge (downstream) was taken down in 1898 and re-erected to widen the road to 6 metres, according to Jervoise. During that widening the stonework was not replaced exactly as it had been, because the inner chamfered arch ring looks to be a new build. There is an engraved stone in the parapet which marks this:

THIS SIDE OF THE BRIDGE WAS
TAKEN DOWN AND REBUILT 7 ½ FEET
FURTHER SOUTH IN THE YEAR 1898
HOWARD HARRIS - MAYOR

The original bridge may have been very narrow for a town bridge, less than 3 metres wide and close examination reveals that there was a second widening operation at the south face. An engraved stone adjacent to the one above marks this event:

THE BRIDGE WAS WIDENED BY A
FURTHER 14 FEET ON ITS SOUTH
SIDE IN THE YEAR 1970
H. RACKHAM CITY ENGINEER

This northern aspect displays this extension, with four segmental arches of different spans, separated by cutwaters capped below the parapets. The arches have double chamfered arch rings in two orders, yet there are prominent keystones that continue across the entire crowns of the soffits of three of the arches, a strange combination.

The river walk that runs along the northeast riverbank is reclaimed land and to accomplish this, an adjoining stream was arched over at the northeast corner and appears suddenly from under Crane Street and runs into the Avon via a small channel.

So, the bridge as it can be viewed is mostly modern. However, when the soffits are viewed, its history can be discerned, and its 15th-century core, which has of course fixed its form, is visible.

At the Bridge: Parking is easy near to the bridge. There is a river walk and parkland area next to the bridge and it can be viewed at both faces without difficulty. Facilities and amenities abound in Salisbury.

Salisbury Crane Bridge – south face

The engraved date stone in the south parapet

3 Harnham Bridge ★★

Bridge Name:	Harnham Bridge
Other Names:	Ayleswade Bridge, Ayleswater Bridge
Location:	Harnham near Salisbury lies to the south of Salisbury city centre on St Nicholas Road, which becomes Ayleswade Road. Use postcode SP1 2SN for your satnav.
Setting:	City / Urban
OS Ref:	SU 14359 29052 and SU 14364 29101
Crosses:	River Salisbury Avon
Orientation:	North / South
County:	Wiltshire
Length:	112 metres (including the island causeway and both bridges)
Bridge Type:	Multiple Arch
Materials:	Stone
Traffic:	Road
Build Date:	1245
Authority:	Wiltshire (Unitary Authority)
Designation:	Grade I Listed and Scheduled Monument
Directions:	From Salisbury Crane Bridge: • Reverse direction and go back eastwards on Crane Street. Follow to Brown Street. • Turn right (south) and follow one block and curve around with it as it becomes St Ann Street. • Follow 1 block to the T junction with Exeter Street. • Turn left (south) and follow back to the big roundabout at the A36. Go all the way around the roundabout to St Nicholas Road. • Follow this as it curves continuously to the left and leads to the bridge.
Driving Time:	From Salisbury Crane Bridge – 20 minutes.

Harnham Bridge – eastern face of the southern bridge

The eastern face of the northern bridge

Harnham Bridge – the date stone in the western parapet

A scene showing the River Avon in the foreground, with the bridge to the left. The painter has captured a domestic scene of a woman from the house filling her bucket with river water whilst a figure watches from the bridge (Artist Unknown, The House on Harnham Bridge, with permission of Salisbury & South Wiltshire Museum)

Information: Harnham Bridge was known as Ayleswade or Ayleswater Bridge until at least the 15th century. Built originally in 1244 by Bishop Bingham across two branches of the Avon, with Saint John's Island between the branches, to protect traffic from the constant inundations of the river. This stone bridge possibly replaced an earlier bridge and is one of three medieval stone bridges in Salisbury including the Milford and Crane bridges.

The northern part of the bridge towards Salisbury, which crosses the smaller branch of the river, has three arches thought to be the original ones of the 13th century. There is a semi-circular pedestrian refuge in the eastern parapet of this bridge, and in the western parapet a commemorative date stone reads:

Built in 1245 by Bishop Bingham – Widened in 1774

The southern portion towards Harnham, crossing the larger branch of the river, has six slightly pointed arches with double arch rings spanning 4.8 metres. There are five piers without cutwaters. The fabric of the bridge is all ashlar stone with solid parapets of a different stone and plain coping. Victorian iron bar reinforcements can be seen in the sides. The bridge was widened on both sides in 1774 and remains of the old bridge are visible inside the outer casing of the newer widening project.

On the island, private houses abut right up to the bridge, making access at river level impossible, but a partial view can be gained from the new road bridge built 100 metres to the east. There is a generous pedestrian walkway on the west side of the roadway but no refuges. The bridge is still in use, but a new four lane diversion takes the main A338 road across the river by a new bridge built a few yards to the east in 1933.

The well-known artist John Constable (1776–1837) painted many works in the Salisbury area, including this bridge in two paintings entitled *Salisbury Cathedral from the Meadows* and *The Bridge of Harnham and Salisbury Cathedral.*

A semi-circular pedestrian refuge in the eastern parapet of the northern bridge

Arch and vaulting of the northern bridge

At the Bridge: A good view of the west face can be had from the back garden of the Rose & Crown Pub Hotel just to the west. Salisbury Cathedral is several hundred metres to the northwest and John Constable famously painted views of Harnham Bridge with the cathedral spire in the background.

4 Coombe Bissett Packhorse Bridge ★

Bridge Name: Coombe Bissett Packhorse Bridge

Other Names: Ponte de Combe

Location: In the village of Coombe Bissett three miles southwest of Salisbury, a short distance downstream (east) of the main road bridge on the A354. Use postcode SP5 4LS for your satnav.

Setting: Village / Rural

OS Ref: SU 10885 26397

Crosses: River Ebble

Orientation: North / South

County: Wiltshire

Length: 11 metres

Bridge Type: Multiple Arch

Materials: Stone and Brick

Traffic: Road

Build Date: 13th century

Authority: Wiltshire (Unitary Authority)

Designation: Grade II Listed and Scheduled Monument

Directions: From Harnham Bridge:

- At the south end of Harnham Bridge, bear right (southwest) onto Harnham Road and follow south to its T junction with the B3094.
- Turn right (west) and follow 75 metres to the next left, Old Blandford Road.
- Turn left and follow ¾ mile to the intersection with the A354, Salisbury Road, signposted Blandford.
- Turn right (southwest) and follow 2 miles into Coombe Bissett.
- Turn left at Homington Road (at the church) and follow for only 100 metres.
- The bridge is accessed via a footpath next to the post office off Homington Road.

Driving Time: From Harnham Bridge – 25 minutes.

Coombe Bissett Packhorse Bridge – west face

The buttress in the central pier – east face

Information: This packhorse bridge crosses the River Ebble, a tributary of the River Avon, a short distance downstream of the main road bridge and probably marks the course of the main road towards Blandford. Historic documents refer to the bridge as Ponte de Cume in 1249.

The original fabric is of dressed stone but widened in brick. This is a very old bridge, mentioned by Leland when he travelled through Wiltshire in the middle of the 16th century. That bridge can just be seen by looking over the east side of the bridge's modern wood parapets.

It is a narrow three-arch bridge, of a length a little less than 11 metres, with pointed arches with double-chamfered arch rings and weathered buttresses to piers on the downstream (east) face. These features could support a very early build-date and would make suggestions of 13th-century origins plausible.

In the 19th century, the bridge was widened by about ½ metre to 1.9 metres in brick on the upstream (west) face, preserving the arch shape, but hiding the old fabric. There are neither cutwaters nor parapets, but modern wooden railings.

The plague stone at Coombe Bissett

At the entrance to the path to the bridge is what is believed to be a plague stone. During the Great Plague in the 17th century, produce for sale outside the village would have been left on the stone and payment would have been made by leaving coins in the 'bowl', which would have been filled with vinegar. This method was used to try and keep the disease out of the village.

At the Bridge: Private gardens occupy the area from where this face could be viewed properly. There is a public green space to the north end of the bridge.

Coombe Bissett Packhorse Bridge – northern arch, eastern face (Raphael Tuck & Sons Ltd., image used with permission of Coombe Bissett & Honnington website)

Coombe Bissett Packhorse Bridge – northern arch, eastern face

5 Fordingbridge Bridge ★★★

Bridge Name: Fordingbridge Bridge

Location: In west Hampshire between Bournemouth and Salisbury in the town of Fordingbridge on Bridge Street, the B3078, off the A338. Use postcode SP6 1AH for your satnav.

Setting: Village / Suburban

OS Ref: SU 14937 14215

Crosses: River Salisbury Avon

Orientation: Northwest to Southeast

County: Hampshire

Length: 40 metres

Bridge Type: Multiple Arch

Materials: Ironstone

Traffic: Road

Build Date: c. 1200

Authority: New Forest (District Authority)

Designation: Grade II* Listed

Directions: From Coombe Bissett Packhorse Bridge:

- Follow the A354 south for 3 miles. At a triangular intersection Rockbourne Road veers off to the left, signposted Rockbourne.
- Take this road to the left (south) and follow for 5½ miles, through Rockbourne, to the intersection with Station Road in the village of Sandleheath.
- Turn left, signposted Fordingbridge and follow for 1½ miles to the bridge.

Driving Time: From Coombe Bissett Bridge – 25 minutes.

Information: Fordingbridge sits just west of New Forest National Park. The first great bridge at Fordingbridge was built before 1252 and is upstream from the original ford. In 1086 the town name was simply recorded as 'Forde' in the Domesday Book. The original bridge at Fordingbridge was built when the bailiff and men of the town received a grant of pontage for one year towards its construction and

Fordingbridge Bridge – south face

Concrete supports for the pedestrian walkway

maintenance. Several similar grants followed, the last being dated in 1452.

The bridge is 40 metres long and consists of seven pointed-segmental stone arches of local ashlar ironstone with single chamfered arch rings and coursed rubble soffits without ribs. The bridge has elevating approaches at each end and short cutwaters protect the piers on both faces. Above the arches is a slightly protruding string course at road level and parapets with weathered triangular coping. At each end of the bridge's parapets are octagonal plinths with heavy stone capstones and corbels below. The approaches have stone retaining walls with a similar parapet butting plinth.

Significant alterations were made in 1841 when both sides were widened and refaced in Chilmark Stone, adding 1.4 metres to the width of the bridge. The new arches sit on the original cutwater starlings, which has reduced the visual impact of the cutwaters. The original arches are still visible from river level, being smaller in span and height than the 19th-century additions. A reinforced concrete footpath on one side was added in 1960 to widen the bridge.

At the Bridge: The George Pub is at the west end of the bridge and affords great views of the bridge's south face. Riverside Park and Recreational Area are to the east of the bridge and also afford good, but distant, views. A bronze statue of Fordingbridge's most famous inhabitant, Augustus John (1878–1961), the well-known portrait painter, can be seen next to the bridge's north side near the river.

New Forest National Park

The area known today as the New Forest was created by William the Conqueror via the Charter of Cnute in Forest Law for the pursuit of the 'beasts of the chase – red, roe and fallow deer and wild pig' *(New Forest National Park Authority, 2022)*. The area was previously known as 'Ytene' the land of the Jutes (an Anglo-Saxon tribe), and it was grouped together as a 'new' forest by William the Conqueror in 1079. 'Nova Forest', as it was originally known, did not refer to a forest in the sense of a wooded area, but rather to a protected royal hunting ground, to which specific, often harsh, laws applied.

The New Forest is in Hampshire located between Southampton and Bournemouth, below Salisbury on the south coast of the UK. The area became a National Park in 2005 in recognition of its outstanding natural beauty, wildlife and cultural heritage, and the opportunities it gives for people to enjoy it. The New Forest National Park's significant landscapes make its 219 square miles a unique national park in southern England and a conserved area that is appreciated internationally. The bridge at Fordingbridge borders the New Forest.

This historic royal hunting forest offers many things to do and places to visit. The New Forest's ancient and ornamental woodland and open heathland make it an exciting place for visitors to explore the land and its culture and arts community. From its 26 miles of beaches on its coastline of shingle, saltmarsh, lagoons, and mudflats, to its vast landscapes, make it a great place for walks and bike rides. The coastline here played an essential role in Britain's shipbuilding past, and you can learn more in the historic village of Buckler's Hard.

The New Forest is said to have the most ancient trees in Western Europe – including 800-year-old oaks and 1000-year-old yews. The New Forest supports sport as well, offering visitors a wide variety of activities to pursue.

The Beaulieu River in the New Forest National Park (© Jim Champion/WikiCommons)

Horse riding is one of the most popular ways to explore the New Forest, and there are at least 10 different stables offering riding lessons and forest rides.

Its maritime heritage allows guests to visit places of historical interest, while various places to grab a bite and a drink are also widely available.

Today, the landscape is mostly heathland, where ponies, deer, wild pigs, and cattle have grazed since William the Conqueror set this land aside for hunting 900 years ago. These animals have shaped the landscape over the years and have made it a great place for people to explore its rivers and valleys as well as its historic villages.

The New Forest has inspired the work of several famous authors who have based their setting descriptions on this captivating location. These include the author of the famous Sherlock Holmes, Sir Arthur Conan Doyle, as well as Lewis Carroll, creator of Alice in Wonderland, and the renowned Florence Nightingale.

Please visit: **https://www.thenewforest.co.uk/.**

Fordingbridge Bridge – the central cutwaters

A Glossary for Medieval Bridges

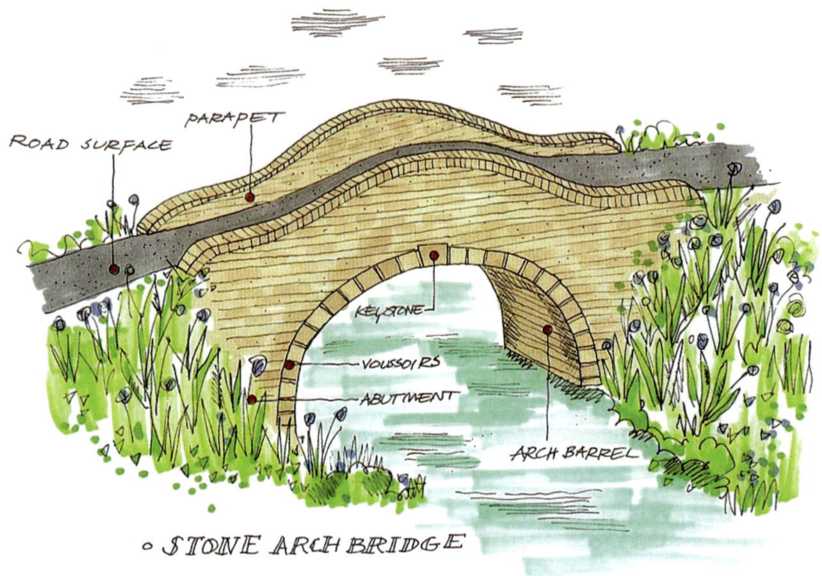

A

Abutment – Abutments carry the vertical and horizontal loads from the bridge superstructure. The ground end-support of a bridge on both sides of a water course especially created to resist the horizontal thrust of an arch.

Ancient Monument – Any scheduled monument, which, in the opinion of the Secretary of State, is of public interest by reason of the historic, architectural, traditional, artistic, or archaeological interest attached to it.

Apron – A device to protect a riverbank or riverbed against scour. A shield of masonry, concrete, or brick.

Aqueduct – A structure carrying water over a river or depression.

Arch – An architectural passageway that controls the pressure from the weight of a bridge and its traffic in a specific way. The arch directs pressure downwards onto the bearings and outwards onto the abutments, creating a strong passage underneath it that can support heavy loads.

Archaeological Interest – There will be archaeological interest in a heritage bridge if it holds, or potentially may hold, evidence of past human activity worthy of expert investigation at some point. Heritage assets with archaeological interest are the primary source of evidence about the substance and evolution of places, and of the people and cultures that made them.

Arch Bridge – A bridge with abutments at each end with structural support elements shaped as a curved arch. Arch bridges work by transferring the weight of the bridge and its load partially into a horizontal thrust restrained by the abutments at either side.

Ashlar – Ashlar is dressed stonework of any type of stone. Ashlar blocks are highly finished, precisely cut blocks of stone. When laid with others in even courses (rows) it creates a uniform face with fine joints. Most often used as a facing on the visible exterior of a bridge, especially as a veneer for the facade. Also called dressed stone. Often used to add classical elements to a bridge.

ASHLAR BLOCK

Assizes – Courts held in the main county towns and presided over by visiting judges from the higher courts.

Asymmetric – Having no balance or symmetry. Without symmetry.

B

Bailey Bridge – A componentised and prefabricated steel bridge developed for use during the Second World War by Sir Donald Bailey. It provided a quick and temporary bridging mechanism for heavy trucks and armoured vehicles that could be transported to the site and erected in a matter of hours. There are Bailey Bridges still in use today.

Ballast – Gravel, broken stone, slag, or other road material used in bridges for fill and to give solidity to the road.

Baluster – A single short post or pillar in a series supporting a rail or coping and thus forming a balustrade of multiple posts.

Balustrade – A row of balusters topped by a rail, serving as an open parapet, as along the edge of a balcony, terrace, bridge, staircase, or the eaves of a building.

Barbican – A defensive outer work, such as a wall or tower, on approach to a castle or walled town to protect the gate or drawbridge of the fortification.

Bargate – A hard, yellow/honey-coloured sandstone, usually found in southwest Surrey. It occurs in several Surrey villages, such as Compton, as well as towns, such as Guildford, and was used extensively during the medieval period. It was often used for rubble work, sometimes squared but largely with a rubble face. Bargate Stone was the choice building material for Godalming and the surrounding Surrey villages. The durable sandstone made for lasting bridges, but all Bargate Stone quarries have closed, and local stonework skills associated with it have declined.

Bascule – A bridge with a movable section hinged about a horizontal axis and counterbalanced by a weight.

Beam – A rigid flat, usually horizontal, structure member, which supports loads and transfers them to its supports by bending resistance.

Beam Bridge – Bridges where beams, usually underneath but sometimes on the sides, carry the loads across the span. Beam bridges can be single span, or multi-span, or continuous multi-span.

Bearing – The components of a bridge, usually located in the substructure, which bear the weight of the bridge and traffic and transfer the load to the earth. Bearings commonly include abutment walls, piers, arches, and wing walls.

Bedrock – The solid rock layer that underlies loose material, such as soil, sand, clay, or gravel.

Belt Course – A moulding or projecting course of brick or stone running horizontally along the face of a bridge placed so as to divert rainwater from the face of the bridge. These may sometimes be ornate to provide decoration. Also known as a 'String Course'.

Benchmark – A benchmark is an Ordnance Survey arrowhead sign found on walls, stone bridges, churches, and specially erected triangulation pillars where the altitude above sea-level has been accurately measured by surveyors. The arrowhead points to a horizontal line above it, which marks the exact altitude.

Bridge Deck – The roadway or surface that carries traffic.

Buttress – A structure built against a wall or bridge to provide support or reinforcement.

C

Caisson – A bridge foundation comprising a watertight open topped box, usually made of timber, embedded in a riverbed by continuously digging out material within it so that the caisson sinks and becomes an integral part of the structure.

Calp Limestone – Comprised of dark grey, fine-grained, graded limestone with interbedded black, poorly fossilised shales.

Camber – This is the gradual slope of the roadway, or along the length of the bridge. Camber is needed to ensure that a bridge deck drains to the sides (or to one side) and does not pond any water.

Cantilever – A beam or member securely fixed at one end and hanging free at the other end.

Capping – Stones or masonry that is placed on the top of a wall or parapet to protect it from damage by the elements. Also called coping stones.

Capstone – The uppermost or finishing stone of a masonry structure.

Carriageway – That part of the bridge deck that includes all traffic lanes, hard shoulders, and pedestrian walkways. The carriageway width is the distance between raised kerbs or parapets if there are any.

Carstone – A sedimentary sandstone from the earliest era of the Cretaceous period, which lasted from about 135 to 65 million years ago. It varies in colour from light to dark rusty ginger. Also known as 'Silsoe' and 'Gingerbread'.

Causeway – A raised path or road across wet ground or water.

Centring – A temporary framework for supporting a masonry arch or vault during construction until it can stand by itself.

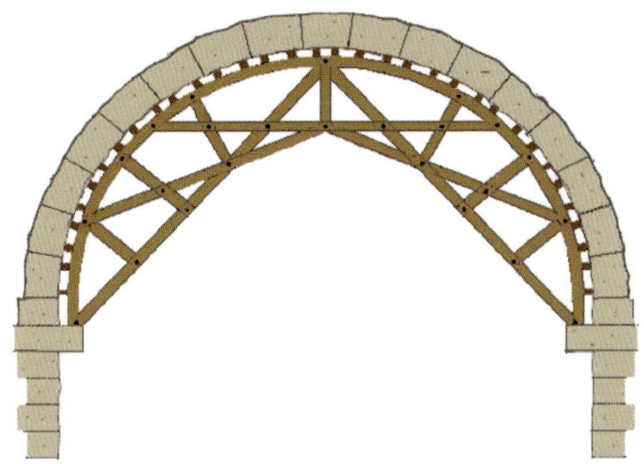

CENTRING

Chamfer – A cut that is made in a material, usually as a 45-degree angle, to produce a flat sloping surface.

Chantry – A chantry, also known as a chantry chapel, is a memorial or even a complete building dedicated to the memory of a person or family, sometimes on bridges. In the medieval period it was common for wealthy patrons of a church to give a grant of money to pay for a priest to say prayers (chants) for themselves and their family. After the dissolution of the monasteries in England, chantries were abolished, and their assets were sold or granted to persons at the discretion of Henry VIII and his son King Edward VI.

Chilmark Stone – A fine grained creamy coloured limestone mined near Tisbury in Wiltshire. It was used historically as a building and masonry stone throughout Wiltshire and Dorset, as well as many other locations in the UK. It is nationally renowned as one of Britain's finest building and masonry stones. This historic stone was used to build Salisbury Cathedral 800 years ago.

Clapper Bridge – Bridges that are formed by large, flat slabs of undressed stone supported on stone piers. A clapper bridge may also be created by placing the slab directly on the banks of the stream and are known as 'cart clappers'.

Cofferdam – A watertight enclosure built within a stream or lake in the early stages of the bridge construction process. Introduced to England by the Romans. A double set of piles were driven into the riverbed and a watertight chamber was constructed. Water is then pumped out exposing the bed and allowing foundations below the waterline to be built in the dry. Rubble and ballast were then poured into the chamber on each receding tide and the cofferdam was then filled with a crude concrete mix, producing a 'starling'. Cofferdams and the resulting starling can take almost any form but under bridges they were most often diamond or egg shaped.

Concrete – An artificial stone made by mixing cement with an aggregate composed of hard, inert particles of varying size from sand to broken stone, water being added to make the cement active.

Coping – A capping or covering to a parapet either flat or sloping to throw off water.

Corbel – A small shelf or single stone cantilevered out from a beam, wall, or column in order to support a beam or a super-incumbent load. A masonry bracket.

Cornice – Any projecting moulding along the top of a building, wall, arch etc., finishing or crowning it.

Course – A horizontal layer of stone in a masonry wall, or pavement. Many courses together form a wall.

COURSED ASHLAR – STONE MASONRY

Cramp – A flattened iron bar that is bent on both ends and used to hold timbers or blocks of stone together. Also called a 'cramp iron'.

Cross-section – A virtual view made possible by a cut plane across the axis of the member, structure, or any construction.

Crown – The highest point of the extrados of an arch. The 'keystone' will always sit at the crown of an arch.

Cruciform – Cross-shaped, as a crucifix.

Culvert – A closed conduit or tunnel used to convey water from one area to another, normally from one side of a road to the other side. Typically, culverts are box shaped, round, or elliptical in cross-section. They are often prefabricated and can be made from pipes, reinforced concrete, or other materials that are embedded within the surrounding landscape.

Cutwater – The triangular or round wedge of a bridge pier, that resists (cuts) the flow of water and ice and helps prevent scouring.

D

Deck – The superstructure component of a bridge that carries the traffic. See also 'Carriageway'.

Dentilation – Embellishment that makes a structure appear as if it had teeth or notches. This is often accomplished by turning bricks or stones with pointed corners exposed outwards. Also written as 'dentillated'.

Designation – The recognition of particular heritage value(s) of a significant place by giving it formal status under law or policy intended to sustain those values.

Diaper Work – A decorative pattern formed by small and repeated geometric motifs set next to one another. These were often used in medieval times to decorate stone surfaces in architecture.

Dissolution – Referring to the dissolution of the monasteries by Henry VIII. In an act of defiance against papal authority, Henry VIII ordered the Act of Supremacy in 1534, which dissolved the Catholic Church in England. Henry declared himself the Supreme Head of the Church of England, dissolved the monasteries and appropriated their income, properties, and lands.

Dovetail – A fan-shaped tenon that forms a tight interlocking joint when fitted into a corresponding mortise.

Drawbridge – A bridge that may be drawn or turned to one side, or lifted, either bodily or in sections, to permit boats to pass under or through it.

E

Eaves – The edge of a roof structure that protrudes out from the structure's walls.

English Bond – A method of laying bricks so that alternate courses on the face of the wall are composed of headers or stretchers only.

Extrados – The outer curve or surface of an arch or vault. The opposite of 'Intrados'.

Eyot – An island formed by the natural flow of a river.

F

Fabric – The material substance of which bridges are formed, including construction material, geology, archaeological deposits, structures and buildings, and flora.

Falsework – Temporary wooden scaffolding or support structures used in arched bridge construction to hold the components (voussoirs and vaulting) in place until the construction is sufficiently advanced to support itself. See also 'Timber Centring'.

Flood Arch – The arched openings in a bridge or viaduct over a valley or lowland through which floodwater may pass during periods of high water. These are used in distinction from a channel arch, which spans the channel and through which water continuously, or usually, flows. Also distinct from a culvert, which is a tube and has a closed bottom side.

Footbridge – A bridge for foot passengers only.

Footing – The spreading course that distributes load at the base of a foundation.

Ford – A shallow spot in the river or stream where people, vehicles, and animals are able to wade across. These were undoubtably the earliest river crossings and many are still in use today.

Formwork – Temporary boarding or sheets of wood used to give shape to poured concrete while it hardens.

Foundation – That portion of a structure, usually below the surface of the ground, which distributes the pressure upon its support. The term is often used interchangeably with 'footing'.

Four-Centred Arch – also known as a depressed arch, it is a low, wide type of arch with a pointed apex. It is much wider than its height and gives the visual effect of having been flattened under pressure.

Freestone – A sedimentary stone without grain that can be shaped, carved, or moulded in any direction without splitting. Some forms of sandstone can be used as freestone masonry. See also 'Oolitic Stone'.

G

Gabions – Large baskets of reeds, rope, saplings (or today galvanised steel wire), which hold rocks together to stabilise embankments and to reduce erosion.

Gangway – A temporary passageway used during construction.

Gault Brick – A brick made of a mixture of a heavy clay soil and sand that when fired produces a colour between white and a pale yellow, sometimes with a slight pinkish tint. It was used extensively in the Victorian period.

Grade I – For bridges, Grade I (one) indicates that the structure is of 'exceptional interest'.

Grade II – For bridges, Grade II (two) indicates that structures are of 'special interest', warranting every effort to preserve them.

Grade II* – For bridges, Grade II* (two star) indicates that structures are 'particularly important … of more than special interest'.

Gradient – A rate of inclination; a slope, expressed as rise related to run. For example, 1 in 5 would be a 20% gradient.

Granite – A rock composed of mica, feldspar, and quartz with a thoroughly crystalline, granular texture. Very hard and durable.

H

Haunching – Material used for filling the part of an arch between its springing and its crown.

Header – A brick or stone laid so that only the end appears on the face of the wall.

Heritage Bridge – Any bridge that makes an important and significant contribution to the heritage of the country in cultural, historic, design and engineering, or political terms.

Historic England – Officially 'The Historic Buildings and Monuments Commission for England', more commonly known as Historic England, established in 1984 by the National Heritage Act of 1983. Historic England is the Government's advisory body on the historic environment in England.

Historic Interest – A classification by Historic England. To be of special historic interest a bridge must illustrate important aspects of the nation's social, economic, cultural, or military history, and/or have close historical associations with nationally important people. There should normally be some quality of interest in the physical fabric of the structure itself to justify the statutory protection afforded by this classification *(Historic England, 2018)*.

Hood Mould – A moulding running around the face of an arch immediately above the opening that projects over the head of an arch. Also called a 'Dripstone course'.

Hook or Crook – Dispensation permitting villagers to gather firewood from woodlands but using only their hook and crook. It effectively permitted the collection of dead branches from the trees.

Hue and Cry – Requirement for all members of a village to pursue a criminal 'with horn and voice'. It was the duty of any person discovering a felony to raise the hue and cry. His neighbours were bound to assist him in pursuit and capture of the offender.

Hydraulics – The science of the mechanics of fluids, which considers water in motion. Bridges will be engineered around the hydraulics of a river crossing point such as flow, quantity, tides, and temperature.

I

Impost – The point on which an arch rests on a wall or column, or the upper part of a pier from which an arch springs. Where the bottom voussoir rests.

Indulgences – A unique characteristic of the medieval Catholic Church in which penitents could reduce their punishment for sin by paying a fee or performing acts of good works, such as the building of bridges. The concept of indulgences emerged in the 11th and 12th centuries when the idea of purgatory took widespread hold.

In-situ – In the original or natural place or site. For example, 'the pottery was left in-situ' means 'the pottery was left where it was found'.

Interlocking – The action of linking into each other, or the joining fast together by mutual or reciprocal action.

Intrados – The interior curve or surface of an arch or vault. The opposite of 'Extrados'.

Iron – An abundant ferrous metal that is strongly attracted by a magnet and has the elemental symbol of Fe. It is very strong and used in making steel. Other forms used in bridge construction are cast iron and wrought iron. It also appears naturally in stone and some historical bridges are constructed of ironstone.

Iron Age – The Iron Age in Britain lasted from around 800 BC until the Roman invasion of AD 43. It is the time when iron first begins to be used. Objects such as tools and weapons were thereafter starting to be made from iron.

Ironwork – Articles or parts of a bridge that are made of iron, especially if made in a decorative way.

J

Joggle – In masonry, to fit together stonework with notches and projections, or with notches and keys, to prevent the slipping of parts upon one another.

K

Keinton Flagstones – A high quality slab-stone used for paving that is sourced from quarries in south Somerset near Keinton.

Keystone – The centre or highest voussoir or arch stone.

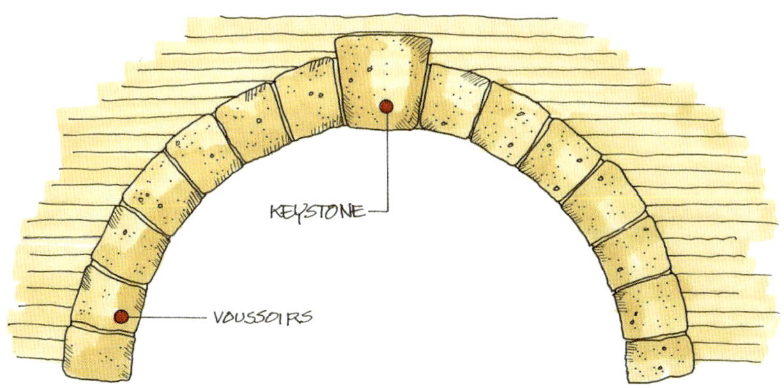

KEYSTONE

L

Leat – An artificially created trench or ditch that conveys water to a mill wheel.

Lias (Blue) – A form of clay limestone known for its greyish blue colouring. The fine-grained stone is formed from a mixture of limestone and shale, laid down during the early Triassic period, and it is renowned for the fossils, especially ammonites, that are contained within it. Lias Stone is also quarried in grey and white and is found in Lyme Regis, Dorset, and Somerset.

Lierne Rib – A secondary or tertiary vault rib that does not spring from the main impost point, but instead connects to, or between, the primary ribs. Used extensively in Gothic vaulting.

Limestone – A white or light grey sedimentary rock consisting mainly of calcium carbonate that is used as an abundant building material and in the making of cement.

Listed Structure – Any structure that is included in a list compiled or approved by the Secretary of State including:

(a) any object or structure fixed to the bridge.

(b) any object or structure within the curtilage of the bridge, which, although not fixed to the building, forms part of the land and has done so since before 1 July 1948.

Load – The weight of bridge components and traffic. Load may be either live (moving) load or dead (stationary) load. The maximum amount of weight any given bridge can carry is called its load limit. The live load limit of a bridge will be greater than its dead load limit.

Lug – Any kind of a projection for carrying or supporting something.

M

Masonry – The craft of building in stone, clay, brick, or concrete. The term may also refer to the finished work of a mason such as a masonry bridge.

Masons' Mark – These were marks incised onto stone blocks as a sign of individual ownership of responsibility for work done. Some marks were utilised as assembly marks to ensure the correct installation of important pieces of stonework. The masons used a variety of chisels and axes to cut their marks and these tools left decipherable patterns in the surface of the stone blocks. The marks were put on the stone for entirely practical reasons, in answer to the specific needs of the industry, but in many grand houses of the era these marks were carefully removed to provide a clean 'dressed' surface.

Mass Concrete – Concrete set without structural reinforcement such as steel rods or mesh.

Medieval – There are really three medieval periods:

1. Early medieval: 410–1066 (started when the Romans left England).
2. Medieval: 1066–1536 (started on the date of the Norman invasion). It is also known as the Middle Ages.
3. Post-medieval: 1536–1901 (started at the dissolution of the monasteries).

Member – Any individual structural component.

Monument – Monument may be defined as:

(a) any building, structure, or work, whether above or below the surface of the land, and any cave or excavation; or

(b) any site comprising the remains of any such building, structure, or work or of any cave or excavation; and

(c) any site comprising, or comprising the remains of, any vehicle, vessel, aircraft or other movable structure or part thereof which neither constitutes nor forms part of any work which is a monument within paragraph (a) above; and

(d) any machinery attached to a monument shall be regarded as part of the monument if it could not be detached without being dismantled (Historic England, 2018).

Moorstone – A type of English granite used as a building material, found mostly in Cornwall.

Mortar – A mixture of cement or lime with sand and water forming a thick paste, used in masonry work for bedding the stones and filling the joints. Cement-based mortar becomes hard when it dries.

Moulding – A shaped strip of masonry that projects out from the bridge face. These may be either for decorative purposes or for use as a drip course.

N

National Importance – The Secretary of State may, on compiling the Schedule of Monuments (scheduling), include therein any monument that appears to him/her to be of national importance.

O

Oolitic Limestone – Limestone that is made up of small spheres called ooliths that are stuck together by lime mud. Known in the vernacular as 'egg stone', they form when calcium carbonate is deposited on the surface of sand grains rolled (by waves) around on a shallow sea floor.

Openwork – Any kind of work, especially ornamental, as of embroidery, lace, metal, stone, or wood, having a lattice-like nature or showing openings through its substance.

Orders of Arches – Receding concentric rings of voussoirs, expressed as first order for the outmost ring and second order for the next, etc.

P

Packhorse Bridge – Packhorse bridges were built so that packhorses and their loads could cross an obstruction, which was almost always a river or fast flowing stream. Packhorse bridges had certain characteristics that separated them from other bridges. A genuine packhorse bridge is defined as being 1.8 metres wide or less, usually built of undressed or roughly dressed stone, have no or very low parapets to allow unhindered passage by animals with pannier packs, and have known packhorse associations, such as being on a known trade route.

Parapet – A low wall placed to protect any spot where there is a sudden drop, for example, at the edge of a bridge.

Pedestrian Bridge – A footbridge designed for pedestrians and in some cases cyclists and animal traffic.

Pediment – A triangle shape used to adorn Grecian architecture. A pediment is often used to form small gables and triangular decorations over niches, doors, and windows.

Pier – The supporting structures built into the ground between the abutments, in the gap, which carry intermediate spans of a multi-span bridge.

Pilaster – A flat rectangular strip attached to a wall (or in our case a bridge face). These may have fluted surface and stand on a base plinth and have a decorative capital. Pilasters are traditionally used for decorative rather than structural purposes and differ from a buttress in that they are not supportive.

Pile – A length of timber, steel, reinforced concrete etc., driven into the ground to carry a vertical load.

Piling – A general term for several piles considered together.

Plague Stone – See 'Vinegar Stones'.

Plinth – The base or platform upon which a column, pedestal, pier, or other structure rests. Bridge piers rest on plinths (or starlings) built into the riverbed using cofferdams.

Pontage – The right to charge tolls to cross a bridge. The right of toll; the Latin term was *pontagium*. In return the toller was required to maintain the bridge – a requirement frequently ignored. Often a small chapel was attached to a bridge. Hermits were known to take residence in such chapels and were givens alms by travellers, though often the hermit was an unlicensed impostor.

Prefabricate – To manufacture (a bridge or section of a bridge) in advance, especially in standard sections that can be easily shipped and assembled.

Prehistoric – The time in history before a written record was kept. In Britain it is the time before the Roman invasion of AD 43. The only evidence of this period is from objects that have survived from then.

Priory – Priories were monasteries run by a prior or prioress. They were usually smaller than abbeys.

Projecting Course – A course of masonry that is set out further from the face of a wall or bridge face. These may be either for decorative purposes or for use as a drip course.

Q

Quatrefoil – A French word meaning four leaves. A conventionalised representation of a flower with four petals or of a leaf with four leaflets. This is a popular motif in bridge architecture.

Quoin – The blocks or bricks forming the corner of a structure. Often these are more visually prominent than the wall material to give a sense of substance or permanence. In bridges, quoins are most obvious along the edge of the arch. Voussoirs act as quoins in this instance.

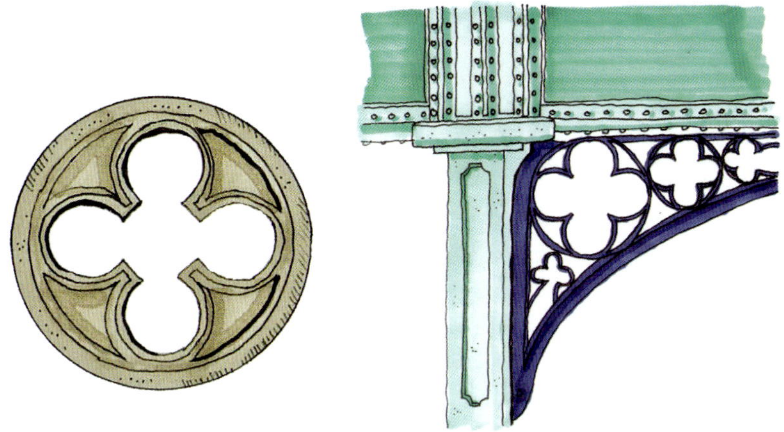

QUATREFOIL

R

Ragstone – A traditional stone building material found in Kent and Dorset quarries that has been used in hundreds of bridges and historical buildings. Kentish Ragstone tends to be grey in colour while Dorset Ragstone is browner. Can be finished as an ashlar stone or used as a rubble walling material.

Reach – A section of river or stream between a defined upstream and downstream location, for which the flow is measured at a point somewhere along that section. Generally, a reach of a river will be representative of conditions in that section of river or stream and will be uniform with respect to discharge, depth, area, and slope.

Repair – Work beyond the scope of maintenance, to remedy defects caused by decay, damage, or use, including minor adaptation to achieve a sustainable outcome, but not involving restoration or alteration.

Revetment – A retaining wall or facing of masonry or other material, supporting, or protecting an embankment or earthworks. Another word for retaining wall. See also 'Apron'.

Rib – A long narrow, usually curved, construction element used to add support and strength. An example would be the supporting stone structural elements, 'ribs', in the vaults of arches in medieval bridges.

Rising – The point at which a river's water 'rises' to the surface of the land and is often qualified with an adverbial expression of place. For example: The River Thames rises in Gloucestershire.

Roll Moulding – Medieval moulding of semi-circular or more than semi-circular section.

Rubble – Masonry bridge construction that uses blocks of stones that are either undressed or comparatively roughly dressed. The opposite of ashlar and usually most visible in the spandrels. The masonry has thick joints since stones of irregular size are used. These can be coursed or uncoursed. There are several methods of building with rubble including square (usually coursed), random (usually uncoursed), and flint.

Rustication – The act of making something look rustic (unfinished). In architecture it is the type of decorative masonry created by chamfering the edges of stone blocks, the use of uncoursed masonry, or tooling worm tracks, vermiculation, in the faces of stone blocks.

S

Sandstone – A sedimentary rock composed of fine grains of compacted quartz sand, felspar, and silica. Sandstone may be any colour, but the most common colours are tan, brown, yellow, red, and pink.

Scheduled Monument – Scheduled Monument means any monument (bridge) that is included in 'the schedule' of historic assets, which is compiled and maintained by the Secretary of State for Culture, Media, and Sport.

Scouring – The washing away of riverbed material and sediment from around a bridge's foundations, undercutting the support of a bridge. This is caused by the constant flow of water and is particularly problematic in tidal rivers. The use of cutwaters helps prevent scouring.

Segmental Arch – A segmental arch, which is also known as a Syrian Arch, forms a partial curve covering less than 180 degrees. It has a small rise in the centre and is semi-elliptical across the top. It is shorter in height than the semi-circular arch.

Sheet Pile – A pile, usually made of timber, driven edge to edge to form an almost watertight sheet, as used in the construction of cofferdams.

Skew Arch – (also known as an Oblique Arch) A method of construction that enables an arch bridge to span an obstacle at some angle other than a right angle. This results in the faces of the arch not being perpendicular to its abutments.

Skewback – The bevelled stone or course of masonry that supports the foot (impost) of an arch ring.

Sluice – An artificial passage for water (as in a millstream) fitted with a valve or gate for stopping or regulating flow.

Sneck – A small, squared stone used in a rubble wall to fill spaces between stones of different height.

Snecked – A process of laying masonry that has a mixture of roughly squared stones of different sizes. It is semi-coursed horizontal masonry with the larger 'rising' stones tying together the courses of smaller stones.

SNECKED MASONRY

Note: Most cornerstones are risers and some snecks are large

Soffit – The horizontal underside of a structural element such as an arch or overhang.

Spalling – Spalling (sometimes incorrectly called 'spaulding' or 'spalding') is the result of water entering brick, concrete, or natural stone. Freezing and thawing forces the surface to peel, pop out, or flake off. It is also known as 'flaking', especially in limestone and soft brick.

Span – The clear distance from face to face of structural supports such as piers or abutments. Span is the length of any bridge segment between its structural supports. There may be one, two, or several spans within a gap.

Spandrel – The roughly triangular area above and on the sides of the arch of a bridge, running below the string course and above the voussoirs.

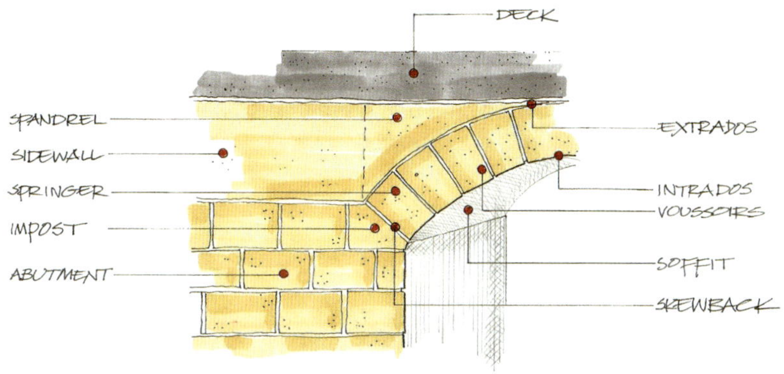

HALF ARCH

Spate – When a river is in 'spate' it contains a lot more water than usual and is flowing very fast.

Splay – A curving face making an angle of less than a right angle with another face, as in the parapets of a bridge splaying outwards.

Springer – The voussoir that meets the impost.

Springing – The point where the end of an arch meets the abutment.

Springing-Line – The level at which an arch springs from its supports. Sometimes referred to as the impost line.

Squinch – An architectural device that runs diagonally across a square corner to provide corbelling support for upper material. In the case of bridges, a squinch may be found between a wing wall and a spandrel to support a parapet.

Stannary – A place where tin is mined or smelted, usually used in relation to Cornwall and Devon.

Starling – Artificial islands on which bridge piers could be built; sometimes called plinths. Their construction was facilitated by a cofferdam. The stone piers of the bridge were built on top of the starling. This arrangement was commonly seen below English bridges and was clearly recorded at Berwick and Exe.

Stress – In building materials, the action within a structural member such as a beam or pier that resists change when an outside force such as weight is acting upon it.

Stretcher – A brick or stone laid so that only the length of one side appears on the face of the wall.

String Course – A moulding or projecting course of brick or stone running horizontally along the face of a bridge placed to divert rainwater from the face of the bridge. These may sometimes be ornate to provide decoration. Also known as a 'belt' course.

Substructure – The components of a bridge that are below the road deck level and bear the load of the bridge downward into the ground.

Sumpter – Packhorse, pony, mule, or other animal used for carrying goods.

Super-incumbent Load – Any load that rests and exerts pressure upon another structural element.

Superstructure – The upper part of a bridge usually defined from the deck upwards. This excludes substructure elements such as the foundations, piers, and abutments.

Swing Bridge or Swivel Bridge – A span that rotates about a vertical axis, to provide openings for the passage of vessels.

Symmetry – A condition of equality or balance of shape, size, and position between similar parts of a figure or body about a central axis. The simplest form of symmetry is reflection.

T

Tensile Strength – The ability of a material to withstand tension *(Burke, 1950).*

Thrust – Outward or lateral stress in a structure, as that exerted horizontally by an arch or vault.

Timber Centring – A wooden framework temporarily built under bridge vaults and ribs to sustain them while under construction. It is removed, and possibly re-used, once the arch is complete. See also 'Falsework'.

Transverse – Extending at a 90-degree angle from something else. Sideways in relationship, i.e., a transverse rib.

Trestle – A trestle is a rigid frame used as a support, especially referring to a bridge composed of a number of short spans supported by such frames. In the context of trestle bridges, each supporting frame is generally referred to as a 'bent'.

Tudor – The Tudor period lasted from 1485 until 1603 when all the kings and queens were from the Tudor family. Timber framed buildings were the most common architectural style in the Tudor period.

U

Uncoursed Stonework – Masonry work that does not form an identifiable layer of stone. Instead, the stone is arranged in a random order.

UNCOURSED RUBBLE-STONE MASONRY

V

Vault – The underside of a stone arch. Sometimes also referred to as the 'barrel'. Often used interchangeably with 'soffits'.

Vermiculation – Stonework that is decorated in such a way to resemble wormlike tracks. Vermiculation can happen naturally *(Wolfpaw, 2018)* in some stone types or it can be tooled by a mason onto the stone surface.

Viaduct – Any elevated passageway, especially a bridge, that carries traffic over a gorge or ravine. The term is most generally applied to railway bridges across low lying floodplains.

NATURAL VERMICULATION

Vinegar Stone – Stones found all across England with hollowed out depressions and positioned at strategic locations around communities such as at the base of stone crosses, bridges, stone fences, and footpaths. Vinegar was placed in the depression to disinfect coins during the plague years. Vinegar was used as a disinfectant in the belief that it prevented the plague from spreading. Residents placed coins in the vinegar and outsiders would place food or goods next to the stone. This practice allowed communities to buy food from outsiders without fear of contagion. Sometimes also called 'plague stones'.

Voussoir – In architecture, any one of the wedge-shaped stones used in forming an arch. The middle-top one is called the keystone.

W

Wing-Walls – The walls either side of abutments that retain the embankment of the roadway and help prevent erosion.

Wrought Iron – A commercial form of iron almost entirely free of carbon, which is malleable, tough, and yet relatively soft. It can be easily magnetised and bent into shapes.

Bridge Index

Acknowledgements

The author would like to gratefully acknowledge the contributions made by the following:

Mark Cowie, *Illustrator*

Marion Townsend, *Photographic Coordinator*

Chris Sims, *Graphic Designer*

Peter Hawkes, *Copy Editor*

The Staff at:

Ashmolean Museum, Oxford

Barnstaple Library, Barnstaple

Bideford Public Library, Bideford

Bodleian Library, Oxford

Bodmin Town Museum, Bodmin

Bradford-on-Avon Museum, Bradford-on-Avon

Buckinghamshire County Museum, Aylesbury

Burton Art Gallery and Museum, Bideford

Burton at Bideford Museum, Burton at Bideford

Canterbury Roman Museum

Dartmouth Library, Dartmouth

Dartmouth Museum, Dartmouth

Dorchester Library and Learning Centre, Dorchester

Dorset County Museum, Dorchester

Faringdon Museum, Faringdon

Kent Museum of Freemasonry, Canterbury

Kingston Museum, Kingston-upon-Thames

Museum of Barnstaple & North Devon, Barnstaple

Lacock Abbey-Fox Talbot Museum and Village, Chippenham

National Portrait Gallery, London

Maidstone Museum, Maidstone

Museum of Gloucester, Gloucester

Museum of Farnham, Farnham

National Waterways Museum, Gloucester

Plymouth City Museum and Art Gallery, Plymouth

Rural Life Centre Living Museum, Farnham

Royal Albert Memorial Museum and Art Gallery, Exeter

Rural Life Living Museum, Farnham

Surrey History Centre, Woking

The Box, Plymouth

The Oxfordshire Museum, Woodstock

Turvey Historical Society, Turvey

University of Exeter Library, Exeter

Wiltshire Museum, Swindon

During the writing of this book, I quickly became aware of a small community of 'pontists' that study each other's works and continue the long tradition of investigating and recording information on bridges. That discovery made this book possible, and all their many helpful resources contributed to the end product. However, there are a few sources that were so integral that they deserve recognition beyond a simple bibliographic reference.

Edwyn Jervoise

I found the books of Edwyn Jervoise a great source of background information. Edwyn Jervoise has been described as both a historian and an architect, but he was also an Associate Member of the Institution of Civil Engineers, and hence aware of engineering as well as architectural history. Jervoise had been asked in 1926 by The Society for the Protection of Ancient Buildings (SPAB) to complete a survey of ancient bridges throughout England and Wales, and he visited more than 5,000 bridges over the course of the next 10 years. In the following years he published a series of three books on ancient bridges in response to his remit by the SAPB:

- *The Ancient Bridges of the South of England – 1930*
- *The Ancient Bridges of the North of England – 1931*
- *The Ancient Bridges of Wales and Western England – 1936*

Today Jervoise is probably the most cited source of information on ancient bridges in England.

The Jervoise books

John Leland

John Leland's New Year's Gift to the King (with permission from Kyra Cornelius Kramer in Blood Will Tell*)*

Much of the earliest work chronicling bridges and their associated documentation comes from John Leland (1503–1552), who in 1538 embarked on a series of journeys on behalf of King Henry VIII, to record English and Welsh antiquities. His five excursions lasted six years, during which he kept extensive notebooks on his observations, details, books, and oral sources. On his return from each trip, Leland organised his notes into what we know today as his 'Itineraries'. In 1544 these were presented as a gift to Henry VIII and subsequently published in 1549 by John Bale under the title *The laboryouse journey & serche of Johan Leylande for Englandes antiquitees.* In addition to bridges, Leland recorded building architecture, the landscape, archaeological finds, Roman ruins, and medieval townscapes. In the 17th century, an amateur historian and gentleman named William Burton collected all of Leland's writings and books that he could find and donated them to the Bodleian Library, where they remain to this day *(Toulmin, 1964)*. Today these serve as an invaluable comparison, a date stamp, for the works of more recent pontists and historians. All of the authors in this work refer to Leland and cite him as a source of information.

Sir Nikolaus Pevsner

Sir Nikolaus Pevsner (Photo by Susie Harris, The Northern Echo*, 2012, used with permission)*

I often electronically referred to, and compared listings of authors with, *The Pevsner Architectural Guides*, a series of 46 volumes noting the architecture of England county by county. These were begun in 1951 by the architectural historian Sir Nikolaus Pevsner (1902–83). His aim was to provide an up-to-date portable guide to the most significant buildings in every part of the country, suitable for both general reader and specialist. These were co-authored by many people and continued after Pevsner's death. Each volume provides an introductory overview of the architecture of the area, followed by a descriptive gazetteer arranged alphabetically by place.

Tom Robertson

Tom Robertson has produced a fantastic website listing of *Historic Bridges of Britain – A Compendium*, which was fundamental in the identification of bridges that fell within the selection criteria. Over the period of five years and many hundreds of miles, he visited nearly 1,000 bridges, photographing and recording vital architectural observations. In my correspondence with him he provided both encouragement and leads on resources that otherwise I would have missed. His website can be found at: **https://drtomsbooks.com/** and the link to his compendium is **https://historicbridgesofbritain.com/**.

David Simpson

David Simpson has written an invaluable website called *Scotland's Oldest Bridges,* which was helpful in many respects but especially around medieval bridge construction methodology. I communicated with David by email and he provided many useful tips on resources.
https://scotlandsoldestbridges.co.uk/

Mark Cowie

Mark Cowie is a UK-based illustrator, his work has appeared at the Cartoon Museum in London. He produces hand drawn maps of cities and towns with an ironic twist.

His work often appears under his alias of Tony Hantz.
Email: **cowieandhantz@gmail.com**
Instagram: **@tonyhantz**

Chris Sims

Chris Sims is a graphic designer and fine artist.
He has worked for over 30 years in the design industry, producing brochures, advertising material, record sleeves, magazines and books. As an abstract fine artist he is gaining a worldwide reputation with his work being collected across several continents.
Email: **studio384@me.com**
Instagram: **@studio384**
Website: **https://web.marcelforart.com/chris_sims**

Bibliography

Addison, S. W., 1980. *The Old Roads of England.* London: Harper Collins.

Albert, W., 1972. *The Turnpike Road System in England 1663–1840.* Cambridge: Cambridge University Press.

Alexander, J., 1937. *Tavistock in the Fifteenth Century. The British Architect,* Volume 69, p. 265.

Alexander, J. S., *2008. Masons' Marks and the Working Practices of Medieval Stone Masons.* Reading: Spire Books.

Andrews, A., 1996. *Unstead Bridge / Trowers Bridge, 1898 and Today.* [Online] Available at: **https://www.andrewsgen.com/photo/godalming/unstead_bridge.htm** [Accessed 6 December 2020].

Beacham, P. & Pevsner, N., 2014. *The Buildings of England: Cornwall.* 3rd edn. London: Yale University Press.

Bellamy, R., 1998. *Postbridge – Heart of the Moor.* Tiverton: Halsgrove Publishing.

Bideford Bridge Trust, 2019. *History.* [Online] Available at: **http://www.bidefordbridgetrust.org.uk/history/** [Accessed 12 September 2020].

Bradford-on-Avon Museum, 1999. *Bradford on Avon Town Bridge.* [Online] Available at: **http://www.bradfordonavonmuseum.co.uk/town-bridge** [Accessed 21 September 2020].

British History Online – Lower Heyford, 1959. *Lower Heyford or Heyford Bridge.* [Online] Available at: **https://www.british-history.ac.uk/vch/oxon/vol6/pp182-195** [Accessed 3 December 2020].

British History Online, 1968. *The Borough of Twekesbury: Introduction. A History of the County of Gloucester,* Volume 8, pp. 110–118.

British History Online – Langford Parish: Radcot, 2000. *Langford Parish: Radcot.* [Online] Available at: **https://www.british-history.ac.uk/vch/oxon/vol17/pp250-269** [Accessed 1 June 2020].

British History Online – The Borough of Abingdon, 2004. *The Borough of Abingdon.* [Online] Available at: **https://www.british-history.ac.uk/vch/berks/vol4/pp430-451#anchorn52** [Accessed 12 August 2020].

Brod, M., Thomas, R. & Smith, J., 2010. *Notes on Abingdon Bridges.* Abingdon: s.n.

Brown, S., 1982. The Medieval Bridge and St Gabriel's Chapel, Bishop's Clyst. *Proceedings of the Devon Archeological Society,* Volume 40, pp. 163–169.

Brown, S., 2019. *The Medieval Exe Bridge, St Edmund's Church, and Excavation of Waterfront Houses.* Exeter: Devon Archaeological Monograph.

Burke, A. E., Dalell, J. R. & Townsend, G., 1950. *Architectural and Building Trades Dictionary.* Chicago (Illinois): American Technical Society.

Burton Art Gallery and Museum, 2017. *Bideford Long Bridge,* Bideford: Burton Art Gallery and Museum.

Carmichael, R., 1991. New Bridge – Oldest Bridge over the Thames. *The Blowing Stone,* Winter, pp. 1–4.

Challis, C. & Savage, T., 1986. *Packhorse Bridge, Aylestone.* Cambridge: Cambridge University Press.

Christie, P. & Whiting, F., 1986. *The Long Bridge of Bideford.* Stroud: Amberly Publishers.

Collcut, E. H., 1929. *Treverbyn Ancient Bridge.* [Online] Available at: **http://www.engineering-timelines.com/scripts/engineering Item.asp?id=850** [Accessed 11 June 2020].

Concrete Renovations, 2019. *What are the Differences Between Grade I and II Listed Buildings?* [Online] Available at: **https://www.concreterenovations.co.uk/news/what-are-the-differences-between-grade-i-and-ii-listed-buildings/** [Accessed 1 August 2020].

Cook, G. H., 1947. *Mediaeval Chantries and Chantry Chapels.* London: Phoenix House.

Cruse, J. B., 1982. *The Long Bridge of Barnstaple & The Long Bridge Trust.* Barnstaple: The Long Bridge Trust.

Culture Trip, *10 Spectacular National Parks In England, South Downs National Park,* [Online] Available at: **https://theculturetrip.com/europe/united-kingdom/england/articles/10-spectacular-national-parks-in-england/** [Accessed 23 September 2020].

Ditchfield, R. P. H., 1910. *Vanishing England.* London: Methuen & Co.

Drew, G., 2001. *Elstead Then and Now.* [Online] Available at: **https://e-voice.org.uk/elsteadnews/elstead-area-articles/elstead-then-now/** [Accessed 3 August 2020].

Elrington, C., 2018. *King John's Bridge.* [Online] Available at: **https://tewkesburyhistory.org/King-Johns-Bridge** [Accessed 12 November 2020].

Green, E., 2002. *Bridge Chapels.* [Online] Available at: **https://www.buildingconservation.com/articles/bridgechapels/bridgechapels.htm** [Accessed 28 November 2020].

Greeves, T. & Stanbrook, E., 2004. *The Clapper Bridge – Postbridge.* Brixham: Quay Publishing.

Harrison, D., 2004. *The Bridges of Medieval England Transport and Society 400–1800.* Oxford: Clarendon Press.

Henderson, C. & Coates, H., 1928. *Old Cornish Bridges and Streams.* London: Simpkin Marshall.

Henderson, C. & Jervoise, E., 1938. *Old Devon Bridges.* London: A. Wheaton & Co.

Hinchcliffe, E., 1994. *A Guide to the Packhorse Bridges of England.* London: Cicerone Press.

Historic England, 2018. *Scheduled Monuments.* [Online] Available at: **https://historicengland.org.uk/listing/what-is-designation/scheduled-monuments/** [Accessed 4 July 2020].

Historic England, 2021. *Clattern Bridge.* [Online] Available at: **https://historicengland.org.uk/listing/the-list/list-entry/1002021?section=official-list-entry** [Accessed 9 April 2022].

History of Bridges, 2020. *Structure, Components and Parts of Bridge.* [Online] Available at: **http://www.historyofbridges.com/facts-about-bridges/bridge-parts/** [Accessed 28 June 2020].

Hudson, K., ed., 1967. Industrial Archeology. *The Journal of the History of Industry & Technology,* Volume 4(1), pp. 60–61.

Ildan, Mehmet Murat, 2005. Available at: **https://www.escritas.org/en/mehmet-murat-ildan**

Jenkinson, T. & Taylor, P., 2009. *The Toll Houses of South Devon.* [Online] Available at: **http://www.turnpikes.org.uk/Devon%20-%20Ashburton%20Road.htm** [Accessed 17 April 2021].

Jervoise, E., 1930. *The Ancient Bridges of the South of England.* London: Architectural Press.

Jones, E., 2019, Hermits and Anchorites of England, 1200–1550 [Online] Available at: **https://www.manchesterhive.com/view/9781526127228/9781526127228.00006.xml**

Lacey, R. & Danzinger, D., 1999. *The Year 1000 – An Englishman's World.* London: Little Brown and Company.

Leland, J. & John, B., 1549. *The Laboryouse Journey & Serche of Johan Leylande for Englandes Antiquitees.* [Online] Available at: **https://archive.org/details/laboryousejourn00balegoog** [Accessed 12 September 2020].

Leeming, J. & Salter, H., 1946. *Burford Bridge, Abingdon.* [Online] Available at: **https://www.oxoniensia.org/oxo_toc.php?title=Burford&author=&range=&s=Search#** [Accessed 12 July 2021]

Lyte, C., 1980. *The Thames.* Hove: Wayland Publishers Ltd..

Malden, H., 1911. *The Victoria History of the County of Surrey.* London: Institute of Historical Research.

Mawrey, G., 2018. An Unsung Arcadia. *Historic Garden Review,* November, Issue 38, pp. 6–10.

McFetrich, D., 2019. *An Encyclopedia of British Bridges.* 2nd edn. Barnsley: Pen & Sword Books.

Muckley, T., 2004. *Ancient Bridges of the Rother Valley.* [Online] Available at: **http://www.simonknott.co.uk/tommuckley/034bridges.htm** [Accessed 12 September 2020].

Naoum, J., ed., 2012. *Parliament of England, Acts of Parliament in the United Kingdom, Greater London.* London: Pearson.

New Forest National Park Authority, 2022. *History and Culture.* [Online] Available at: **https://www.newforestnpa.gov.uk/discover/history-culture/** [Accessed 12 April 2022].

Page, W., 2017. *The Victoria History of the County of Wiltshire.* [Online] Available at: **https://www.history.ac.uk/research/victoria-county-history/county-histories-progress/wiltshire** [Accessed 17 November 2020].

Page, W., Proby, G. & Ladds, S. I., 1936. *The Victoria History of the County of Huntingdon.* London: Institute of Historical Research.

Parsons, J., 1973. *Excavations of Yalding 'Town Bridge' Site, Kent.* [Online] Available at: **http://cka.moon-demon.co.uk/KAR031/KAR031_Yalding.htm** [Accessed 15 August 2020].

Penn, D., 1974. Report on the Eashing Bridges. *Research Volume of the Archeological Society,* Volume 1, p. 167.

Pevsner, N., 1958. *The Buildings of England: South and West Somerset.* London: Hamondsworth.

Pevsner, N., 1971. *The Buildings of England: Surrey.* 2nd edn. London: Penguin Books.

Pevsner, N. & Cherry, B., 1989. *The Buildings of England: Devon.* London: Harmondsworth.

Pevsner, N. & Newman, J., 1972. *The Buildings of England: Dorset.* 3rd edn. London: Yale University Press.

Pevsner, N. & Sherwood, J., 1974. *The Buildings of England: Oxfordshire.* London: Yale University Press.

Philpotts, E., 1921 *Orphan Dinah.* New York: Macmillan Co.

Polsue, J., 1965. Lakes Parochial History of the County of Cornwall – 1872. *Country Life,* 7 January. pp. 12-17.

Renn, D., 1974. The River Wey Bridges Between Farnham and Guildford. *Research Volume of the Surrey Archaeological Society,* Volume 1, pp. 77–78.

Richards, J., 1984. *The National Trust Book of Bridges. London:* National Trust.

Robertson, T., 2020. *Historic Bridges of Britain – A Compendium.* [Online] Available at: **https://historicbridgesofbritain.com/** [Accessed 11 November 2020].

Salzman, L. F., 1953. *A History of the County of Sussex.* London: Institute of Historical Research.

Salzman, L. F., 1972. *The Victoria History of the County of Oxford.* London: Institute of Historical Research.

Sandles, T., 2016. Dart Bridge. [Online] Available at: **https://www.legendarydartmoor.co.uk/dart_bridge.htm** [Accessed 19 December 2020].

Sheldon, G., 1928. *From Trackway to Turnpike.* Oxford: Oxford University Press.

Simpson, D., 2020. *Early Bridge Building.* [Online] Available at: **http://scotlandsoldestbridges.co.uk/early-bridge-building.html** [Accessed June–December 2020].

Simpson, D., 2020. *Construction Methods.* [Online] Available at: **http://scotlandsoldestbridges.co.uk/history.html** [Accessed 28 November 2020].

Slocombe, Graham, 2019. *What is Landscape Aesthetics and Environmental Psychology?* [Online] Available at: **https://landarchconcepts.wordpress.com/what-is-landscape-aesthetics-and-environmental-psychology/**

Taylor, C., 1979. *Roads and Tracks of Britain.* London: J. M. Dent & Sons Ltd..

Toulmin Smith, L., 1964. *The Itinerary of John Leland in or about the Years 1553–1554.* s.l.: s.n.

Urban Dictionary, 2010. *Pontist.* [Online] Available at: **https://www.urbandictionary.com/define.php?term=pontist** [Accessed 11 September 2019].

Whiting, F. & Christie, P., 1945. *The Long Bridge of Bideford Through the Centuries.* Bideford: The Bideford Bridge Trust.

Williamson, T., 2004. *Shaping Medieval Landscapes: Settlement, Society, Environment.* Oxford: Windgather Press.

Wolfpaw, 2018. *The Medieval Exe Bridge.* [Online] Available at: **http://demolition-exeter.blogspot.com/2013/03/the-medieval-exe-bridge.html** [Accessed 12 June 2021].

On the Cover: The Gough Map

The cover of this book includes an image of the Gough Map, so named after Richard Gough who bequeathed it in 1809 to the Bodleian Library, Oxford, where it still resides. Richard Gough acquired it for half-a-crown on 20 May 1774 at the sale of the collection of Thomas Martin of Palgrave, where it was offered as Lot 405 and described as 'a curious and most ancient map of Great Britain'. It is one of the oldest surviving maps of Great Britain and shows the medieval trade networks from the perspective of someone living in that time. Conventionally the map has been dated to around 1360, though lately one researcher has suggested instead that an early 15th-century date is more likely. There is certainly evidence that portions of the map were redone and that work on it probably continued into the 15th century. The cartographer (or cartographers) is unknown. The map is drawn on the flesh-side of two pieces of sheepskin parchment, joined vertically. The lap-join was held together originally with a plain running-stitch, clearly identifiable by sewing-holes and thread-indentations along the join. The map is 115 cm x 56 cm in size on vellum and consists of the coastline of the island of Great Britain (depicted horizontally), several smaller islands and parts of the coastlines of Ireland and the Continent. Rivers are shown, and over 600 cities, towns, and smaller settlements are represented by churches, fortifications, or simple houses.

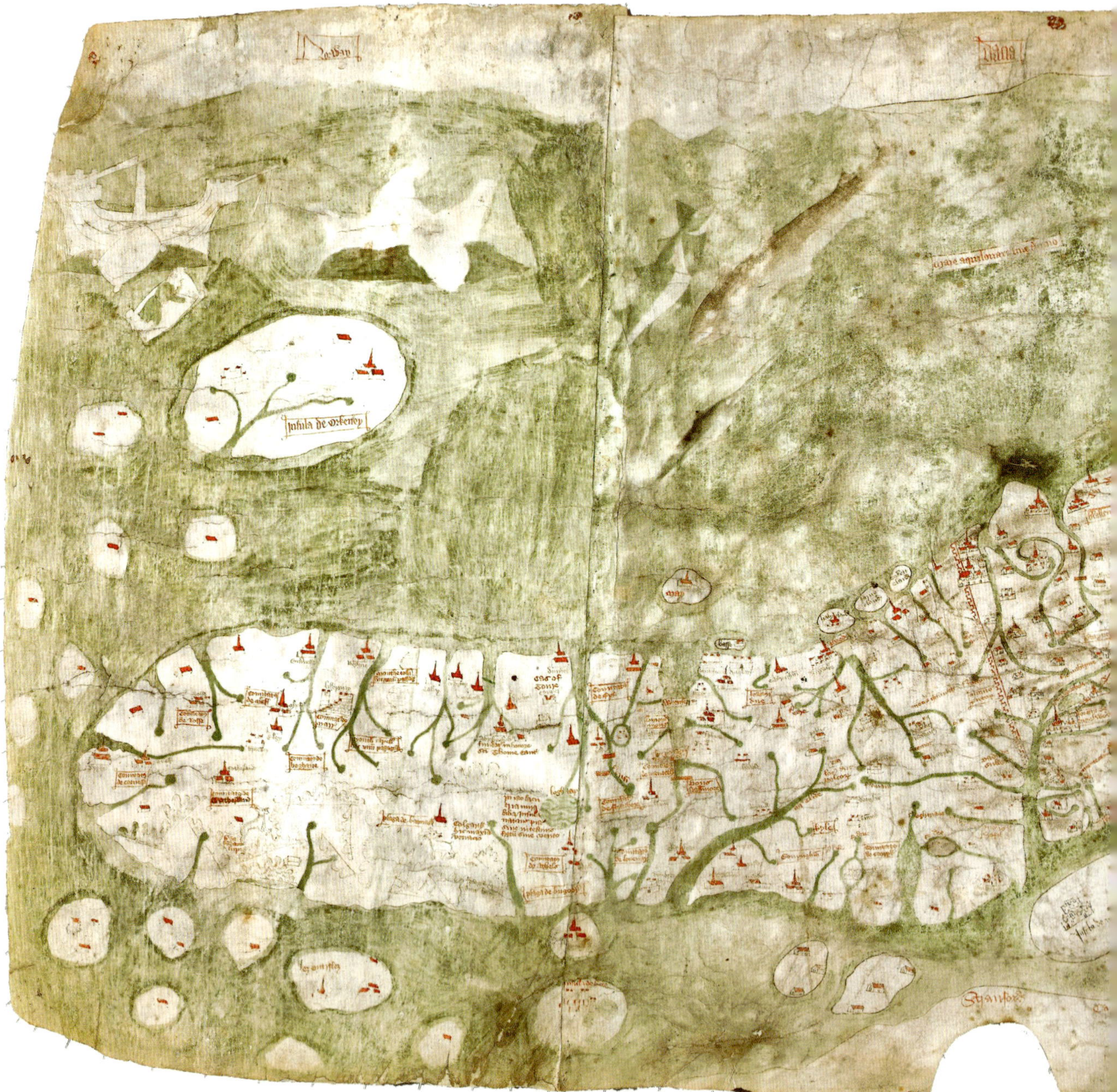

The Gough Map of the British Isles, c. 1400, ink on vellum (Held by the Bodleian Library, University of Oxford, www.goughmap.org, used with permission)

The Gough Map is considerably more detailed than earlier 13th-century maps of Great Britain and, in the context of studying the medieval travel and communications networks, its particular value lies in the web of red lines, almost 5,000 kilometres in length, marked as linking various settlements in England and Wales. These lines seem to represent major roads and are, in most cases, accompanied by a Roman numeral indicating the mileage between two settlements. There is some debate as to whether the lines indicate actual roads or merely estimates of the distance between select towns. But given that the lines chart out significant sections of such important thoroughfares as the Great North Road, and the medieval Watling Street, and also given the Gough Map's remarkable correspondences to the roads in John Ogilby's *Atlas Britannia* from 1675, it may be concluded that the Gough Map does contain a representation of the English medieval transport network in the 14th century. The map is not comprehensive significant omissions include Watling Street between Canterbury and London, and the route from London to East Anglia via Colchester – but the map is nevertheless a unique survivor, predating the next major mapwork of overland routes by some 300 years. Further detail and a digital version of the map can be found at: **http://www.goughmap.org/** and the interesting story of its conservation is at **https://www.bodleian.ox.ac.uk/about/libraries/our-work/gough-map-conservation**.